VIE

INTONEX

THE SECRET
HARMONY OF LIFE

A Mystical and Sacred Journey Unveiled

Intonex: The Secret Harmony of Life
Copyright © 2023 **VIE**

ISBN (Paperback): 979-8-9897589-3-7
ISBN (Hardback): 979-8-9897589-4-4
ISBN (Ebook):   979-8-9897589-5-1

Printed in the United States of America

"Love beyond Passion"

Our love is here to transform humanity from slavery to freedom.
It must be understood that there is no true liberation without love.
Love is an energy resonant frequency and
the carrier wave silent language.
Love generates the body's most powerful and most
extensive rhythmic electromagnetic field. Sixty
times greater in amplitude than the brain.
Love is the key to your home frequency.
Intuition and discernment is needed.

VIE

Trinity Oneness
The Triad, the Trilogy of Creation inside the Human Body

The Recovery of Important Past Knowledge Lost
with the Burning of the Alexandria Library
Frequency, Energy, Color and Sound, Light, and Divine Life

The Link between Color Harmonic and Sound Frequency

Earth (crystal onyx)—Rainbow (power
of color)—Frequency (energy)

Illness is when you are resonating in a low frequency or wrong frequency.

To successfully rebalance the energy the technique of the forty-ninth vibration begins at the highest vibratory level.

Cure is nothing else than frequency.

Harmonic Resonance Frequency

The Tesla Harmonic Technology manipulated matter, metals, rocks, wood, anything made of matter at the atomic level.

Understand that harmony is the sixth plane. Humans have a wave pattern for everything on your side of the veil. Each wave has a frequency to it, as it travels up and down, forward or backward. That is the frequency of your wave, or your tone. Every part of your body has a slightly different wave and vibration, and yet you have a signature vibration, which you send out into the world at all times. And it can be altered; by just having different thoughts can help to open those waves so that you can more easily harmonize with other people.

3: Trinity
and the human body function
6: Creator
in the form of the Son of the living world,
coming in the Messiah (3 + 3)
9: Universe
the full enlightenment, the completion.

The 3 represents the body, the 6 represents the Savior Christ Consciousness, and the 9 is the full evolution of the soul to total consciousness.

The 3 is a number that our body relates to, the vibration of 3. After three minutes without blood circulating in the brain, death occurs. The body can't live longer than three minutes without oxygen. After three days, humans can't live without water, and three weeks without food based on essential vital energy that keeps you alive.

Six is the Christ Consciousness. (But 666 is an insult to the Christ.)

Nine is the Nirvana. (The number 9 symbolize the concepts of completeness and also represented the *Nine Lords of Time*. They were the original galactic masters that have come to Earth to present Earth humans with a key to understanding the universe and our place within it.)

The number 144 as a significant sacred number has esoteric associations with the concept of Light.

Nikola Tesla was understanding the all spirituality. There are three steps to reach completion. The human (3), God and Jesus Christ (6), and the ultimate consciousness (9).

Tesla was understanding the all spirituality.

"If you wish to understand the universe, think energy, frequency, and vibration."—Nikola Tesla

Important Powerful Steps toward Personal and Spiritual Growth

"Faith comes by hearing, and hearing by the word of God."

—Romans 10:17

Even though it has happened to me over and over, in this collection of fascinating journeys and stories, the Intonex (volume 5 of the series) makes out another case for the introduction of a new genre of tale. A shamanic story is a journey containing elements that are representative of such. I have to say that I am always amazed because I could be struggling with something for some times, then I'll get my guide's help from behind the veil. And you'll see that I have many. Confusion is the feeling we get when our brain is searching for an answer. Within a few short minutes, I get a complete different understanding of the situation. I have full clarity.

As I said, I have been chosen and work directly under the father for the father, our infinite Creator.

A shaman is a harmonizer and a healer. A shamanic journey is one that generally takes place in a trance for divination. A shamanic journey occurs by shifting awareness or consciousness. Through a change in consciousness, shamans enter unordinary reality. A shamanic story has either been based on or inspired by a shamanic journey, or one that contains a number of the elements typical of such a journey. A venture into invisible realms and the access to loving and compassionate helping spirits who can give advice on how to move forward in lives, how to heal, and how to let go of hurts and disappointments.

The One Infinite Creator wanted to understand duality from every perceivable point of view. Wanted to know everything about duality. The experience of duality. So it exploded into innumerable sparks of which all human beings are. Everyone is a piece of the One it dispensed itself in this creation, this universe that is an electric universe, and we are all one. We are the One Infinite Creator having simultaneous experience to understand duality.

And when you understand this, and if you have a trauma (as the perpetrator, or a witness, or as a victim, as the duality), you go back to that time period and you reexperience that trauma and experience it in all facets, the energy of that trauma begins to leave as you realize we are One.

But I then enter in connection with out of space entities.

The Apocalypse, or in the revelation to John in the Bible, says, "Wisdom is needed here, one who understand can calculate the number of the beast, for it is a number that stands for a person. His number is six hundred and sixty six," (Rom. 13:18).

This revelation part in the Bible applies to our new era, today. We are living the last part of the Bible. Yes, you all have been lied to, dumbed down, and manipulated in too many ways to categorize, the additive in your water, the universe pollution in one product "biosluge," the new recycling technology "cannibalism," food, GMOs, Big Pharma, the inoculations, chemtrails, about the climate change, the endless wars and disease…by the elite in power that control the planet and now the Klebsi plague. Through these shamanic journeys, I narrate, I offer you some noninvasive alternative help to the body, like the Bio-Qi Therapy™ that I created, for the mind and the spirit. They will help you awaken to see the truth, enable you to see the reality, and to spiritually grow. Opening yourself to compassion and love toward each other and finally get aligned with your path and destiny. For that there is no need of pundit, whistles, and belts, No need for high expenses and time-consuming hours of research. I bring it all to you, helped by my blue flame. Because the ascension is a consciousness shift and when the consciousness goes through the shift, we see everything from a completely different aspect. You'll start to understand Oneness and you connect with each other a different way and understand how all is one, plus you begin to pool together in assisting each other.

It is a fact that the awakening can't happen with fake news on current climate that triggers division of political parties among the population, fear in hearts, stress, and hate. The awakening won't happen with the division among population and relentless pressures of politics of greed and petitions of outrage marches and demonstration. It can't happen while the elites in strategic places are pedophiles, killers, rapists, and cannibals. Not only the ignorance but the denial to open up to the truth, combined by the trance-induced state of mindful obedience has enable large part of the cabal to plunder, rape, pillage a large part of the world's resources that makes them rich. The world is in a prison planet. There is division among human beings, fear induced and relentless draining pressures of the politics of greed. There is more than psychological and Reiki and energy healing to fully heal and protect if you want to get to higher frequency and reach the fifth dimension (5-D). There is more than one holographic reality; there is other unheard frequencies that also unbalance you. There is some hidden technology, some hidden knowledge also that goes back to the Egyptian time and link now to the UFO. There is one most important ingredient left out—Oneness and the reconnection to the divine. You cannot get it with psychotropic drugs, drinking hallucinatory plant/vine tea blend or any pills manufactured by a state's government agency administration responsible for science and technology.

This is why we, the God Duo, CHADD and VIE, came to show you the path of Oneness and to reconnect you to the Divine and higher frequency DNA programming. We are metaphysical and spiritual teachers and healers, and we came back on earth to help you at that time of transition. We have a long history of living on earth. Egypt, Atlantis, Lemuria. Sacred Tibetan texts remember it as Ra-Mu; inscriptions on the American continents refer to it as the

Lost Motherland of Mu; and Edgar Cayce, who had access to the Akashic records, names it Muri, or Lemuria.

The vibrational transformation energy is the higher frequency DNA programming. It is a special package for encoding the DNA and only carried by us. As the God Duo, we have the higher frequency DNA programming, which we had before coming within the third dimension. We chose to use the vast knowledge gathered in past lifetimes when we practiced the arts of higher communication to aid humanity in raising the collective frequency. This is what you currently term the ascension. The knowledge of these arts encoded in our DNA requires that we shift our energy to much higher frequencies than the masses. This has been true even during those past times when all humanity's collective frequency range was much lower than it is now.

With this method, we are able to share the knowledge and information we have to assist you in your evolution. The energy we send streams to the human receiver who then translates it into words. Other humans receive pure energy transmission and interpret them as sound, such as music or tones for healing the physical body. Yet others receive our transmission energy as visions, which their special encoding translates into images with meaning for them. Each of these methods is part of special encoding within human DNA.

Not to be confused with Reiki energy that is occult 100 percent because anything that takes God and Jesus out of the equation is from Satan. Reiki can't reconnect you to the Divine. And a true healer receive their power from God.

To perceive the reality you deserve, try and treat your brain with only mindful and creative information and become a conscious reader. Be aware that there are new methods and different ways to perceive the vast humans knowledge of the new era.

Alternative medicine, herbal medicine, psychic healing by hand laying, healing remotely, self-healing, and psychic surgery have been rejected by global Illuminati establishments because these cures do not benefit the Illuminati-controlled pharmaceutical cartel and impact the foundations of the medical academy that serves the chemical medicine of the pharmaceutical cartel.

Other Books by VIE Loriot de Rouvray

E ach volume of the books takes you on a spiritual trip for your growth and well-being, which are powerful steps to personal growth presented to you in a pleasant way and must be read in chronological sequence.

9.1.1. Complete Guide to Natural Healing
Destiny of the doG—Volume 1
Time Is Ticking: The Fifth Amendment—Volume 2
Karma through the Window of Time—Volume 3
New Century, New Age, New Experiences—Volume 4
Intonex—Volume 5

Bio-music *Frequency of Sound* is a color vibrational balancing CD imprinted of the language of the Light and on a sonic base.

Note for the Reader

In writing this book, I am conscious that my purpose, our mission, and our work as the God Duo might be criticized by unfaithful or by unawakened beings. And it's OK. I am sure that they will still give them some reflection and help them be opened, awakened, and grow. To skeptics, I have found when you have an audience of metaphysical-minded people, the science qualifiers are not necessary. Those persons accept the teachings without the science because they feel they are true. Our new therapy is a bridge between science and spirituality, some ancient texts, and the way Christians have experienced the Bible, which is an abridged and changed version. But some of these ancient texts written years ago and even centuries before the Bible were not included in the book, or original text, and has been since changed. Many of these documents have been stored in Egypt and Tibet.

Be aware that not every human receives the special package of encoding higher frequencies than the masses, frequency DNA programing within the DNA. We are and we choose to use our vast knowledge gathered in past lifetimes to help you. The knowledge of these arts encoded in our DNA requires that we shift our energy to much higher frequencies than the masses. With this method, we are able to share the knowledge and information we have to assist you in your evolution.

Humanity is living its last battle between good and evil and entering the Aquarius era. The world is not what you have been told. Truth has been hidden to you. Division has been created among you because of withheld, twisted, or fake information. We are bringing you the secrets of the spoken light language, the sound and Sacred Geometry that have been kept hidden to you by the Grays and more. Human rights abuse is their food. Your suffering is their food. In 3-D, you eat food in D, your food is energy, and they eat that loosh soup.

Your body is a holographic body of Light made of 70 percent water. You are spirit in manifested form. You must know about the DNA—.666 or .618? 440 Hz or 432 Hz organic?

I am Catholic and very close to the Creator, and I work directly under God's guidance. I am also very close to the Blessed Mother Mary, and she is always with me, as well as Archangel Michael. All my books has been guided from another realm, sometimes by my higher self and others, by entities I am familiar with or gotten in contact with. This book is another book that is part of a series of lessons in expanding the mind and opening up the consciousness, taking the reader on a journey. The first book was guided by Archangel Michael and this one initiated by Cassia, then others.

To understand and benefit completely from my books, read them in chronological sequence. Please begin with *Destiny of the doG*.

Thanks to Archangel Michael, all my life was transformed.

Dedication

I dedicate this book to the
Blessed Holy Trinity
and
Archangel Michael.

I want to thanks my coworker, all my guides, all the entities on the other realms that have offered me their help and supported me.

Of course, Archangel Michael, who trained, initiated, and protected me. Our Father God for whom I work. Jesus, Mother Mary that guides me, Archangel Gabriel, Archangel Raphael, Archangel Metatron, Saint Faustina, Saint Hildegard of Bingen, Saint Therese of Lisieux, Saint Mother Theresa, Saint Anthony, Saint Dymphna, Archbishop Fulton Sheen, Monk Thomas Merton, Padre Pio, Nikola Tesla, my great, great, great ancestor Pierre Montour de Laroue, who came to help with its chevron. My ancestor the Sun King Louis Dieudonne, known as the Great King, Ignatz, and Flour. People of the star, solar beings. Asuba, most particularly, and all the people of his planet, Zeta Reticulan. The Pleiadians. Earth's Divine sacred lady Kaala Likilaki, who honored me of her protection with King Kamehameha from Hawaii, Grey Wolf, Malmo. All the wise ones entities, the Council of Twelve with Asuba, Grand Ambassador Solon, Altire, Ascended Master Ahshundrah, Commandant Ashtar Sheran, and our Lady of Guadalupe, the Radiant Star Unity Group, Patricia, Dave and Jerry, Shaman Light Bear, Saint Germain, Divine

Sister A., the eight blurry faces, and my wonderful friend astrologist Ron, who was of a great help when it was needed the most. A beautiful, faithful, and gifted soul.

Introduction

You are about to embark on a most powerful, unusual, and spiritual journey. A quest to your path and your destiny that is now at hand. It is about individuals assuming more power. Steps to personal growth without whistles, belts, and gurus but through short series of writings. An easier, quicker, and more economical way and the fastest way for you to grow spiritually and find answers to your questions maybe. To become your own master with no time-consuming hours of research. No expenses of flights, hotel rooms, and conventions to attend.

I have been chosen, and I am told to let it be known. You must hear it. I am the chosen one. *I am the door to the Divine.* I have lived many lives before that one, but I have come back to help you and to accomplish my mission, which is to help you grow spiritually and become your own master. You came here to search for the creator and to be reconnected to the Divine.

This book volume 5 is mainly about frequencies. Everything is energy. Frequencies of colors, Light, and Sound. I am bringing you back in this book, the knowledge that was content in the Alexandria Library, *destroyed by fire*, actually located in the Vatican Library.

What the cabal have always known but hidden to you—the truth about energy, frequencies, and your body of Light activated by Sound. To successful rebalance the energy, the cause of all illnesses, the technique of the forty-ninth vibration begins at the highest levels. Sound frequencies of low intensity and acoustic energy can induce strong effects on human behavior. Sound and Light are forms of resonant vibrations that change the human brain and body.

The Archons are psychopaths, parasites, liars, and have the ability to create an illusionary world to keep you in a fake world and feed of your energy.

"You are the energy renewable. Love frequency is the Divine healing energy."

My name is VIE. I am your guide into the Light.

I will raise your vibration to the optimum level, reconnect your so-called junk DNA through different ways of using my Light energy. Using the Sound frequency of my voice and the *language of the Light* or by sending energy from my heart in quantum. Just ask me.

I was led to write this book for you by an entity named Ignatz. Ignatz was granted the authorization to access my files and to give it to me. Then Flour, also from the Akasha, came to guide me and recover some previous knowledge.

A little bit later, Asuba from Zeta Reticulan planet will also come to help.

As a spiritual teacher, I am bringing you information that, in my opinion, my understanding, are real, some of them you may be aware of, and some others that you are not. Use your intuition and discernment. To be able to master your life path, and reach your growth goal, you have to understand that there are technologies used that keep you denying the truth and keep you unawakened. I have met many in my journey and even those who think are aware of everything are not totally. That is how and when they take advantage.

At the time of the beginning of the Aquarius era, there is wars, and many atrocities going on, at your expenses on planet earth. The world that we are living in is a world of control on the population by all means. It is all about making money on human beings. Human trafficking, tortures, rapes of adults and children, kidnappings, forced ingestion of prescription psychotropics and drugs in general. Beds for profit in governmental institutions with altered mental states and a mind control program. All is made to trap you in the system for money purposes, keeping you with false information.

Beware: these people worship Lucifer. The cabal is here to destroy your soul. Not only they enslave you and deprive you of freedom, they also kidnap, sell, trade, rape, torture, kill, drink the blood, and eat the flesh of babies. They sell organs for profit, and they are cannibals and delight in orgies and deliver fake news.

Your body is a holographic body of Light made of energy, water, and colors. Your aura has colors, and each of your organs corresponds to one color. When you are sick, your body has an unbalance of energy (your vibration is too low), of color, of frequency. Diseases are implanted, lately through vaccines, viruses are also created, and it is all to control you for money purposes and reduce you to slavery.

The final battle uses advanced technologies that you are not aware of to keep you in a loop, controlling you, in poverty and poverty consciousness, sickness, and unwanted emotions, disabling you to grow and find your freedom.

I have been viciously attacked by the enluminades, trying to stop my new gift from opening up to a much, much greater energy that will flow through me.

As my body is being prepared to be a sort of broadcasting channel of greater healing energy to others, they viciously attacked my body under both arms on the lymph location. Like they did by the past on my front body and legs that left me with scars. This new energy can even be sent to faraway locations.

These satanic energies also used the heat at night, which kept me awake all nights.

Then forty-four of them invaded my body in an effort to introduce a disease in it while I was grieving the loss of my dog. Then they assaulted my physical body and inserted a stinger into my back, attacking my shoulders and my knees in an effort to refrain me from flexibility, and it weakened my energy as my body had to fight these attachments.

My body tones was received by Asuba from a solar star being. Asuba my guide, him, and other Zetan alien people received the tone of my body. From this tone, they could read all I was going through and knew everything of my life.

They knew all about me and my coworker's mission and what the system is doing to him.

The Zetan people have evolved for half a million years. Upon reception of my body tone, Asuba entered in contact with me, asking me to allow them to help me heal my own body and help me in my mission to have my destiny and path back and centered. They asked me permission to make what they call a correct life path alignment.

My new gift allows me to become a broadcast where the flow through me can be projected from my palms, third eye, heart, and throat. My crown chakra being the open canal of reception.

The new energy will come into my body and get out from these four places. When to give clarity of mind to others, it flows then from my third eye. When deep emotional wounds need to be healed, it is then projected from my heart and it will balance the Love energy. When someone is unable to speak up, make a decision, or need a part of its body to be healed then, it is coming from the palms of my hands.

This flowing energy from me to others heals people. A healing energy that has nothing to do with Reiki or anything already known on this planet. It has nothing to do with any of these methods that takes God and Jesus out of the equation.

It is rays on energy with sparking gold-glittering flakes of little suns entering me.

An energy that the satanic forces did not expect or want on the planet. While my coworker, CHADD, expert of Sound, is forcibly retained in a retention home, declared incompetent to appear in court, and forced to ingest psychotropic drugs and receiving injection of psychotropic drugs every three weeks. It is through these inoculations that they inject you with a nanochip, then they manipulate your brain while making money on you.

As they know everything of me, they know very well about the most troubling woman. A diabolic archon energy, the Surrogate, which Asuba, the Wiser Ones, and the Council of Twelve describe as a harsh worker woman, and some others refer to her as the voodoo woman as she use similar tools, and also describe her as a psychic vampire.

Prologue

Now remember that I told you that this adventure began with the first volume, *Destiny of the doG*, a theory thriller book. VIE met CHADD in a wheelchair, felt a deep and strong connection, inexplicable. They had lived together in a previous life, and her memory awakened. She got to know him better and became enveloped in a world of mysticism, government conspiracies, religions, and upcoming prophesied events. Entered a world of lies, deception, hope, and pain. Her spiritual journey began when she joined forces with her blue flame, CHADD, to bring the words of Jesus.

Henri, a professor who lived near an Indian tribal reservation, had a son, Edward, with his wife, Martha. Edward married Ethel, and they had a son CHADD, who was diagnosed with several behavior and mental problems, after his dad took him to the government hospital that his father, Edward, used at the request of the NSA. At the age of five, they started to do testing on CHADD to understand his unique ability. Though he was never sick, CHADD was given multiple drugs at the age of five. Then Edward divorced, and during the time of Edward and Ethel's separation, he started dating a coworker named Katherine, an archon known as the harsh woman, or surnamed the Surrogate, working hand in hand with CHADD's half-brother, Paul. Katherine's son, Paul, was a deputy sheriff at that time. Paul, Carlos, and Katherine were all involved with the corrupt government.

The government would take the drug from the drug dealers at west, send them to Miami for sale in Florida, and generate money for the government's clandestine operations.

CHADD spent times in hospitals and medical centers, and during his stay in the hospital, a group called Guardians revealed themselves. They were the Cathari. There were two elements to them, the Perfecti and the Believers. The Perfecti were the helpful and wanted to bring people closer to God. They defeated Hitler. The Believers were the Nazis and are the serial killers of today and the many world leaders that destroyed rather than created. Extremely intelligent and hypnotizing at the same time, some of the Believers had guidance in genetic reproduction thousands of years ago, before and after the great flood, to create creatures seen throughout history as vampires, werewolves, Bigfoot, and reptilians.

I suddenly feel a gigantic power approaching, and I know I am being called once again to another time and place.

By now I am so accustomed. My mind works differently now. I look around in an attempt to piece together what is happening, and I see clearly in a book title a series of numbers and phrases appearing.

"Intonex, 432 Hz organic, 432 cycles, 440Hz a creating broadcasting, (.666 counterfeit DNA), (3.6.9.), (555), 0010110 algorithm platform, pictography radiation, heliosphere, the benevolent physics, the triad, the violet code…"

Then a familiar voice is talking to me, saying, "This is another part of a series of writing stories, that I am bringing up to your consciousness already written by you."

All these started when CHADD met VIE, and their meet up that set the thing in motion. Then all this series of writing continued to happen in vision.

How can CHADD and VIE explain to the unprepared person the meeting, reunion of two angels with one common mission? Their humanitarian mission is spiritual and somewhat holistic and also a shamanic journey, and that's how it's described.

They are both reconnected to the Divine and are here on this humanitarian mission sent by the higher government of the universe.

Two gifted souls, blessed with special gifts from God, who came together for the same purpose.

"CHADD and VIE are the keepers of the secret contained in His hands."

But CHADD has been kept away by the Cabal with the collaboration of the harsh woman, unable to defend himself from the trap. He was given an archon to defend him in court!

At the very, very beginning, Archangel Michael guided VIE to put together a *complete guide to natural healing*. Giving access to withheld facts about drugs and their real effects on your health and what some supplements can do to keep you healthy. Because spiritual growth, vitality, and wellness are being linked to the primary purpose.

That's when then the mystical journey launched with VIE, the metaphysical light and vibration healer, from her unexpected meeting with her blue flame, the gifted CHADD, and about how the culmination of historical events interact with the prophecies of the future days. In the theory thriller book is the Messiah, the Christ Wavoka, and the ancient city of Antioch, fallen angels, ancient Indian legends, and secret religious sect created in the days of Jesus. A modern adventure lived by CHADD and VIE with tribulations, through which Christianity is introduced to the world. It follows a fascinating and historical adventure that includes the return of Jesus and Mary Magdalene. And CHADD and VIE who demonstrate the path of Divine love. It's about the matrix and the ascension process: the connection between Sacred Geometry and modern physics. A never ending battle of good and evil: the modern world is a literal and figurative warzone. All narrated in the first volume of a series called *Destiny of the doG* that brings a powerful message to the world, with warnings and future prediction that you not want to hear, but have to hear it.

The journey continues in the second volume, *The Time Is Ticking: The Fifth Amendment*. CHADD has been Baker Acted and drugged, but he holds the key to the divine wisdom while VIE brings humanity into the light of God, just when it seems all lost. But all of this was a treat to the Anunnaki who wanted the earth for themselves. The Thuggee medical doctors from India reincarnated. They keep CHADD by court orders, in drugs, and in a foggy state between mental hospitals and an asylum. They drug him with dangerous drugs, brainwash, program, and manipulate him, beat him, steal from him, and deprive him of all his rights to a fair trial of freedom. He was beaten by several people, like a black pastor under the shower, Carlos, a well-known man by the court though, broke his sternum and left him in front of a hospital. CHADD tried to play his fifth but rapidly understood that only politicians have this right. The government controls the population through the false information they diffuse. The Illuminati are in key places, and all institutions are corrupted. They sent an Asian couple to steal the Vajra from VIE, a galactic tool given by a Tibetan monk. That's what has been told to VIE but in fact been given by Christ, delivered his bloodline, His star codes through the Goddess and brought the instrument of ultimate creativity that could transmute violence, "the Eucharist," True Christ.

In the third volume, *Karma through the Window of Time*, VIE is now in a different life to see the transformation from Pisces to the age of Aquarius. Now she works with transformation energy and is bringing knowledge to the masses of people. CHADD is gifted of sound frequencies and is a messenger of God. The black government with the support of Katherine, the Surrogate,, Paul, her son, the lost case, the court system, a social worker, and the Indian Thuggees keep not only Baker Acting him but also depriving him of sleep, rights, money, identity, and freedom in Chateau USHI Asylum. Where he is kept on psychotropic drugs, disabling his brain's ability to filter information and perception, blocking signals to his conscious mind. They are keeping him in delusion and making him seem incompetent. Drugs are demons and give a false feeling, causing addiction to the DNA that is compromised, making spirituality vulnerable. But VIE sees and understand everything. She used the language of the Light. She knows that they have received the knowledge that can be used to enlighten the world that will help resolve the difference that separates you on earth.

New Century, New Era, New Experiences is the forth volume of the series. Now while CHADD is kept on drugs under an illegal program experiment mind control, the MK-Ultra, initiated by the CIA, VIE is helped by entities from other realms and aliens. The UN thinks of eliminating all borders and genders to create an atheist human field human race since they realized that Christianity was based on the Essene teaching. There is something that is of big preoccupation happening right now, and it's in CERN in Switzerland that change human's DNA. The global heating has nothing to do with what you have been told but with the excavation in the underground of Antarctica by the cabal.

The reality is not what you think. Everything is energy; everything is an illusion.

The Roman Empire stepped to eliminate the teaching from the Essene, the human ascension. The transformation of your body into a body of light or the rainbow body.

The volume five is *Intonex*. This book tells you that there is no ascension without spirituality, or Divine reconnection. The Alexandria Library linked today's affliction of the world and the secret cabal. It is why CHADD and VIE are going through all these tribulations. They lived during the Egyptian time and came back. The New Template is here, the algorithm 0010110 platform of freedom and renaissance, and when you awaken and become a serious cocreator, the cabal will have no more power over the world.

And as failing has never been an option for CHADD and VIE, the battle is ultimately won, and the Light enlighten the dark.

VIE received the key that unlocked all the chains to the renaissance and freedom of the algorithmic platform 0010110 and a powerful tool from her ancestor Pierre to defeat the unclean trying to stop her in her mission with CHADD. The key Pierre received directly from Louis XIV, the Sun King.

Contents

CHAPTER 1

And I began a New Shamanic Adventure with Intonex

"Shamans were the first healers and teachers. Eventually the wisdoms of the shamans were lost through the trials and travails of humanity. Now in modern age, with technology that grants access to knowledge from around the world, the old wisdom is back, and the most is stunning of ways. Science has actually come to parallel the ancient practice of shamanism. Shamans work with the spirit or the soul, and they work with energy. In the case of shamanic extraction, they are working with misplaced energy. No energy is truly bad from a shamanic perspective. Energy can be misplaced or it isn't in accord with the environment. There are a number of connections between the ancient practice of shamanism and what we understand today. Shamanism was an integral part of humanity for thousands of years. Eventually the wisdoms of the shamans were lost through the trials and travails of humanity."

As the veil keeps thinning, people are becoming more aware that something else exists. You can now gain insights that will give you a full understanding by reading this new book of the series. It will unlock hidden and kept secrets. The answer to who you are, why you are here, what you have been looking for, what has been kept hidden to you by the elite in control, all the lies you have been told, and why they keep you in division and fights for political ideology.

While the time begins, and continues, to collapse, the concept of remembering is gradually replaced with the concept of knowing. At first, *knowing* feels similar to remembering, but you increasingly realize that remembering had doubt, whereas knowing is. In other words, when you know, you are free of all doubt.

I have in front of my eyes, in vision, a big screen appearing on which is written some interesting facts and shown also interesting images at the same time: Planet earth's first civilization was etheric intelligence and was designated to be the guardians of earth, but this ethereal intelligence also needed the help of physical guardians of earth. Dinoids from the Bellatrix system in the constellation of Orion and Reptoid colonies from the constellation of Sagittarius arrived later to inhabit the earth. The Reptoid and Dinoids allowed a mammalian species to evolve to sentiency. These mammals were called the pre-cetaceans. The pre-cetaceans provided food for all three colonies in exchange for technology, which in turn improved their production rate further. These three civilizations coexisted in harmony, trading among one another for over eight million years. All three civilizations developed advanced forms of space-time travel. The pre-cetaceans developed their spiritual side, such as psychic abilities, extensively.

A Dinoid-Reptoid alliance from Bellatrix, believing they were superior to the pre-cetaceans, came to earth to cease all cooperation with the pre-cetaceans and wanted to put them under their control. Over time, the earth Dinoids and Reptoids became more and more influenced by the Bellatrix Dinoid-Reptoid alliance. The pre-cetaceans, through their high psychic abilities, began sensing the aggression against them and came to see the threat presented by the Dinoid/Reptoid civilizations. Being given permission for the earth spiritual hierarchies, the pre-cetaceans decided to implode their fusion reactors located in the Ural Mountain Range. The pre-cetaceans divided into two groups.

One group evacuated out of our solar system to the constellations of Pegasus and Cetus, and the other group altered themselves physically so that they could enter the oceans and find haven. This group is now our present-day cetaceans such as the dolphins and whales. The entire transformation process occurred over a period of four million years.

When the transformation was complete and the later sector was safe, the first sector imploded the fusion reactors, destroying 98 percent of the Dinoid/Reptoid civilizations. The survivors evacuated to the planet in our solar system, Maldek. Now with the Dinoid/Reptoid no longer present on Earth, the Earth's spiritual hierarchies and the cetaceans had to find a suitable guardian for the land. They searched the galaxy for two to three million years before finding what they were looking for. They found, on the fourth planet of the Vega system, a primitive aquatic species that was starting to emerge from the oceans. This species had creation myths, a language, and a hunting and gathering culture.

The spiritual hierarchies of the Vega system were then asked if they would permit this species to be vastly altered genetically to accelerate their evolution so that they may become a guardian species. Vega's spiritual hierarchies agreed. So the traces of the first humans came from the Vega star system. Their technology improved very quickly, and once they had developed star travel technology, they started to migrate into nearby star systems for a period of 2.5 million years.

During this time, the Galactic Federation was formed, Sirius B was colonized, and Earth was selected for seeding. Later Mars and Venus were colonized, and the Hybornea colony was founded on Earth. Dinoid-Reptoids in the meantime had built up their forces and were invading the various colonies throughout the solar system. Hyborean Earth, Mars, and Venus were victims to these attacks, and the Dinoids and Reptoids gained control over the solar system for a period of approximately eighty thousand years.

In response to this, the Galactic Federation planned a counterattack to reintroduce humans into this system. They arranged for a battle planet (four times the diameter of the Earth) to come into the solar system and destroy the planet Maldek, which was the Dinoid-Reptoid stronghold. The remains of the planet Maldek are what we can now see as the asteroid belt. After the destruction of Maldek and the defeat of the Dinoid/Reptoids, a human colony was again established on Earth. It is what we know today as Lemuria. Over the next 850,000 years, the Lemurians spread across the face of the planet. They founded daughter colonies such as Atlantis, Yu, which is now Central China and Tibet, and the Libyan/Egyptian colonies.

The Atlanteans began to acquire a feeling of uniqueness about their culture and wanted to eliminate Lemuria so that they could become the mother country. The Atlanteans began forming alliances with renegade Pleiadians and Alpha Centaurians, which had hierarchical systems of government. They accomplished the destruction of Lemuria by taking the Earth's moon (Earth had two moons in those times).

Out of orbit by using force fields until it was as close as possible to the Lemurian Empire, and then the moon was destroyed, resulting in a catastrophic shower of meteors. This destroyed much of Lemuria, but this also resulted in many pressures being inflicted upon the tectonic plates: resulting in the gas chambers under Lemuria to implode and thus sink most of the Lemurian continent.

Yu Empire would not bow down to the hierarchical rule of Atlantis and Libyan/Egyptian empires and was thus forced to literally go underground. Today, they form what is known as the Kingdom of Agartha or Shambhala.

Then autocracy was born. Atlantis formed ten ruling districts, each with their own king. These kings together formed the governing council of Atlantis. The royal governing council of Atlantis decided that a new form of government was desperately needed in which a superior ruling class could be established and sustained by their pretense that they had been empowered by a god force. Autocracy was thus born and was in full control, enforcing a period of peace and stability. To achieve control over the populace, they started experimenting with the people's DNA and genetics. This resulted in the people's consciousness being reduced, life spans contracted, and psychic/spiritual abilities dramatically decreasing.

Throughout the years, there were many wars among the various empires due to underground movements of people that wanted to have the Lemurian *philosophy* back in place (i.e., no hierarchy). These wars led to vast destruction. As a last resort, the warring empires decided to attack the opponent's crystal temples (which were responsible for maintaining two frozen layers of water about fifteen to thirty thousand feet above ground, which protected people on earth from the harmful sun's rays and also ensured a stable weather pattern at all times).

Unfortunately, the attacks were made simultaneously and caused the firmament (the water layers) to be broken down, and thus millions of gallons of water thus poured down onto the surface, causing what is known biblically as the Great Flood. The breakdown of the firmament also resulted in the polar icecaps freezing and also the many climatic variations we have today to form.

After the flood, only about two million people survived the flood from an original sixty-five known million. Unfortunately, many of the survivors were the mutant humans who had been genetically altered by the Atlanteans into a much lower state of consciousness. Also, the fact that the firmament was now no longer in existence resulted in the DNA and thus consciousness breaking down even further. A few different renegades from Pleiades, Alpha and Beta Centauri came to different places on Earth after the flood, seeing it as an opportune time to establish their own desired ideologies and also be seen as "godlike" and thus reverenced. Being already genetically altered, the surviving humans were therefore easily controlled by these renegades.

Since no form of disobedience to these new "gods" was allowed, the concept of ruling by "divine right" became inculcated on earth. This concept of worshipping an elite has continued through to modern times. Culture would rise against culture in wars claiming that the elite they themselves worshipped were superior to the elite of the opposing faction.

We are now in times, though, that will finally bring to an end an approximate ten thousand years of "semi-consciousness" and regain our full consciousness that we deserve. This will be due to our entire solar system coming into contact with what is known as the Photon Belt.

Then this text appeared from the federation on Lumeria (translated by Sheldon Nidel).

You were mutated into limited conscious beings, and your cluster of realities was also affected. Suddenly, a new paradigm was adopted that favored lack, limitation, power, and division. You lost your connection to your history and to a sacred set of beliefs, which the Anunnaki and their carefully chosen minions replaced with a new conception. As a result, they ruled you as your "gods and goddesses." They brainwashed you to believe that they were your "creators" and that the past wonders of Lemuria and Atlantis were myths. They ordered their minions to institute *writing* as an agent of their own glorification. These acts are recorded in the ancient tablets of Sumer, in the steles of ancient India and in carvings found throughout Europe, Australia, Oceania, Asia, and the Americas. Now as your consciousness expands more quickly, you are coming to see these tales for the elaborate fiction they truly are.

Your origins are not of this world, but are extraterrestrial in nature, and are to be found on a planet that circles the star Vega in the Lyra constellation. Yet you have achieved more than to travel a mere twenty-six light-years to reach your present home. Many millions of years ago, you became part of a vast rebellion by the Light against the dark in this galaxy. The uprising began in Lyra, Cancer, Gemini, and Orion, as well as in many other lesser-known star groupings (constellations). Eventually, this rebellion led to the formation of the Galactic Federation of Light, over four million years ago. At the very core of this battle were the Star League of the Pleiades, the Andromedan Confederation, the Lyra Light League, and the Sirian star-nation. Of these, Sirius is most sacred and the place where the Great Blue Lodge of Creation has chosen to enter this galaxy. Originally, it was defended by Lion people who decided to settle only on two planets in the Sirius A star system. Later, with their permission, humans from Lyra were first to colonize Sirius B and, in time, Sirius C and D.

The Sirian star system is filled with the great energy bestowed by the Great Blue Lodge. This energy obscures its exact configuration. The system is an anomaly. Sirius's energy defies the physics of a star's normal construction. Sirius A and its companions seem to be what they are not. Thus, to your scientists, they appear, incorrectly, to be exceedingly dense. This seeming density is due to the energy exerted upon them by the Blue Light of Creation. From within this Light, Sirius gathers up the great energy and disperses it to the galaxy. This energy also transforms the way in which those who dwell here see themselves and their sacred mission. It has led Sirius to assist in spreading the energy of its galactic society to a multitude of solar systems throughout this galaxy. The "Four Great Laws" were presented, long ago, to humanity on Vega and reached their fullest potential on Sirius. Your ancient Lemurian civilization brought them to Earth, and they were anchored here by its descendants—the Inner Earth realm known as Agartha (Shambhala).

In the language of Sirius B, our star-nation is known as Akonowai, meaning "sacred path of Creation's Light." The third and fourth planets in our system circle a blueish-white star. Its light forms a pattern in our atmosphere that creates a red-orange sky filled with the rare blueish cloud. Most of our vegetation is quite purple-blue in color. Infrequently, it is green, orange, or brown. On our main world, Sirius B's third planet, there is one interconnected sea that contains cetaceans, fish, and many creatures unrelated to any aquatic species existing on your world. We dwell in this land of lush forests, huge mountains, enormous prairies, and very high mountains. Our main cities are located some 50 to 200 miles (80 to 320 kilometers) beneath all this beauty. On the surface are only 144 main temple sites. The largest is the grand temple of Atar, dedicated to the spiritual warrior clan named after our largest bird—a six-foot-tall eagle that we call an Atar.

The dimensions of the grand temple of Atar are astonishing. Its main hall contains 576 columns, each exactly 288 perdums or 312 feet (94.8 meters) in height. Its roof is covered with a special lacework of pure gold to let in the majesty of our sun. Its floor tiles are inscribed with the text of the Great Book of Understanding, in which the Creator bestowed upon humanity the blueprint for physicality and the wisdom to fulfill its potential.

The main hall is most sacred. The remainder of the temple complex is designed to support and accommodate the rituals practiced within. In the exact center of this very large hall is our planet's main node. The temple is situated on a huge cliff that looks out over our one great sea. The energy that emanates from it each day forms a ring of golden light around it. At night, when viewed from the ocean, this light seems like a strong beacon signaling to a ship far out at sea.

The beauty of our world is sacred. Soon, the limitless glories of your world will be apparent once again. Despite all that you have done to her, Mother Earth's magnificence is clearly visible from space. This water-world of yours is utterly exquisite. Soon, most of its deserts and the fierce heat that envelops them will be transformed. Ice caps will vanish and the wonders of your most southern continent will be revealed. As you help to return your world to its original, pristine condition, recall what we have ever so briefly told you about our home. Like the two water planets of Akonowai, your solar system embodies much that is sacred. In a short time, Mars will bloom once more, and the desolation on Venus will metamorphose into a land of abundant oceans that teem with life. Such a destiny awaits you and is truly not as distant as you may imagine.

This realm is shifting in accordance with the sacred decrees of the divine plan, which have established a timetable for your transformation into fully conscious beings. As a result of this process, we have come from all sectors of this galaxy to form your first contact team. We are totally dedicated to completion of the mission that heaven has entrusted to us. Right now, dear hearts, when much is unfolding in your world, you must continue to focus closely upon your sacred intentions. Be firm in your commitment. Know that your victory is inevitable. Know also that you are not alone. Heaven has sent many to assist you. They have come from this and many nearby galaxies, and from the vast orders and life streams of heaven. The will of the Divine will manifest upon this realm, dear ones. Feel it in your heart and remain united in your intentions.

Today, we have examined the elements that are transforming your reality. In doing so, we have given you a brief glimpse of our beautiful realm, which we all deeply love. We in this most sacred organization of Light salute you and fully support what you are actively accomplishing. We now take our leave. Blessings, dear hearts! Know in your hearts and souls that the countless abundance and prosperity of heaven is yours!

Then this is what I heard:

"What are the ascended masters? Well, ascended masters are camouflaged light beings. A few of these Light beings are present today among us in disguised human form. Their energy can transmute eons of psychic layers carried by us within seconds.

'Foxes have dens and birds have nests, but the Son of Man has no place to lay his head' (Matt. 8:19–20; Luke 9:57–58).

Such was the life I led with my beloved, said Mary Magdalene, no. It only was there no stable 'home' for us...there was not much privacy. There were always thongs of people wanting His help.

Add to that...many of the other disciples were jealous of any time Jesus spent with me.

We made it because I knew in my heart that our destinies were intertwined.

I knew He needed my strength to be able to complete His mission.

Yes, there was some sadness and even aggravation, yet the joy so fully overcame any fears I had.

I had faith and then I trusted."

Ascended Master Jesus, his working with the Cosmic Master Omega. He has become the second ray, the yellow ray of wisdom, joy, and lightness of being. As the Chohan of the ray, he focuses the Christ consciousness of the ray onto humanity. He holds this position as he fully embodies the qualities of the second ray. Jesus works with the energies of teaching, unconditional love, joy, forgiveness, and devotion to the Christ within. He has a lot of humor. He has mastered the Lightness of being, He can be serious, as we can all, but his innate being is Lightness and Light. Christ is the name of Jesus's higher self. So when talking about Jesus the Ascended Master, it's really talking about Christ. Master Jesus is aligned with the state of joy and works with the Deva of Joy. The Deva is the animating force of the act of joy and is also aligned with the Deva of Devotion. All the knowledge of the world is not enough to get closer to God but only devotion will get you there. So you need to call on Master Jesus.

And the *Ascended Master Mary Magdalene* works with the energies of the Divine feminine. She is the quintessence of the "female instructor" of paramount important in the dialogue with Jesus in *Pistis Sophia* on the nature of purification and ascension, with his post-resurrection disciples. She stands with those who need warrior energy to deal with issues in their environment. She is best known for the life she spent with Jesus. Mary Magdalene has been both a revered and despised woman of Christianity. She truly is a warrior woman; she coped and through her adversity learned to love all of humanity, and so ascended. She is a master who is strong, yet gentle. There is humor and laughter, yet show her injustice and she stands ready to give her support. If there is an external battle, bullying, abuse any type of external attack, and she will help when asked. Mary Magdalene is working with the Elohim Aloha. Mary Magdalene has recently also formed a working relationship with the Ascended Master El Morya to help erase those who are in personal crisis, finding their personal power, fighting external battles, and have chosen God's will over their own free will. Mary Magdalene's aura colors are mid to strong pink aura with some magenta. She is working with the third ray, the pink ray of unconditional love. If she is your teacher and you are third ray soul, then you will have the qualities of inner strength, openness, and compassion. Your soul color will be pink.

An amazing find was unearthed in the dig of one of the oldest churches in all of Christendom. Inside the church is a 580-foot mosaic with the image of fish and an inscription that reads, "The god-loving Akeptous has offered the table to God Jesus Christ as a memorial." This inscription is the earliest anywhere to mention Jesus and refer to Jesus as God.

The life and times of Jesus continues to fascinate—whether unearthed in an archaeological dig or discovered through the study of the testaments.

Both of them, Jesus and Mary Magdalene were ascended masters but also time travelers. As time travelers and masters, they came in order to assist and direct the trajectory (path) of humanity and assist how to consciously work with the light body and ascension work. Linear time being an illusion. The idea that Jesus and Mary Magdalene were actually married has been a hot topic and, of course, is still being disputed today by religion. Though the Gospel called Mary Magdalene, Jesus's companion. The Gospel says that Jesus has preferred the companion of Mary over any other disciple, and Jesus would kiss Mary on the mouth.

Like the important part of the Bible missing: The Book of Enoch!

Here is the Psalm 23 and its important meaning:

The Lord is my shepherd; I shall not want. There is nothing I lack—The Lord takes us into the Light.

In green pastures he makes me lie down—Green represents the heart chakra. We are to open our hearts to love.

To still waters he leads me—Our hearts become still in love. (Be still and now that it's me.)

He restores my soul and he guides me along right paths for the sake of his name—Karmic debts are released and makes us move toward the Light.

Even though I walk through the valley of the shadow of death, I will fear no evil, for you are with me: your rod and your staff comfort me—With God's protection, we understand that death is an illusion; once fear is transcended, we now live according to a deeper and more expansive new Life.

You set a table before me in front of my enemies—The enemies eat with us because we no longer fear them. God's generosity extends toward all.

You anoint my head with oil—*The oil of sanctification.* The anointing is the sign that we are children of God who belong to the Risen savior.

My cup runneth over. My cup overflows—Abundance is promised, after our initiation along the paths of God. Since our consciousness has shifted, we no longer experience the world as a place of deprivation; rather, the world overflows like a cup of prosperity.

Surely goodness and mercy shall follow me all the days of my life. Indeed goodness and mercy will pursue me all the days of my life—Peace, joy, and freedom are our birthright, which we discover through this anointing.

And I will dwell in the house of the Lord forever. I will dwell in the house of the Lord for endless days—There are many mansions in God's house. All of us have the chance to live there in peace and happiness.

Mary Magdalene was a temple priestess, and four pieces of Gospel evidence strongly point to Mary Magdalene as a temple priestess of the Goddess. Literally Mary of Magdala signifies Mary of the Goddess temple. Christian tradition has said that Mary is of the town of Migdal, which was known as the village of the Doves, a place where sacred doves were bred for the Goddess temple.

Mary Magdalene works with the grid changes of the Earth that support etheric reconnection to Lemuria and Atlantis. In doing this, she supports the Earth and the rapid ascension process of her corresponding body and consciousness back with the fifth dimension. The master symbol "sacred symbol of activation of the sacred lineage" located on Mary Magdalene's third eye consist of the consciousness—the crescent moon and the cosmic symbol of Venus. These symbols represent a sacred lineage of priestess teachings that bestow the Goddess powers of the feminine principles into the consciousness of one's faith. It symbolizes the way of Mary Magdalene.

Mariamene e Maria—Mariamene, also called master. An ossuary is a chest, box, or site to serve as the final resting place of human skeletal remains often used where burial space is scarce. The ossuary of an elite, a *Mara*, or Master.

The *Mara* added at the end of her name, in Aramaic, means "master" or "teacher." Mariamene was performing duties usually restricted to men authority of Jesus.

Mary Magdalene was a woman of means, helping to fund Jesus and his ministry. She went with Jesus on his fateful journey to Jerusalem. From *The Book of Enoch* texts such the *Pistis Sophia* and the *Gospel of Philip*, we glean that Mariamene Magdalene was called "chosen among women," and she performed miracles and baptized converts.

She died at the Jordan River *near Jerusalem*, not in France or Ephesus as later tradition suggests. Mariamene, Mary Magdalene was indeed a Mara.

CHAPTER 2

Ignatz

One day an entity named Ignatz told me that I will write about the link between Color and Sound and Love and the Love beyond passion. And you will see that it is all about Love, which was Jesus teaching.

Intonex is a revelatory guidance of the hidden truth for your growth if you seriously want to get align to your destiny that I, VIE, received through sometimes bizarre, others magical, or unexpected ways of experiences and channeling knowledge that I can share with you through my series of writings like this fifth volume. Though it is necessary to begin with volume 1 to be able to understand and to take the necessary steps to your personal growth, as it may be a lot to learn for some.

But it all began in that life for him, my blue flame, from the surrogate womb to the psychiatric ward. She, the surrogate mother, knew what she was doing. She wanted him for herself and also to stop his mission and twist his destiny. The archon, the harsh worker, wanted to keep him in an altered state to suck his energy because archons live on human energy. To make money from him but also use this money to pay others to control him.

She gave the opportunity to three women working for the cabal, one in justice that is also an archon, a legal worker, and one in health to keep him away in drugs and control him.

Though he is the catalyst for this all adventure, and for the beginning of the rest of our life.

Then my right ear became deaf for ten days to stop others from coming to me. I could not hear them, my left eye sight went briefly bad, and the optometrist thought that I was losing sight and even suggested me to have surgery. This was for me not to see people that needed me. Then I got the flu with bone pains, runny nose, followed by the throat and postnasal. The postnasal was the worst, it lasted the longest, and it was giving me the feeling that I could not breathe many times. The mouth being the vehicle of the soul.

This all fight goes back more than two centuries. It started to the times the force was trying to stop the Messiah to be born and trying to kill Mother Mary.

There was also a primary energy to stop the Jews from receiving the Messiah.

The first hard attack started to go against the Virgin Mary, so that the child was to be born dead or for her to die. But the Angels were strong and powerful to protect us. I am connected to the Virgin Mary, so I was under great attack back then and baby Jesus had to be taken to Egypt.

My body still has a genetic link to the Virgin Mary. I am here to introduce you to the seventh ray used by the highest lords, like the Lords of Light, to combine the mathematical frequencies of color within ranges that are inaudible to the ears. I came forth with immense love for you and for humanity. Love is my role, purpose, and gift that I am here to give to you, inspired by my connection and Divine relationship with the Creator.

Memories of limitations, lack, suffering, and fear are often acknowledged by you as being, or creating, pain and anguish.

Now is the time to realize that your journey continues. You are called to wake up to a new paradigm of freedom and in authenticity.

"As the energy of our universe flows, it resonates in complex geometric patterns. When you begin to understand this geometry, you begin to understand the underlining of all reality. This is why many mystery schools try to keep this all a secret."—David Wilcock

We, the God Duo, came to demonstrate the path of Divine Love. The end results of infinite growth is to realize oneness. The meaning of Light, being growth in consciousness through mental, physical, and mind experiences, like pain, stress, anger, fear, illnesses, and diseases that many of you are actually subjected to. Once you understand and have acknowledged it, you should be able to move ahead and find your way.

But remember that you do not need any whistles and belts, gurus, or "DNA pills" to get you reconnected and ascend.

CHAPTER 3

The Zero Point

As I started my next phase of my spiritual work while CHADD is kept away, the guardian person from the Akasha appeared in the room to start me on my next spiritual work. His name is Ignatz, and he was assigned at the task in the records. He received the permission to pull the file for me; I was now given the gift to receive from the Akashic all of the lost past information.

The Akashic record is where all information are stored in. This sort of universal filing system contains every action and thought, every word and deed, every idea and imaging that has ever was or will be. The Akashic field, also called zero-point field. The hall, or library, of the Akashic records also contain our collective wisdom.

Another entity named Ignatz was coming to me now to permanently work with me because of my next phase and task. He received the authorization to pull and open the file for me. But he did not pull and opened my files as some very poisonous alien parasites were immediately put in my body, not only to unbalance my body and weaken me maybe to death, but also to be able to see and hear everything. And I had to receive it another way. But what God wants, God always gets and I surely did receive.

So my next spiritual work is to rewrite information lost from the past.

The rediscovery of the past knowledge lost with the burning of the Alexandria Library was never burned but kept hidden in the Vatican Library about the link between colors and sound. It has to be with the beginning of the rest of our life. While we have to go through a series of bittersweet events before reunion can show and arise.

Am I to ignore the bittersweet and just focus on the book information I am asking myself? Because I was told of some bittersweet events that will happen soon.

And I saw a big mouth from which information flow out of it. Then I saw the ear that receives the information. I quickly said, "Arise, O Lord! And let thine enemies be scattered!" and I heard voices saying, "And let those that hate thee flee before thy eyes. Amen."

Now as Mary Magdalene, I am inviting you all to prayer for protection and say this powerful protection prayer given by Saint Germain: "I am now calling for the activation of the Violet Flame Grid of Light of transformation and protection, with the legions of Michael as well as the Melchizedec Lords of Light to form around my body, my home, my office, my works in general, my car, my computers, website, business, books, music, loved ones, my coworkers, and my friends. To protect my personal environment and help alleviate harmful energies from earth and all humankind, visualizing it spiraling and spinning around everyone and everything."

And to defeat the devil, repeat days and nights: "Lord Jesus Christ, have mercy on me and the entire world. Amen." This is for the benefit of the whole world. Repeat it again and again. (It will burn the devil.)

CHAPTER 4

The Gnostic View of Early Christianity (Alexandria)

That time, I came in connection with an entity called Flour. This entity wanted to lead me to some and the most important part recovery knowledge of the Alexandria Library and at the same time show me the connection with CHADD's tribulations in his journey. The link to his familiar environment, why his relatives sold him to a mind control program initiated by the Nazi, and recovered by the CIA. To understand clearer how and what happened to him, and also how and what it has to do with the system, the era, why the fake news, the pharmaceutical companies, drugs, vaccinations, chemtrails, implanted virus Klebsi plague, created pollution, human disappearance, the kidnaping and the raping of children, tortures, wars, the terrorists, the banking system, and the poverty in the world etc., the archons, the Illuminati elites in power and key places around the world and the link with the disparition of the Alexandria Library's documents and the importance of it to understand this "modern day."

It all goes back to the Egyptian world and Babylon. It has to do with the Illuminati elites, the controllers of this world, the Roman Church, the Rosicrucian, the Jesuit, the banking system, the

MK-Ultra, the melting of the Ross Ice Shelf, pre-Adamite, and the Phoenician alphabet.

In 1945, a sealed jar was discovered in Egypt, north of Luxor with loads of documents in leather-bound. The suppression, as banned documents and their burial on the cliff at Nag Hammadi, turned out were both part of a struggle critical for the formation of early Christianity. The Nag Hammadi texts and others like them were denounced as heresy by the Orthodox Christians in the middle of the second century. Many early followers of Christ were condemned by other Christians as heretics.

The Nag Hammadi Gnostic texts told about the beliefs and the perceptions of the people called the Gnostics. And the Gnostics had a completely different view of reality than religion. Which is why the Roman Catholic Church and the Romans tried to destroy them whenever they got any strength in any foothold. The Great Library of Alexandria had like half a million scrolls detailing the beliefs and the history of the ancient world part by the Roman Church. The most important part is hidden from the public eyes in the inaccessible to the public Vatican Library. The Cathars were also destroyed by the Roman Church. The religious establishment wanted these "dangerous" (to them) people destroyed because they had the truth hidden to the people, and they did not want them to know.

One-fifth of the Nag Hammadi texts were about a force called the archons. They say they created our physical universe, and they equated them with the Judeo-Christian Yahweh Jehovah God. And in these texts, it says that archon means "prime ruler authorities," also the lord of the archon named Demiurge was a fake God that created our physical, or material, reality as we perceive it.

It said that the Demiurge archon had no creativity, no imagination, and envied the humans. All archons are like a robotic race that can imitate and mimic but not innovate. They are parasites and possess humanity; they are deception and inversion. They can even possess your body. They are very good at twisting what exists. They are deceivers and deception is known to be from the devil. They are satanic and worship Lucifer. What they do in the world is that they create an inversion of the natural order; invert the word *evil*, and you have *live*, which is the inversion and distortion of life. They are obsessed about killing and destroying. Distortion of the natural order that is about life and abundance. Take a look at the system with the elite archons in power; they destroy life through wars, created pollution, environmental devastation, and the melting of the Ross Ice Shelf. They created political terrorism by dividing the people with their illusionary world.

The archon world described by the Gnostics is of a death cult with no creative imagination and a psychotic mind. They are in fact psychopaths, have no empathy, no remorse, no shame, are parasites of the society, and target the population. They are pathological liars, have no feelings for others and for whatever others can go through, and do whatever it takes to get their end goal achieved. They have no limits because they are deprived of emotions. These people manifested in world leaders, are pathological liars, and have the ability to create virtual realities controlling perception. Inducing a virtual reality experience, manipulating humanity, human minds, by creating illusions. They make something appear to happen that does not, programming a distortion of our perception. So they are retaining CHADD in psychotropic drugs in Chateau Ushi Asylum to parasite his mind under MK-Ultra programming. The idea is to disconnect the human brain and lock into in this tiny set of frequencies, which he'll then perceive as that there is to see.

The Gnostics text also say, "The archons made a bad copy of our original reality." Their idea was to create an illusionary reality and replace the old reality by tuning human into that bad copy, then you think that it's real because that's the only reality you can perceive. Then they can feed them a different information source, tune into it, and the human brain decodes a different reality. The modern human history. Now it becomes dominant frequency, and when you can create a dominant frequency, you can start to entrain the human decoding system into that frequency, and suddenly many are decoding a completely different reality. That's how they control and enslave people. It is the actual control by the system to keep people in a fake reality and keep them into slavery by ignorance, if you do not realize what is happening. We could compare it to a computer virus introducing into the original file fake information, distort, damage, slow the system, show messages, and take control. They can't create but can distort what already exists. The world leaders, which are the system, are vampires.

There is another main reason why they do that. They need to feed themselves, and they can only be fed by your energy. They feed on low energy, which is the human emotions like fear, anxiety, frustration, anger, grief, conflict, and wars. All that is distortion of the natural order. All these emotions are essential to them and their energetic survival.

The archons are inorganic and artificial. They created the inorganic parts of the solar system but the sun, the moon, and the earth were a system that were of itself and different of the rest. There are many different names around the ancient world for the archons, for the same force seen all over the world.

The pre-Gnostic people that ran the Great Library of Alexandria also manifested in the Cathars in Southern France. And they say that the archons are made from luminous fire, are called jinn according from Islamic and pre-Islamic belief, and are made from smokeless. They are also called serpent of gods, or Chitauri, or children on the serpent, or Anunnaki in Sumer (Irak) Babylon. Like they are known as snake brothers to the Hopi, demons to the Christians, and archons to the Gnostics.

The Nag Hammadi library, called chenoboskion manuscripts or the Gnostic Gospels, is a collection of thirteen ancient books called codices containing over fifty texts discovered in upper Egypt in 1945. The fifty texts discovered in Nag Hammadi, Egypt, include secret gospels, poems, and myths attributing to Jesus sayings, beliefs, which are very different from today's New Testament.

"These are secret words of the living Jesus spoke, and which the twin, Judas Thomas, wrote down"—fragments of Greek Gospel of Thomas. Did Jesus have a twin brother as implied?

According to Thomas, this text identified itself as a secret gospel and contained many sayings known from the New Testament but placed in unfamiliar contexts, suggesting other dimensions of meaning. Jesus said, "If you bring forth what is within you, what you bring forth will save you. If you do not bring forth what is within you, what you do not bring forth will destroy you."

The reconnection to the heart chakra and of the DNA.

The companion of the Savior, Mary Magdalene, but Christ loved her more than all the disciples and used to kiss her often on her mouth, and the rest of the disciples were offended and said to him, "Why do you love her more than all of us?"

Besides the Gospel of Thomas and the Gospel of Philip were found included the Gospel of Truth and the Gospel of the Egyptians (the sacred book) of the Great invisible James, the Apocalypse of Paul, the letter of Peter to Philip, and the Apocalypse of Peter.

The Thunder Perfect Mind offers an extraordinary poem in the voice of a feminine Divine power.

> For I am the first and the last. I am the honored
> one and the scorned one.
> I am the whore and the Holy one.
> I am the wife and the virgin…
> I am the barren one, and many are her sons…
> I am the silence that is incomprehensible.
> I am the utterance of my name.

CHAPTER 5

The Importance of Colors, the Etheric Body, Your Holographic and Energetic Body of Light

Now that the same entity, Ignatz, gave me these information that I shared above with you, you must be aware of the importance of predominant colors on our behavior, but also on our organism, and our spiritual life is now recognized. Colors open doors to other worlds and influence us.

If you take green for example, it is not only known to be healing color, but it will help you when you are discouraged and with depression. In creativity time, it will stimulate the spirit of invention, but excess of green will engender a sensation of cold and will provoke the lack of self-esteem. Violet is good for meditation and brings intuition and Divine inspiration. Too much violet and you could lose sense of reality. But when you applied it the right amount of time within a month, you will higher your energy.

Aura is also called the etheric body and reflects the color of the moment. The aura is the mirror of the soul. Colors change if you are tired, stressed, happy… It is in the aura that are the signs of the symptoms before illness appears. Each color has its specific characteristic and a very precise function. When not in sync at short-term, the body and spirit of the individual will slowly begin to degrade and degenerate. There is a direct relationship between the aspect of the color of your aura and the function of the endocrines glands that are linked to the chakras. Each layer of light in the composition of the aura corresponds to one of the seven vital centers of the body or chakras, and of the good balance of each chakra depends the good function of the various physical organs and the mental clarity.

The human body is a wonderful machine in which all elements are interdependent. Like the rainbow that is birthed from the rain and the sun reflect the perfection of Divine creation. But the rainbow of the human body very often presents some irregularities, dysfunctions, but nothing is ever impossible to cure because the human cells renew itself every seven years.

There are seven colors to the rainbow, like in the body. Red is the first ray, or the will. The father energy that is anchored through red, through the red organ that is the pituitary gland.

Blue is love and wisdom, the healing energy, the sun energy, the Christ energy, and is anchored through the heart. Everything related to blue relates to that energy at one point.

Green represents the thyroid gland and is the female, it's the Holy Ghost, a synthesis of the red and blue. Red, blue, and green are the primary forces.

Orange or the yellow region, there you get into the synthesis of other energies. It's the mental power that the Pleiadians call the array of concrete science. It is the mental power.

When you are getting into the dark blue, you are getting into the astral plane. The emotional body. Where you go to sleep at night, the emotional plane of energy.

Violet, or the base of the spine, down at reproduction, which then rotates up and down around the top of your body and also causes creation.

It is scientifically verified that 7 is when the universe is connecting with you and 777 means synchronistic is happening to you. Universal is that source energy communicating with you.

All these energies are not just static in the body. They are moving all the time.

You can break substances into one of those forces. Vitamin A is very powerful in the immune system and a red force; it's the will-power. B complex is the fourth energy, which is compassion energy and a yellow force. And when you relate vitamin to a feeling that you do or do not have, like when you do not want to do something, you do not have the will to do something, then your body needs something in the immune system related to red, the will, and you need vitamin and need chromium. Chromium is also the first element to take when you start to have a runny nose or a scratchy throat, like with any sign of any kind of physical symptoms coming. Chromium also produces helper T-cells. Many make the mistake when they have a cold or runny nose of jamming in large amounts of vitamin C, but it's wrong because the life force in the body is now being directed toward the virus that is giving you the cold or runny nose. Like with antibiotics, it will fight bacteria but not fight viruses. It will instead feed them.

Dots found in the aura are generally, for most, coming from negative thoughts and emotions, and it can result from discomfort to diseases.

One of the principal objective of the application of light in chromotherapy consists in regenerating the aura to allow it to regain its initial, absolute perfection of the seven rays of light that compose it. The more the human being grows in harmony and symphony with its spirituality, the more the aura grows in power and Light.

You are holographic and energetic body of Light. Illness is when you are resonating in a low frequency. There is disharmony; some of the organs are out of sync.

Sound is universal language. Love and Light are the universal healers. Water is the universal solvent. Sacred Geometry is the knowledge key. The fabric of the universe is vibration and colors.

Musical notes open all the doors for spiritual renaissance. Love is the universal healer, and the heart is a resonating magnet.

Music Sound is the universal language. Words are sound that are frequency.

Love is the universal healer, and nothing can replace the human heart to heal.

Water is the universal solvent. Water is a conduit.

Sacred Geometry is a universal language that unites all forms of life, human, animals, plants…and a knowledge key for shifting to a new paradigm of universal wholeness and loving interconnectedness.

On this planet, at that time, I am your gateway of Light that encourages you to explore my synthesis with the Creator as well as your own and my vibratory transformation energy. My name is VIE, which means life and is the Egyptian ankh.

I am here to activate your DNA, attune your light frequency, and initiate your power energy. I came to also give you very important information hidden to you.

"The DNA can be adjusted to accommodate higher frequencies of Light. By combining Light radiations in a neutral zone coupled with a sacred Geometry form. I am than able to cooperate in the connecting of the DNA-RNA nuclei to chromosomes of another evolutionary inheritance. It is all about attuning, balancing, and reconnecting the body. This process enables to go into equivalent bodies of different Light thresholds and selectively breed to obtain positive characteristic from the gene pool of advanced galactic civilizations. Along with this I use the Light language, which is a language coded of Life which is beyond the biological language of acid denaturation." (J. J. Hurtak)

Once your DNA is loaded into a robot or implants embedded within you, and you accept artificial intelligence into your physical body, you are a robot. The decision whether or not you will be your own sovereign being begins with a firm intention to eliminate technology as best as you can from your world. Keep it out your skin and by no means allow it to enter the tissues and bloodstream. The chip, tattoo, nanoparticles in the bloodstream, bionic body parts, the holographic brain implants. This is not who you came to be nor who you are.

We all carry two different genes. The physical genes from our ancestors, our family, and the spiritual genes. The spiritual genes for me go way back before the time that I was Mother Mary. It goes back to the Atlantis time. My name was Megali Thoosa-Row. I was a scientist and invented a form of synthetic skin for burned people and deformed areas in the body. An antidote for skin deformity, burns, acne…

I asked my ancestor Pierre, who has a very powerful chevron, to use his chevron and help me go back to that time before I was attacked. It only took him seventeen seconds to do it.

And now, today, I am a doorway, a vortex. I am the portal of spiritual knowledge, awareness, and practice delivered into the daily lives of human beings. I am a point of vortex to be transformed into this physical lives. Where spirit converted into matter. I am bringing work information. I am the point, where the point is coming through me. This writing work is also flowing through me.

The same dark force, before Pierre my ancestor used his powerful chevron, implanted in me some alien parasites. These parasites were sucking my energy by depleting me of all my nutrients and making me sweat all nights and unable to sleep. This was also their way to change my blueprint and separate me from my Divine husband and our reunion for our commune mission.

They wanted to stop my work and tried to block the information on the link between the Light and the Sound vibration burned in the fire that has destroyed part of the Alexandria Library.

But I am not alone. I did not come alone, but with my blue flame, like we have for thousands of years. We travel together. We also astral project and travel in the past, present, and future.

I am here with him like we were together in Atlantis and in Egypt.

I was then Megali…and we still share, now in this journey, the same great Love that we did as a Divine married couple can.

We are the chosen ones. I am his Light and he is completing me with his Sound. He is the Sound.

We are sharing one mutual mission and we are called the God Duo.

We are CHADD and VIE. Like we were Christ and Mary Magdalene. Our spiritual love for each other has never stopped. We are here so that you can awaken to a new reality and remember who you are to reach your ultimate goal, to reach the promised land.

To reach the promised land, you need to travel with us, under our guidance, through Colors, Light, Sound, and Sacred Geometry forms and receive Divine reconnection. Reconnection of the heart and at the heart center.

We are here to show you the path of Oneness.

Alchemy and Atlantis: CHADD and I were already working together in Atlantis, and I was an alchemist, like CHADD was a high priest and working with me. Alchemy is not about making gold from lead. Alchemy is about an ancient process that stems from a civilization, which was far more advanced than ours: Atlantis. The magical healing waters used come from underground caves.

CHAPTER 6

Maria Prophetissa

know now that I am also known as Maria Prophetissa, or the Lady of the Lake in the Arthurian legend. Notre-Dame or Our Lady in Masonic and Templar tradition. I was one of the greatest teachers of mankind. A troubadour and a messenger who thought to bring the truth and light into the world of men. I and my beloved family of friends, along with my descendants and ancestors, kept this simple truth and method alive for generations dating back to times immemorial, "the gospel of peace." The very DNA itself and the emerald of Thoth, the mighty chlorophyll, wherein all of life's wisdom resides. These are the door and lock, through which all will be admitted, to the tantric wedding chamber, where the light, power, and majesty of the mitochondria are made manifest. I have come back to tell you the truth. I am the companion and wife of Jesus. I am a gifted visionary teacher, vibrational transformation healer, and the best qualified disciple to lead Jesus's movement as I was before. I experienced a reunion, reuniting vision with Jesus and received advanced teaching about the fate of the soul and the meaning of salvation. I am his feminine part and was an alchemist.

.666 is the counterfeit DNA and the Pauline Christianity referred to in the twentieth century by scholars who noted historical references from the second century to differences in the teaching of Paul with the teachings of Jesus. These differences were attributed as being the foundations of Christian Gnosticism, which is a pagan version.

.618 is the original DNA replication and original Jesus movement, opposed to those counterfeit commands issued by a virus and other parasitic entities that exist at microscopic and subatomic levels, the .666.

Mitochondria are the cell's power producers. They are the sites of cellular respiration and convert energy into forms that are usable by the cell.

The chakras must be tuned and they must each learn to recognize one another and differentiate between commands issued by the conductor, the Master Architect. Chakras are the seven nexus within the human body, when the subtle nervous system interface.

Search for deeper understanding often leads beyond the Bible itself. The reincarnation is yet misunderstood of how RNA-DNA operates as a superconductive memory storage and processing apparatus.

RNA-DNA is an organization's data passed along for use by future generations through (hardwired) reproductive process and through (wireless and subconscious) utilizing the superconductive resources of (ORMEs) ORMUS nanoparticles that are bound naturally occurring in nature. RNA-DNA operates as superconductive memory storage processing apparatus.

Mary Magdalene's role in the dispensation of the truth has enjoyed a fair amount of scrutiny and ridicule. "But wasn't I a leader among the Apostle, and that is why I have been portrayed down through the ages as a repentant prostitute?"

It has taken two thousand years for the true message to resurface. Didn't I told you that I came back with a gift for you that will take two thousand years for humanity to process? Here it is.

Wisdom and knowledge of the Christ teaching have resurfaced now, two thousand years later. My ultimate purpose in my teaching is to support the world as it moves forward.

If you had found a path to *immortality*, you would surely want to share your discovery with other good people. The only problem would then be convincing others that your method works. Because this is bad for business where slave traders and authoritarian rulers are concerned. From their point of view, it is better that you should die young and leave a new collection of slaves to take your place. Your children before you had lived enough to figure it all out and rebel.

Welcome to your actual system managed and conducted by the unclean, *the cabal.*

Gold is classified as a chemical element. Its chemical symbol is Au and its atomic number is 79. And thus, it will be easy to manipulate with harmonic resonance frequency technology. It will be the mixing of certain elements with a spoon made of radio waves. The India Scientific Community is already working on isolating all the different frequencies needed to manipulate matter into whatever they want, and they are teaching it to their college students. This technology does nothing more than point radio waves at a certain object using a certain frequency. It's all done with nothing more than *radio waves.*

Gold is a powerful electrical conductor and tends to bring the golden you to the surface.

Alchemy is not about transmutation of metals. It's not about making gold from lead. It's an ancient process that stems from a civilization that was far more advanced: Atlantis. The ancient tribes of Moses's time were taught by the Akhenaten priests to make powerful, revitalizing elixirs that restored the breath of life and opened the devotee to talk to God. One such elixir was manna, which in dried form was called the Bread of the Light of God. The tradition for making this substance goes way back in history along with its amazing vessel: the Holy Grail. The effects are profoundly spiritual, stimulating vibrant life force and promoting an extended life span.

Thoth, named the father of alchemy, taught humans how to extend their lifetime to one thousand years and beyond. His Atlantean alchemy was the foundation of the "fountain of youth" myth.

Moses attempted to feed those just liberated slaves of Egypt, with the manna, which would have set them free, and he returns with the ORMUS from the Temple of Hathor to discover that the majority of those people had unwittingly rendered themselves unworthy of the sacrament. Does history repeat itself?

The Israelites come to the wilderness of sin. They murmur for food, God promises bread from heaven, God sends quails and manna. Particulars respecting the manna (22–31). An omer of manna to be preserved (322–36).

At evening, the quails fell out and the manna was rained from heaven.

God hears all the murmurings. God promises a speedy and constant supply. He tried whether they would trust him, and rest satisfied with bread of the day in its day. Thus he tried if they would serve him, and it appeared how ungrateful they were. When God plagued the Egyptians, it was to make them know he was their Lord; when he provided for the Israelites, it was to make them know he was their God.

"The word of God is the manna by which our souls are nourished" (Matt. 4:4).

"The comforts of the Spirit are hidden manna" (Rev. 2:17).

The manna must not be hoarded up, but eaten; those who have received Christ, must by faith live upon him; and not receive his grace in vain.

Seek earnestly for the grace of the Holy Spirit, to turn all the knowledge of the doctrine of Christ crucified, into the spiritual nourishment of your souls by faith and love.

See here the folly of hoarding. The manna laid up by some, who thought themselves wiser, and better managers, than their neighbors, and who would provide lest it should fail next day, bred worms, and became nothing. That will provide to be most wasted, which is covetously and distrustfully spared.

"Such riches are corrupted" (James 5:2).

CHAPTER 7

Then I had a dream...to Warn You to Awaken to the Truth or You Will Be Held Accountable

My Mystical Journey Continues

Ten days later, I had an important and informative dream. I was driving the car and my coworker is in the back of the car behind me. Suddenly two small, round little things with big ears appear in front of the car. They were looking like two animated hedgehog toys with pointed ears, and the car stopped running. The driver of the car behind us came to the window. I saw that a tall and strong man was approaching the car, and I wanted to be careful and asked my passenger not to roll its window down, but it was too late; his window was rolled a quarter down. Luckily the man stared at us without a word, then turned around and went back to his car. Then the car started working and running very slowly though, again. What was that for? Who was he? Was it to slow our work?

I was given the vision of what they did when they operated the CERN again. The scientists looking at accessing heaven with the CERN accessing a portal to hell, and they released these small demonic creatures. And my spirit guide is telling me:

"The discovery of the so-called particle was first announced love the Higgs boson, so far an elusive theory that holds matter together. Crash two proton beams into each other three times more force than ever before. Then scientists wanted to build a machine ten times the size of the Large Hadron Collider, "recreating" the process of creation itself, they said. They wanted a large future collider needed to explore these fundamental mysteries more deeply, possibly revealing the need for a paradigm shift. Because if you get to even higher dimensional energy, it could be possible to make higher dimensional black holes. Talking about a machine that will take right back at the beginning of time itself, sharing information between scientists around the world supposedly, but making decision that could affect people outside the laboratory when work is done behind closed doors and virtually all of science is kept secret from everybody. Because the incentive system is set up such that if you tell somebody else your genius idea, some other lab is going to do it.

So rush it, publish first, and get all the credit, and you get none. This is an insane way to set up scientific system. No one in their right mind building it from scratch would say, "We should do it this way." Why would you do that if you want to engage with a community?

When you start talking about opening portals and demons and the awakening of Osiris or the Antichrist, people are going to want to know how they know these things if it's not apparent to them as it is to the scientists involved in the experiment. So for those people who do not really believe in those things, the only concern should be if the events, the experiments conducted at CERN, are dangerous or not. And CERN knows that the most common concern about the public is that they may open up some black hole that sucks us all in or destroy the earth. So they have taken measures to assure all people that their experiments are perfectly safe. But they are producing cosmic rays in our planet, and what they have to say to the public about the safety of this is that the fact that the earth and the sun are still here rules out the possibility that cosmic rays were due to the LLC and could produce charged microscopic black holes."

The big athletic looking man that appeared in my vision was one of the Guardians sent to make sure that these small creatures are doing correctly their demonic work.

I received this dream because their plan is based on evil, and I am here to warn you to awaken yourself.

The small interdimensional creator, realized into the world, cannot be seen. They are here to destroy machinery, trains, airplanes… They are here to stop many electronics. They are responsible for the failing computers on airplanes. They are the one behind the airplanes that are stuck on the ground due to failing computers and the incident that happen with the Chinese doctor on surbooking a US plane.

You must know and understand that when one comes into a physical body, many times they are locked into layers of matter. But the Spirit is still alive, and so those of you that are stuck in it, it is important that you get in touch with who you are. No matter how hard, you will be free of it by emphasizing the power inside of you, the power of your Soul.

The enluminades (the cabal) like to control, and it's a matter of creating with labs. This is not your fault; it's what is happening on the planet now. But you will be held accountable for not helping, for not making the effort to reconnect with the Divine.

Because this is the answer to your question, why am I here for?

CHAPTER 8

This Dream Was Followed by an Event a Few Days Later in Park Avenue

A few days later, as I was having a coffee with my friend Mila in Park Avenue, I saw a black man approaching our table but in a very funny way. It was one of these few but perfect weather. Not hot, not cold, blue sky. Families were out with their children walking on the pavement or eating outside restaurants and small cafés. People were happy, and you could feel the energy of happiness and joy. The black man was kind of hiding himself from my view, obviously trying to take pictures of me. First behind a small tree, then passed in front of us, hiding within the flow of the people walking. He was wearing a skirt with long short under it, and it was hard not to notice him. *What was that for?* I thought. Then he disappeared behind the wall to come back, and while he passed me, I heard him saying, "The Owl is the symbol of the Illuminati domination. They have nowhere to go. It's the moment of truth for science. Reincarnation is an established scientific fact. Clues are scattered throughout the Bible and many other ancient teaching. The New Template is here."

Then followed a Japanese couple, and the man began to take pictures of me, quickly passing me. Came back from the back, crossed the road, faced us again, and he took several other pictures. One of these weird experiences in my journey. Another weird experience. Where is that going to lead me now?

On my way driving back home, the phone rang and I heard an angelic voice saying, "Do you know that *Bible* stands for basic information before leaving earth and that *CIA* stands for Catholic Intelligence Agency? They gave their time machine to the CIA to look at the past and future. Goddess Hathor was the goddess of music and transformation. Toth, the oldest son of Ra hatched the world egg—he is an ibis bird," then the phone went dead.

I suddenly found myself driving in a place I had no idea where it was, somewhere in the middle of nowhere. The vegetation was untouched, growing wild. My coworker was sitting next to me with a big smile on his face. The music was loud and pure. I was out of my body driving the car and had no idea where and why I was there. But the music was surely hypnotic, and it felt great. It was pure harmony and balance. Reflecting joy and perfection. No one was on the road or on the side of the road. I could not see any houses or any people around. We were riding the music of the sphere, and I heard, "Do not forget what you just received about the owl symbol, the Bible, and what it means, and everything else you just heard."

Then I woke up.

CHAPTER 9

The Illuminades and the Dinosaurs

I woke up and glanced at my phone and saw a strange text. "Good morning. I am able to travel under your ocean, and I leave in your underground. Signed, Illuminades."

As soon as I had finished reading, the text disappeared from the screen.

Another weird and incomprehensible event, I thought.

Then I called for the activation of the violet flame grid of transformation and protection, and I heard this name, Flour, saying, "I am here to answer your questions."

"On this planet, dinosaurs were human being like us and were killed by the advent of a rock 6,500 years ago that hit the earth. But not of all them. Some of them could not stand the Light and went to leave underground and advanced themselves and survived.

Not only have the dinosaurs not been extinct, but there is plenty of evidence the many are still alive. The deception comes with the wealthy Croesus dynasty, who owns many excavation sites around the globe and rules the financial world. They are an Illuminati family who wants to keep many as unsecured and unaware of mankind's beginning as possible. If you do not know where you come from, how on earth can you know where you are going?

They are many references to living dinosaurs in the Bible. They are referred to Leviathan in some part, and there are countless passages that refer to "dragons" as well as "dinosaurs" that is a relatively modern term, which means "awful lizard." And there are numerous ancient writings where dragons were referred as living at the same times as humans.

They conspire to control the world affairs, by master minding events and by planting agents in government and corporations in order to influence and establish a new world order, pulling the strings levels in dozens of novels, films, television shows, comics, video games, and music videos.

The evolution is a fact for every creature, and they became scientific, from reptile to one time the group evolved to human forms.

They came, creatures that now want to control the planet. This is part of the UFO that can be seen. Not all, but they control one particular UFO. They can shapeshift. They do not come from another planet and do not want human beings anymore.

There is more than a war between Syria, Afghanistan, and other countries; their purpose is to kill as many as human beings.

Their planet is been based on evil, and it is time that people realize it. People have to stop thinking that they are coming from another planet, from the cosmos, and look like humans.

The Illuminades know the power of appearance, they are looking like humans, though they shapeshift, and human beings must be aware of it.

When one that is not from the Illuminades comes into a physical body, many times they are locked into layers of matter. But the Spirit is still alive, and so those of you that are stuck in it, it is important that you get in touch with who you are. No matter how hard, you will be free of it by emphasizing the power inside of you. The power of your Soul."

Wow! That gave me a lot to reflect on and, on what my coworker is going through living on this planet.

CHAPTER 10

The Ascended Masters, the Brotherwoods, and the Galactic Command

And Flour continues, "Ascended Master Mary Magdalene works with the energies of the Divine feminine. She is the quintessence of the *female instructor* of paramount important in the dialogue with Jesus in *Pistis Sophia* on the nature of purification and ascension, with his post-resurrection disciples. She stands with those who need warrior energy to deal with issues in their environment. She is best known for the life she spent with Jesus. Mary Magdalene has been both a revered and despised woman of Christianity. She truly is a warrior woman; she coped and through her adversity learned to love all of humanity, and so ascend. She is a master who is strong, yet gentle. There is humor and laughter, yet show her injustice and she stands ready to give her support. If there is an external battle, bullying, abuse any type of external attack, and she will help when asked. Mary Magdalene is working with the Elohim Aloha. Mary Magdalene has recently also formed a working relationship with the Ascended Master El Morya to help erase those who are in personal crisis, finding their personal power, fighting external battles, and have chosen Gods will over their own free will. Mary Magdalene's aura colors are mid to strong pink aura with some magenta. She is working with the third ray, the pink ray of unconditional love. If she is your teacher and you are third ray soul, then you will have the qualities of inner strength, openness, and compassion. Your soul color will be pink.

Ascended Master Jesus is working with the Cosmic Master Omega. He has become the second ray, the Yellow Ray of Wisdom, Joy, and Lightness of Being. As the Chohan of the ray, he focuses the Christ consciousness of the ray onto humanity. He holds this position as he fully embodies the qualities of the second ray. Jesus works with the energies of teaching, unconditional love, joy, forgiveness, and devotion to the Christ within. He has a lot of humor. He has mastered lightness of being, He can be serious, as we can all, but his innate being is lightness and Light. Christ is the name of Jesus's Higher Self. So when talked about Jesus the Ascended Master, it's really talking about Christ. Master Jesus is aligned with the state of joy and works with the Deva of Joy. The Deva is the animating force of the act of joy and is also aligned with the Deva of Devotion. All the knowledge of the world is not enough to get closer to God, but only devotion will get you there. So you need to call on Master Jesus."

Thank you!

CHAPTER 11

A Rapid Glimpse to the Fifth Dimension

I began my Tuesday morning like usual. I sat in my private spot and got into a deep meditative state, lost track of time, and left my body to access another dimension.

Foremost for a meeting. I found myself in a beautiful conference room. The building is made of pure crystal and gold, I smell the essential oil burning; the feeling of harmony in the room gets me in an unexpected, because never experienced before, well-being state. It is a "still" kind of state. I am warmly greeted by the people that I know, whom I already met, somewhere. Faces are familiar.

I am apparently in this meeting for a briefing on the timing, with my galactic friends, and they are giving me all these information for you because you have been kept in the dark, lied to by the politicians for a long time. It is time now to unveil to you the truth. And when you, then, have full knowledge, you will able to help to liberate my coworker. You become cocreator and are closer to getting into the fifth.

Does it begin to make sense now this all journey of CHADD and VIE's time traveling, and at the same time journeying with you for you, in five periods (volumes) so far!

"Prescription drugs kills 380 people a day just in the US, but they also use the frequency. Time to hear about the truth, time to tell the truth. They are all in, the Thuggees, the Illuminades, the small creators. They are all about killing human beings. They control the world wealth.

Then I shifted into the fifth to Archturus, or Arcturus. It is the fifth dimensional civilization, and it is one of the most advanced civilizations in the galaxy. In fact, it is a prototype of earth future. Its energy works as an emotional, mental, and spiritual healer for humanity, and Edgar Cayce said that it is also a gateway through which humans pass during death and rebirth.

They work in close connection with the ascended masters, the brotherhood of all, and very closely the Galactic Command.

They are guardians, protectors of higher consciousness in the universe. The Arcturians teach that the primary ingredient for living in the fifth dimension is Love and that the fear and guilt must be overcome and exchanged for Light and Love. Arcturians came to educate humanity but have had a difficult time dealing with the government and the military, who are primary interested in military technology and not spiritual enlightenment.

The United States and the world are so materialistically and egoistically oriented that they resist the help of these incredibly advanced beings that could help in greater and more open capacity than they are now. But the very selfish Gray beings are only interested in taking over the world for their own greedy purpose and made a deal with the US government.

The Illuminati, the Grays, want a one-world government, and they selected electronics to bring to planet earth just for that. That is how they keep human beings from seeing and understanding that they have an agenda to control them. Very few are able to see the manipulation that is going through. That is how they are actually dividing the human beings. By keeping humans with unclear minds.

Sound, Light, or thought, everything has a frequency and thus a resonance.

The government has a new ground-based *star wars* weapon in Alaska. It turns Lights never intended to be artificially manipulated. The new system manipulates the environment in a way that can disrupt the human mental process, can jam all global communication systems, change weather patterns over large areas, interfere with wildlife migration patterns, negatively affect your health, unnaturally impacted by the negative breakdown of the old magnetic frequency.

The Arcturians have been working with earth since life first started on this planet and have many bases on earth as well as three bases on the moon. Many of the bases are inside mountains. They are here to assist humanity entering the other dimension of reality and in raising their vibrational frequencies."

I opened my eyes thinking that we have a lot to be thankful to them.

Then I suddenly understood something about harmony. Harmony is the sixth plane. Humans have a wave pattern for everything on your side of the veil. Each wave has a frequency to it, as it travels up and down, forward or backward. That is the frequency of your wave, or your tone. Every part of your body has a slightly different wave and vibration, and yet you have a signature vibration, which you send out into the world at all times. And it can be altered; just by having different thoughts can help to open those waves so that you can more easily harmonize with other people.

CHAPTER 12

Trained to the Language of the Light

We are, that time, in a beautiful early spring, and I went for a walk. Perhaps it is the bright sunlight doing something in my vision. There are some flashes of light from my right and left and then all around. I realize that a star is turning around its axis. Immediately I fell into another reality. Before I know what is happening to me, I am already standing comfortably within this new reality where I found myself back home in another place and time.

One member of my spiritual family begins to talk.

"Here is something you must know and let others be aware of.

The Pleiades represents the key to physical procreation, and the chosen ones have received the knowledge of how to use the codes of biochemical creation on this planet to mutate a species. It is from the Pleiades that will come the cross of redemption through the image of the lamb. Various galactic councils have been trained in the language of the Light to synchronize the time cells of their administration with the right knowledge within the turning of the wheel of the Law. It will then dispense the correct knowledge for soul evolution.

The Egyptian documents of Light are keys to the grids of the earth, and if fused together with a pulsating geometry of a thought form with a given color and placed together on the right vibrations of consciousness, then the experience of going into other words through the pyramid is revealed.

We will have the power to enter into higher unity of being.

But be careful, the spiritual power is not sufficient to be in the presence of the Almighty.

Reincarnation was a hidden secret of Christianity, though we keep reincarnating after each lifetime until we have grown enough and are ready for the next level of human evolution. We have then graduated. Reincarnation is a scientific provable fact.

There is an organized war going on in science between materialistic theory and anything that could be termed *spiritual* or *metaphysical*.

Fallen angels, that like to call themselves the Illuminades these days, have abused the physical creations, and therefore they come down from the higher to the lower level of intelligence. As they cannot have their own bodies, they take advantage of human beings that do not believe the power of God and have unprotected frequencies.

The nonbelievers of God are used by other intelligence that walk upon the earth. They become then possessed and their vehicule occupied.

They are puppets for mind control or real demonic possession. They are hearing a given assignment. They assault innocent victim, and like all humans possessed by demons, it takes more than one person to deliver the innocent person assaulted.

When these Illuminati and Archon, who have not the love of the Father, arrive on the planet, they cannot cope with their own form of energy, and they can be very destructive to all families and nations upon the planet.

This is what we see happening now with the Islamic radical extremists, the terrorists. They also deliver fake news, twisting and changing the real information. They lie very easily without shame. They have no feelings, no emotions. They like to create confusion.

The actual controllers of the planet in various countries and places want deep-seated cultural codes, religious beliefs, and structural biases to be changed. They would like Catholic and Christians to deny their faith through the enforcement law and political will and even went to say that Christians' belief is the unfinished business of the twenty-first century and partial abortion up to three days before birth should be authorized. They are characterized by low-profile corporate approach interlocking global networks and connections (Women's World Summit speech). I confirm it.

The Vatican and the Orthodox would like to see you worship an underground God and demigods."

The voice and the dream dissolved, and I was awake.

CHAPTER 13

Back to Egypt to Visit My Past

I do not usually hide things to my family on earth, but so far I hadn't found the words to explain even to myself what had happened. They have already labeled me "different." I knew I had to return to a different person. I looked at myself in the mirror, hoping to find the clue to regain the reassuring security of my old familiar self. But here we go again, another entity voice is suddenly guiding me, saying, "VIE, now listen very carefully. I want you to imagine a bright light coming down from above and entering the top of your head. Filling your entire body. See it, feel it, and it becomes reality. Now imagine an aura of pure white light emanating from your heart region. Again surrounding your body and protecting you. Now only your higher self, masters and guides, and highly evolved loving entities who mean you well will be able to influence you during this trip back."

And I found myself back in time into the Egyptian era, when I was living and as was with my blue flame.

Thoth, the son of Ra, hatched the world egg, and he is an ibis bird. Ra is the guide of Osiris and Isis, accomplishing the work of creation by the sound of his voice. He is said to be the most powerful friend of the soul, and through the trueness of his voice, he is contributing to the soul's resurrection.

Through the purity and trueness of my own voice, I am resurrected. This happened through my chanting, tonic, meditative prayers, by releasing my voice becoming clearer, and it becomes a healing balm for the world and others when I speak the language of the Light.

The Egyptian temple music is guided by Thoth and his beloved Ma'at, goddess of truth. They teach that by continual singing of harmonious chants, humans grew like unto the gods. And I see when we sing in nature, the trees expand their force field and the stones increase their energy field with sacred sound, or song, with well-intentional tones. Two Greek twins conquered Thebes, which fell to them by the power of music. And it was the sound that causes big stones to slide effortlessly into place.

The singing on earth is the reflection of heavenly harmony and the hymns of Hermes, which can also be read. It states that sacred sounds pour forth blessings and open a path throughout nature, straight to the Divine, and it is through the sacred sound the fastest way to enlighten and awaken.

Isis is considered to be the queen of heaven, and she received the secret of Ra, which she tripped out of him while he was dying, after he has been bitten by a venomous snake. Isis now with the name of Ra had the sound codes of creation. Ra, our Great Central Sun that is also the energy behind the brilliance in the sun.

Isis then used the green language and alchemy of the birds. Enchanting the sky, the earth, the abyss, the mountains, and the sea.

The body of Isis changed, and she swallowed and cried and whistled as she circled the dead body of her beloved Osiris. The swallow Egyptian language hieroglyph meaning to anoint, with this key, Isis chanted the dismembered parts together after he was cut into fourteen pieces by Set. So Isis enchanted and infused Osiris with life and gave also birth to their child, their creation Horus.

The temple of Isis, like the Temple of Mary Magdalene, has swallows circumambulating and whistling every day in season. Their whistling creates a beat frequency, creating and altering an altered state. And also each temple in Egypt is tuned to a unique language, unique musical scale based on its dimension and sacred proportions.

In the temple, singers used specific tones to create healing in the body, mind, and soul. As our voice is an instrument for healing and also is the barometer of our state of being. Musical instruments were used by all prophets in order to enter into an ecstatic mood before receiving the spirit of prophecy. This were the shamanic use, using musing to altered state and expand the energy field opening up to greater possibility.

The vision continues, and I see and hear the bird singing two dominant notes. In my vision, there is an Egyptian harp with seven colored strings, matching musical notes. Then appears Egyptian manuscripts of musical notation using seven notes and seven colors. Now I am shown what I already knew, that it corresponds to the seven tones and colors in the human system.

In the temple I am inside now, an Egyptian harp is playing a seven rhythm, making evident that rhythms and tones are both obviously important. I can feel it entering my body; I merge or rather the music merge in me. The toning and chanting increases my sensory perception, clarity, and intuition. Releasing limiting beliefs and dissolving my stress. Then it changed and altered my brain state, inducing in me an alpha-theta state. Synchronizing my heart-brain-body rhythms and producing a state of centeredness, balance, and integrity. The veils dissolved, and it opened a gateway to free my soul.

At that point, I entered an altered state and I lost track of time. An Egyptian entity tells me that it is so resonating to me that music. It is regulating the material and immaterial world, and the string is resonating with the macroscope of the universe and the macroscope of the human Soul. And says that as the word of Jesus became flesh in Jesus, so did the heavenly voice bath-kol, the daughter of the voice flesh in Mary Sophia, the bride of Christ.

The journey continues, and I am now visiting the Tibetan monk Sanassinian in Tibet. He is showing me around and wants me to see how they can levitate things. I see some Lamas using trumpets and drums to concentrate laser-like beams of Sound energy and levitating huge blocks of stone up. Sanassinian explains that Sound science can be found in the roots of Christianity with the Latin chanting monks and in mass, in Islam and Judaism as well as Buddhism, and most of the indigenous cultures (the indigenous Australians like to use the didgeridoo) around the earth. The mystical set of all use these traditions, used purification with sound to build a diamond body of light to become Christ.

Then I awakened.

CHAPTER 14

The Key to the Nature of Life

decided to center myself so that my energies are as focused as they can be. Being raised Catholic, I also pray the rosary and the Divine Mercy prayer like Saint Faustina received it. I pray that I will be able to accomplish my mission the way I have been chosen to carry for the benefit of everyone and that people will be receptive to what I am here for to share. I started doing this more and more, even in the dark in my bed, in the middle of the night, when for some reason I would be awakened, after many, many entities appeared to deliver messages that I had to share with the world. That day it was all about the secret behind the 432 Hz.

It's about the key to the nature of life. Five hundred years ago, a mathematical system was born that still serve us today based on the Sumerian 1260 counting system. In the sixth-century BC, on the Greek Island of Samos, the mathematician Pythagoras led a school of thought that married philosophy, mathematics, music, and geometry. And while Pythagoras did not discover advanced geometry, he applied it in new ways, especially to music. He discovered that when a taut and spring was plucked, it would create a tone, and when that string was divided in half, it would make the same tone only twice high in pitch. Then Pythagoras came up with numerical ratios based on harmonic fifth, and this led to the creation of the musical scale found at the root of most modern music. According to Pythagoras, all musical notes were found by using mathematics and as such were given number values. By using fifth, beginning from note number 1, Pythagoras was from note number 1, Pythagoras was eventually guided to note 27 and to find the same note twice as high in pitch to simply keep doing it to 54, 108, 216, 432, and so on up the scale. In Pythagorean tuning, the number 432 is quite important to Pythagoras himself. In the quest to find a universal language based on mathematics and frequency, this particular note represents a significant piece of coincidental evidence. 432 Hz raise positive vibrations and heals. Many ancient musical instruments from Tibetan bowls to Native American flutes happen to produce the same tone. A tone that vibrates at 432 cycles per second. What is the most intriguing is the fact that he was not calculating vibration cycles to find tone 432. It just happened to be the same fourth octave with a value of 432 cycles.

The circle, triangle, square, and pentagon, in each of them are angles and degree that, if were added together, always total a specific number relative to that particular shape. It seems to be something about them that reaches beyond a simple sum of angles. They happen to be in the same neighborhood as tone 432, they just add up to 9 just like 432.

If you take a look at the numbers found in basic geometry shapes and apply then those numbers as vibration cycles to hear the tones they produce, their tones are F-sharp and it is perfect harmonic fifth sharp. A seven-side septagon, which total 900 is an A-sharp, which happens to be the note required to complete an F-sharp major chord three-part harmony.

For Plato, who advanced the study of two-dimensional geometry into three-dimensional geometry and who began to recognize that nature whether expressed as a tone, the petal design of a flower or a spiraling design of a seashell seems to follow a 3-D mathematical pattern. Plato's quest ultimately revealed what was what we now call the Platonic solids. And these forms represent the most elemental construction found in both human made and natural forms. It actually fit into our geometry tone grid. We can see that two- and three-dimensional geometry can be expressed by the notes found in an F-sharp major chord, and that could be true with what is known as sacred geometry.

But musical instruments are no longer tuned to 432 cycles per second and no longer adhere to Pythagoras. Whole numbers' simplicity and the tuning method required to reveal geometric shapes is based on a mathematical grid rather than mathematical ratios.

CHAPTER 15

Eight Hertz, the Double Helix in DNA Replication

Though my coworker, CHADD, is still retained in Chateau Ushi Asylum by the MK-Ultra control program, we continue to communicate telepathically, and these are some important information he provided me with for you.

"Tune yourselves to the tuning to the heartbeat of the planet OM."

Then CHADD continued saying,

"It is a musically evolved creation from 432 used by the musicians to an impose 440 hertz is a modern change creation by the Illuminati. 432 Hz organic vs. 440 Hz is an MK-Ultra broadcasting.

Music prior to 1939 was mainly tuned in 432 hertz. For the most part, this was natural, or seen by researchers as an organic evolution of music through the ages in which classical music was tuned to 432 hertz. This frequency is said to be synonymous with organic projections from nature beings, being a projection of course of nature.

So 432 hertz was the frequency in which instruments pre-1939 for the most part was used in Europe and around the world. But that was all changed in 1939, when an international held in London recommended strongly that the world frequency, at least in regards to tuning instruments, be changed to 440 hertz, after the state the BBC among many other around the world, required their orchestras to tune to 440 hertz to slowly change the tuning mechanics now being used as an industrial standard to 440 hertz. A major change from the organic 432 hertz to 440 hertz.

Only fourteen years later, in 1955, 440 hertz became what was adopted by industrial standards worldwide. And people are now asking was there a sinister reason for the change since the number of researchers has stated that people feel differently under the long-term influence of music broadcast at 440 Hz, then they actually do at natural-organic broadcast, 432 Hz.

So we start with the difference itself, seeing how music played at 432 hertz forms different particle path means that it does when played at 440 hertz on cymatics tonoscope. 432 hertz is less broken and more symmetrical while 440 hertz is more broken and more distorted. The effect that this would have on the human being over a long time period of time of course is unknown. But with logic and scientific principle, we can know that because there is a measurable change and a visual one, that then it must be indeed a change to humans as humans are physical creatures whose physiology affects your overall psychological well-being.

Does it come down to small thoughts leading a response in a subtle almost immeasurable way, or is it large and maybe even have physiological effects on cells or the nervous system?

Study proves that classical music tuned to 432 hertz frequency help plants grow faster. They found that the music helped plants, the crops grown at a faster pace, and it's evident that plants have genes that enable them to hear. This affecting the plants in significant way, the actual DNA of the plants and its ability to absorb the light. And we have now clear evidence that actual frequencies affect the DNA on living structures and human beings.

To understand the healing power behind 432 Hz, it is necessary to first learn another frequency—8 Hz. 8 HZ is the fundamental 432 Hz beat of the planet. The heartbeat of the earth, which is better known a Schumann resonance. The Schumann resonance is a global electromagnetic resonance, which has its origin in electrical discharges of lightning within the cavity existing between the earth's surface of the ionosphere. The cavity with electromagnetic waves in the extremely low frequencies of approximately 7.86 Hz to 8 Hz. The ordinary thought waves created by the human brain range from 14 Hz to 40 Hz. This range only includes certain types of dendrites belonging to brain cells, predominantly within the left, the more rational hemispheres of the brain, which is the center of activity.

8 Hz is also the frequency of the double helix in DNA replication. Melatonin and pinoline work on the DNA, inducing an 8 Hz signal to enable metasis and DNA replication. A form of body temperature superconductivity is evident in this process, 432 Hz resonates with the frequency of 8 Hz. On the musical scale where A has a frequency of 440 Hz, the note C is about 261.656 Hz. On the other hand, if we take 8 Hz as a starting point and work upward by five octaves, we reach a frequency of 256 Hz in whose scale the note A has a frequency of 432 Hz."

CHAPTER 16

I Was Launched on Another Unexpected Trip of Revelation

I am looking at some of the lower rulers who are said to be those who have kept humanity in bondage, in a meeting right now.

What I am sure of is that the power of negation governs the body, the clay people, which confused the rational minds and the spiritual minds. These are the influences of the fallen angels. They suffer the illusion of being separated from the Divine and therefore have neither the knowledge nor the wisdom.

Those who are subject to the vibrations of the lower dimensions, the earthbound games of the male who never grows up and still desires playful technologies, which become technologies of death, will not understand how Christ will appear and assist the soul to reach the Virgin of Light, who prepares the soul for ascension.

Human beings are subject to external forces until they remember their own essence and awaken a commitment to the Light of the Savior.

But I found myself in a meeting room where there is a circular table with ten beings, most probably Archons, seated around. Nine human beings and one ET. I am in the room observing the scene. In the middle of the round table is a giant globe, the earth. On top of this earth globe rests a pyramid. I see a pyramid on which is a giant eye.

The energy is heavy, not a good feeling. I don't want to stay, but I have to.

They actually control the earth environment through High Frequency Active Auroral Research Program, HAARP.

It is a target of conspiracy theorists who claim that it is capable of weaponizing weather. It is perturbing the ionosphere with radio waves and generating catastrophes of floods, hurricanes, droughts, earthquakes, thunderstorms, power outages, downing of airplanes, Gulf War syndrome, and chronic fatigue syndrome. It's founded by the US Navy and the US Air Force, and it covers technology that can allow US military to communicate with its fleet of submarines through very long distances.

There is an instrument in the center, called Rack research laboratory, focusing on the development and the investigation of molecular photoswitches for new photoactive or photoresponsive materials. Spanning the traditional subdisciplines of physical and inorganic chemistry and material science. It's a facility that transmits high-power radio frequency directed into a limited area of the ionosphere. This instrument manipulates the ionosphere, the place where free electrons exists, and has a potential to create radio waves that manipulate the earth's magnetic field. You get yourself a control of the earth's magnetic field and you control the earth. And what is frightening is the fact that HAARP has the potential to control your emotions through wave frequencies, and they manipulate human minds with sudden mood swings.

Also they control and rule human population with fluoride in tap water that makes people poor. There is no need for a fluoride in tap water for the ones who want to control the world, and they make sure no one rises above them. So fluoride in tap water is an essential element to keep you under their control. Fluoride is a chemical that has an effect on the pineal gland, and about the brain. The third eye gland is responsible for majority of human emotions as well, and they know it. So they use the fluoride to damage this human being's gland, and it promotes apathy, depression, low vibrations, resulting in a lack of motivation, bad health, boredom, and unconcern. Brain is the survival organ, and the pineal gland is the intuition. They are all laughing around the table by the fact that to survive in the world today, humans must earn money to buy the necessary things. Their food, water, shelter, medicine instead of following their dream or escaping the system. People are depressed and unmotivated, which forces them to work for someone, just so they can survive. These two forces, the survival instinct and apathy, limit humans to follow this system and never rise above it. Humans are scared for their survival but unmotivated to go their own way, so they let others, the controllers of the planet, lead them to "safety." Making humans look at chemtrail and doubt about it, or say there is nothing we can do about it, so let's ignore. But these controllers are spraying humans with aluminium, arsenic, barium, boron, and fluoride. They want humans not to ask too many questions, and fluoride is now also being added to almost every food product made with water. Fluoride is in insecticides and other products like toothpaste, mouthwash, cleaning products, shampoos, creams, cosmetics…and many psychotropic medicines.

The rulers add the use of GMO to destroy all humanity. Genetically modified organisms, or GMOs, are plants or animals created through the gene splicing techniques of biotechnology. This experimental technology merges DNA from different species, unstable combinations of plant, animal, bacterial, and viral genes that cannot occur in nature or in traditional crossbreeding. It is the greatest discipline nature has ever seen.

The universe is one divine ruling that is whatever happens, it must always keep rebalance. Every action has its own opposite reaction. Humans make this balance to nature, but the universes will always find balance. The combination of elements like shape, color, size that phrases the senses of sight, and music has a beauty also, and beauty is a harmony between elements and forces. Sacred geometry is found where elements meet the golden ratio, and it exists through all the universe, between gravity planets, nature design of flowers, shape of animals, proportions of land, crop circles. It also exists in many man-made objects arts. In famous artists' work in painting and music, or Greek architecture. Almost everything that is found harmonious, beautiful. It has been kept a secret. No one think there's any relation with the golden ratio because it's like a magic show found magic. No one knows why or how the magician knows the trick, and in order to manipulate the audience, nobody else is allowed to know how it's done.

There is one other thing the controllers do not want you to know, the international standardization organization made the change in 1955 from 432 Hz to 440 Hz the general standard to musical pitch. Because sound of music, when it's more harmonious, can promote happiness. Music touches where nothing else can, where the essence of human emotional being is. So they decided to control with 440 Hz what emotions that the music promote, then the work on controlling the world is 99 percent done. These uncleaned world rulers of the planet don't want people to understand their true nature and your higher self. They want humans to be in a hurry to believe only what they see and be competitive about material things. This way, 99 percent will be in reality the 1 percent will create for them. The 1 percent, that is the shape, the reality of the 99 percent, and through various things they have accomplished that. And they are very good in keeping the control.

But Jesus pointed out to his disciples how his work is to provide a flow plan for recycling of souls, the transformation of the rulers (Archons) of the spheres.

Jesus is proclaimed as the one who is able to work through all the realms in the ineffable, from the highest of the Light worlds to the realms of chaos and affect a plan of salvation.

CHAPTER 17

The True Nature of International Terrorism

just had a few days break from any experiences, and I am back into another traveling experience. I went into a hotel meeting room one Thursday night in May. I was earlier and sat on a chair in a little corner from where I could see the entrance of the room. I wanted to make sure to see when they would begin to let us enter so could get not too far in the back. Someone started to come through very clearly. A young man started to tell me that for twenty-three years, there was a district attorney. He was a solid man with a tough reputation. One day the district attorney phoned his wife and told her he was driving in the countryside and would be back soon. He never returned. But he was bound to make enemies due to his tough reputation as a district attorney. He was probably making that call under pressure from some gang member or something. That is pretty much what the cops must have figured out when the district attorney's car was found outside a pound shop. Pretty much everything but his cell phone was missing. There were no signs of struggle. A search ensured; the attorney's credit cards and accounts were monitored, with no signs of activity, and his laptop was retrieved from a river nearby river, too damaged to recover any files.

The man stopped for a few seconds and looked at me to make sure that I was listening to him and continued his story.

They are kidnapping and raping the children, are into human and children trafficking for sex, make the population addicted to all forms of drugs that poison the body and destroy the neurons. They have transformed jail, prison, hospitals, and all kinds of state places into beds for profit. They do not hesitate to lie for their own benefit. Through false information, and fake news by the press and the media, they are dividing the people. Fortunately they cannot create their own reality but only twist and delay our own creation, and this is why humans have to get clarity of mind quicker because these dark and evil spirits are the biggest liars there is, and they have an agenda that is to keep reducing and controlling the population. They do not have your best interest in mind. Reducing the population to slavery for their own profit. They have created all forms of diseases and implanted illnesses. Alzheimer's, autism, cancer, flu viruses...all for their own profit. They have their own army underground, and all these profits goes toward it. These people have no emotions and are all about money and control.

But you are different and you came here for another reason. Human beings came to graduate.

The education of the soul takes planes through energy fields established by colors and separated by threshold colors of evolution. From a continual succession of colors with all of their intermediate degrees. A garment of colors emerges from the seventy divine names. The restoration of all colors within the human spectrum get back into the white Light, allowing the inner vehicules to proceed from the biochemical shell when the meridians of time changes.

This is the true nature of the international terrorism. It finances itself, buys and sells officials.

Separately from my astral projection for a briefing with my galactic friends and collaborators, and the meeting with this young man, I kept going back and forth teleporting myself for rejuvenation to my earthly spiritual guide, my husband and mentor on the spiritual realm. In fact my Divine husband for thousands of lives. We have been together for years and years. So I kept teleporting myself all the time for rejuvenation on time and space continuum, as we feed and charge ourselves on each other's energy. Something that the controlling dark energies did not quite understood. They fear our power when we are together, and they kept separating us, but it would not stop our commune spiritual and galactic mission. So after labelling him with ADD, they added pyromaniac. We are here to help, guide, teach, and educate you. And we are experts of Light and Sound frequency and vibrations working in collaboration with Nikola Tesla.

It is through the spoken Light language, Sound, and the transformative vibratory energy that human bodies can be re-encoded, reactivated and re-attuned to their original vibrations and energy and be prepared to take their body of Light. Emotions are held in the body and in the etheric field (the aura), and when not addressed on time, discomfort like symptoms appear.

The body is crystalline in nature, and it is only through what has been not recognized yet and brought back to you under the name of Bio-Qi Therapy™ that stress, emotions, discomfort, traumas are erased, vibrations are raised to the appropriate and necessary level at this time, DNA cleaned, chakras are balanced giving now clarity of mind for spiritual growth and enlightenment. And the heart chakra reconnected, "Divine Reconnection." And it takes the trinity: the Light, the Sound, and the Holy Spirit.

The Two Chosen Ones and the Trinity

Bio-Qi Therapy™ is an angelic advanced system of energy (chi) based on the knowledge from the being of Light of the fifth and higher dimension. Pleiadian *angels* have in their mission to support and assist mankind in their evolution, to get prepared for the higher frequencies directed to them, respecting their free will. In providing session of holistic healing, activating the thirty-four various channels (chakras) using the Light language that is spoken, hand signs, tones, or chants with biostimulation Light waves. New information from the fifth level dimension helps people to expand their consciousness and grow spiritually above the manipulated duality world of 3-D and 4-D, and help mankind to discover their purpose and destiny in life. It is a unique and exclusive therapy to bridge the gap of this new era, while drugs poison your body and keep you in a loop. This therapy helps you restore yourself in the face of personal and global challenges.

Many people into alternative medicine try to bring the news to the public, but scientists resist. Scientists these days understand Light vibrations and offered many theories, but when it comes to the functions of the human bodies, this knowledge seems to have deviated to technologies that would increase death at the expense of wellness and healing. It is most painful to see that all these substances ingested are applied to the human body in the supposed name of healing, and it is disturbing to see the abuse upon the human beings and that humans still believe in drugs and would not acknowledge anything else. These people are trapped into unclarity of mind. The world has been under control of false information but also bombarded with new technology to keep them in a walking sleep.

The abuse upon the human body and upon its mind by different vibrational frequencies created by the black government elites are directly responsible for all the human distress upon the earth at this time.

There is more than one vibrational frequency of Light. All the different hues seen by the human eye operate at different frequencies. The only information scientists are willing to admit is that Light has a frequency and it also appears as particles. Humans are misled into believing false information, and education today teach everything except about Light frequency. Because we are living in a world where many want power over others, and this is not an information to spread and there are various frequencies of Light. Human thought has its own vibration, feelings and emotions have its own vibration, memory has also its own vibration, and electricity is Light vibration.

We are made of Light, all things are made of Light, and different colors possess different properties. The transformation of the species occurs through the infusion of Light crystals.

Each organ in the body corresponds to a specific meridian point, acupuncture point if you will, and each organ has a specific color. Colors are frequencies. All musical notes correspond to a color; notes are colors frequency. Chakras are wheels of energy placed in various places in your body and have a specific color. When your body is unattuned, depleted of the right vibration or energy, first the symptoms appear. All these symptoms are stored in your aura, and when left for too long, illnesses and diseases unfold. The problem is that all this is unknown to physicians. Medical schools teach orthodox methods that utilize drugs, surgery, and endovascular procedures to "improve" body function. Physicians are formed to diagnose, give a name to the discomfort happening in your body that corresponds to specific drugs, and write you a prescription for drugs that unbalance your body even more. Proof is from one prescription drug, you need another one from the side effects, then another side effect arises, and it goes on and on. It is a vicious circle. But some refuse to recognize it.

It is important for scientists to recognize that even in our biological realm of creation, matter is created by Light and that it is taught in medical schools about the multidimensional human anatomy and the etheric body. It is time to use methods that address illness and promote wellness at every level.

But to heal there is more. It is linked to the balance and connection to the whole. It goes first with the reconnection to the heart chakra.

Looking at the Pythagorean law, you see the application of the rays of Music, Sound, and geomancy.

The energy of seven goes all the way into the planet. I see that we have seven continents, seven human races, seven days in a week… and the seven rays can be understood in relationship to color, have also an application to the Sound of seven tones of an octave and the qualities of geometric forms. All these relationships enhance the energy of reality when it comes down to spirituality.

When you use vibration like the bio-sound, or a mantra or pray the Rosary, when we work with the vibration of healing, it implies a quality of healing that brings Divine order.

When we pray or listen to aspiring and harmonious music of right nature and right tone, when we listen, speak, and communicate and share the right vibration and energy, it brings about healing energy to our environment. It heals.

The Seven Rays and the Vibrational Healing of Virtue

The influence of the rays around the throne of God are the seven rays, or the seven archangels that are respectively called the cosmic celestial rays, and it makes up everything.

Saint Germain has now a message for you.

"I have a special interest in everyone who has fallen under the influence of drugs. This love which I practice towards them is born out of the consciousness of knowing that all these beings, who have fallen into the abyss can still be saved from there, and brought to a new world of light and harmony."

I was doing my best to understand and integrate my experiences at that point.

CHAPTER 18

The Seventh Ray that Comes to Transmute

That time I was guided to work closer with the seventh ray, with my business, then to send it through my eyes to heal, then to repaint one wall of the room in violet.

The seventh ray is the Ray of Synthesis, it is the ray which closes a circle, it is the ray that precedes the new era. This violet ray, for being the seventh, is consequently the ray of the highest vibration; it comes transmuting everything, which has already been achieved by the active work of the other six rays.

This is the Ray of Transmutation par excellence, this is the ray of ceremony and ritual, it is the ray of white magic, the magic that all the followers of the Light employ when they arrange their lives in line to God's purpose; then their surroundings start to change in a magical way and go down on their knees before the one who has arranged their life in such a way.

True white magic does not require candles, uniforms, and power objects; true white magic is of the same irradiation as the disciple who is aligned with the Divine purpose, who, wherever he passes, is transmuting the environment around him. Even the universe itself goes down on its knees and aligns itself to this Divine plan of which the conscious being is an active part.

Do you want to help the world to change? Do you really want to step forward as active collaborators of the divine plan, which the Father has prepared for this humanity? If your answer is positive, be assured then that the simple continual use of the Violet Flame of Transmutation will empower you in the course of time to alter everything that is not in accordance with this Divine plan; you will be given the power that your simple presence, even if you don't even notice, transforms in a radical way your surrounding environment.

And here we are, I am hearing this now that I must share with you.

May your daily prayer always be:

> My Father and Almighty Creator, may Your will be done in heaven and earth. My almighty Father, allow me to be an active collaborator in this, Your Divine plan. My eternal and loving Father God, may my hands move through the inspiration of Your will. May my steps always lead me to the place You want me to be. My all powerful Father, allow me to be the same for all Your children what you are for me. *So be it.*

When you say this prayer with all your heart, you will feel that inside of you, a light of such proportions will appear, that you will, indeed, want to surrender yourself to humanity in order to teach, which is the way that leads to the Father.

Because if you don't pray daily to your Father Almighty Creator, be assured that the controllers are diligently worshipping Lucifer.

Therefore, nourish the serenity of your being, eliminate the fury, which often causes a mission to fail, and in this peace, which is obtained by knowing that you are consciously working in the Father's will. Walk with firm steps and savely on the ways he wants you to walk.

And to those who are under the influence of alcohol or drugs, if you direct the violet flame directly on the laryngeal chakra, the heart chakra, and the front chakra, this will bring immediate help to the persons who are under the influence of these ennervators. If it is your task to bring the beginnings of spiritual teachings to these groups, invoke the violet flame upon which I will come to help you whenever you face a difficult case. This was it for that time.

CHAPTER 19

My Encounter with Shamina

The rain finally stopped and the clouds cleared quickly away. It is a beautiful spring day. I am sitting on the sand under the shade of a tree, meditating. I am in total harmony with nature; stillness invade my body. A little breeze caresses my cheek, I am breathing a soft fragrant air, and it surprised me when an older woman appears next to me. She is not very tall and her energy is very calming and sweet. She looks familiar though I do not know her.

"Who are you?" I asks.

"I am Shamina," she says. She stays there for a while, smiling at me, then said,

The children would like to talk to you through me regarding the children on earth. They are mistreated and suffering.

The children of all earth nations, all races, and many planets, children of the fire, the storm, the rain. Met you in your dream and as they journey across time and space in all colors of the rainbow to join you. They sit next to you or at your feet while you guide them.

These children stand with the Divine host and broadcast you a vibrating energy. As your inner knowingness picks up the frequency, they ask you to feel the pulse of our energies in your soul. As you all sing together after that you have felt the melody of the song that caresses your soul, you all sing and create new songs. The legions of angels and the whales join you with the solar wind.

Listen to the tones that they send you. They are contacting you in your soul, making you recognize the frequency in your everyday life. You may hear a buzz, a ringing chime, a soft voice in the background, it may last an instant or much longer. They are training your ears and mind to once again recognize and communicate this vibration.

These children that are entering into incarnation today already possess the new structures and already have an innate understanding of the world beyond duality. The buildup of heavy metals in their system is a major contribution to their hyperactivity. The water they ingest is harmful, the toxic chemicals, drugs, and fluoride too. The solution is not to medicate them, but to correct the imbalances created by them. We suggest instead that you take the child to a healer, shaman, or holistic therapist. It is counterproductive to recognize the symptom but to refuse to admit and address the underlying causes.

Vibrational therapy, like the energy that you carry, VIE, is a vibrational transformation energy and involves the use of resonance and vibration. It stimulates the five senses and restores the balance. It tunes the body up and tune up life, by realigning to the spirituality and destiny. By consciously stimulating the five senses with color, light, sound, essential oils, aroma, food, art, and touch, the body can then be healed of trauma and pain.

Everything you need to help these children are available without the assistance of the pharmaceutical drugs. These drugs are adding to the poison ingested in their body. There is no need to give them psychotropic drugs and pollute their system with drugs. Psychotropic drugs are addictive to their DNA."

And Shamina was gone.

CHAPTER 20

A Spiritual Gathering of the Light and the Sound

A few weeks passed since my meeting with Shamina, then that day, I was at the chapel praying the Rosary when I heard the voice of my Divine husband. He got me confirmation in a vision created by his voice, of what I already knew from previous incarnations.

"Sound is the vibration of molecules and travels through a vocal cord, the messenger or *speaker*, while Light is a distinct physical entity that behaves as both particle and a wave and can be transmitted through empty space where there is no sound. The primary similarity between Light and Sound are their behavior as waves and both be reflected, have frequencies of oscillation while can be measured as color of Light of pitch of the sound."

And this is what happened next: Father Peter had so many of his parishioners that talked about the alignment to their path and destiny but also that they found their way to spiritual growth after sessions of Light and Sound that he wanted to see by himself.

He requested an appointment with the experts of Light and Sound and prayed and meditated a lot before asking Saint Michael to protect him.

He entered the office and was relieved when he felt the harmonious, not to say loving energy, that was in the place. The smell of the incense, to which he was very familiar.

The spiritual counselors and energy therapist experts of Light and Sound he came to see asked him to close his eyes, center himself, forget them, and just be.

The melodious music got him rapidly out of reality, and he began to feel the warmth of the color Light bathing different parts of his body.

He had flashes of Lights, colors, and received visions. He heard the angels singing.

He traveled in colors and Sound, played with the colors, and even approached and played with the whales that were gently talking to him. He visited a pure crystalline pyramid. Was greeted by beautiful angels and experienced different feelings in various chambers. Sat on a flower seat for rejuvenation and continued to travel. He saw the expert of the Sound working on him, morphing and becoming the Sound and the Light expert, morphing into the Light. He felt the unity with the Father.

Suddenly he hears an angelic voice singing and speaking a language to which his body reacted very well. It seems that his body understood it well. His subconscious understood it, and his pain in the knees was magically gone. He felt a quick and sudden pain that disappeared as quick as it came in his upper body. This was from his car accident years ago. And the Sound is guiding him now saying,

"Those who hide in the darkness, and veil their actions, are perceiving this web of Light and love that is created across and around the planet. Tell your parishioners that their Light has become their greatest fear. The beings controlling the planet propose to stop the enlightenment at all costs. But you have been promised by your Creator you will be allowed in this lifetime to manifest the fullness of your divinity and spiritual gifts that were veiled from you for a very long time. New governments and new collectives are becoming visible. Allow the children of the hand of God to play their magic. If you wish to be of serving you are the way showers, the nucleus of many small groups. Become the pillars of peace for all in fears, Father Peter. And when it finally shifts and miracles will take place, your political leaders will experience a serious reduction of their powers because Divine laws do not allow interference with free will. But know that your church has been divided. The devil, Lucifer, hides everywhere and in your high authority. He is a wolf in a sheep's clothing. Children must be given a balanced and clean environment. They live in a high level of toxicity, and this is not conducive for their evolution, the way it should be for them to accomplish the goals they have come to accomplish. It is a major contribution to their hyperactivity and other nervous and systematic conditions. They have all volunteered to be here.

The use of drugs prevents a completely positive mutation, the main factor in the cellular mutation is Love vibration, and the drugs help to lower vibrations, and the low vibrations is not conductive to the raising of love and light frequencies.

No technology, any holistic or alternative, herbs, or elixir can replace the Light and the Sound that brings a different awareness of oneself and brings you a new level of consciousness."

When Father Peter opened his eyes, he understood what he was told when he arrived to his appointment, after beings greeted, "You will not feel grounded for a while."

He opened his eyes and everything looked and felt surreal. He was in great peace. He was in joy. He felt intensively like he was outside his body and were floating for quite a long time. He then had to sleep right after leaving the office location. He awakened from his nap feeling completely rejuvenated and kept telling everyone, "Don't disbelieve until you experience it. This will align you with the will of God."

CHAPTER 21

The Harmony in the Body and Another Out of Body Projection

Two weeks later, I suddenly was aware of the presence of some very evolved beings. An enormous spiritual presence. I was being transformed into rainbow wheel of Light when an energy began to speak. The voice asked me to feel the bubble that just formed itself. I was stepped outside of my body, and my ordinary awareness faded.

And I was asked to describe what people can expect from a Color and Sound session and what it does. I chose to talk about my client Alice.

Alice entered the room and began to ask a lot of questions. She was looking pale, uncomfortable, and very nervous. Then Alice sat, her purse on her lap, and explained in an angry voice that she was in pain, her stress and emotions were at the top, that she could not get mental clarity of mind, and was looking for her purpose. Because nothing seemed to mean anything for her but that she was determined to find out and grow spiritually, to self-heal and get out of pain.

"I think," Alice says, "that all this is interrelated."

"Alice," I said, posed and calmed, "yes all is interrelated and even more than you think. When the Lord's Prayer is prayed, it opens the pineal gland, thyroid gland, solar plexus, Lyden cells and gonads. It produces an organic response on the mental and acts on the physical body. And the 144 elected people symbolize the cellular structure of the twelve principal parts of the human bodies. Edgar Cayce also mentions that it's based on this, that medical astrology work, and that the trumpet of the seven angels symbolize the experience in the physical body in the purification process.

The body is an electrical system of sorts, and we are the generators of our own destiny. Our own reality is a holographic grid program, a matrix of Color, Light, and Sound, that our thought creates in repeating cycles. It is through Color, Light, and Sound that we experience emotions. Consider what we call emotion in all forms to be unknowing expressions of our prime energy drive. The creative force inherent in each of us. Joy, happiness, fun, anger, hate, sadness, nostalgia, ego, greed, guilt, anxiety, worry…and emotion is the key and the driving force. We all think we love and break our hearts when we discover we were mistaken. Or laugh rejoicing and become depressed when the moment fades away.

At physical birth, we are bound by our previous experience but also by the genetic structure of our physical body we inhabit, therefore we are bound to operate and maintain our physical bodies within the limitations they impose.

Sound and sonic vibration construct reality, realm of sound that crosses the lines between the seen and unseen. That is why sound has played a vital role in our lives. Acoustic resonance influence the body's organ and cells and the functioning of the brain. Sonic vibration affects the human body and stimulate the DNA. When your ears hear a certain type of sound, the brain responds.

In addition to Sound, Light can be applied at a particular frequency, through a particular color frequency, and will cause your brain to perceive images, geometric patterns, shapes, colors, and objects, but also you could simply feel warmth or cool air, an emotion could arise, and it is perfectly alright. If you see colors, please do not stare at it but just merge with it.

You see, Alice, if the light and the sound chosen are the correct ones, and used at a particular time for a specific good reason, it will trigger in you a new sense of awareness into another layer of reality. A change of brain wave patterns that will create also a deep meditative state, increasing calm, and a shift in mood and attitude, and an increased awareness.

Sound, Light vibration changes the human body and brain. The idea that the body responds to different Light and Sound frequencies is far from new and one of the oldest treatment modalities that exist. It was already known in the Egyptian time and used in Atlantis. In fact, it attunes the body, heals physical diseases, mental, emotional, and spiritual diseases. The necessary strands of DNA will be reconnected and your chakras balanced and activated. But this is what some people does not want you to find out.

Some sick people of our time are unfortunately involved in the manipulation of high-tech weapons of resonance, using it for lethal and nonlethal means, for the wrong reasons. That's the ones that are trafficking, raping, and abusing the children in sex. But luckily there also is the living Light language that I speak that can't be used by these dark egoistic controllers, also my blue flame expert of the sound, and we have an energy exchange at the heart center.

At the beginning was the word, and out of the divine mind proceeded the Light pictures, combined with the sacred geometry forms producing the spectrum of all forms coming out from the alphabet of creation. The Light language. It is the language of future mathematics.

Light pictographs and ideographic cybernetics, coming out from the Light language spoken, serve the Father's will. The pictographs are energized image shapes symbolizing the meeting of ideas, which produce pictures and sounds in mental language. Pictographs of Light are essential for communication exchange between the human body and its overself body. Therefore, pictographs not only communicate higher spiritual wisdom to the brain, but also provide us with a new circulatory system for linkage with our higher self. The transmission of pictograph cybernetics work through a holistic love process.

Then the pictographic radiations reach the brain during session that is ready to participate in an infinitely expanding scale of knowledge throughout its universe. The, what I call holistic love process, is necessary. The love energy is part of the unfolding. All is created by love. This is why some have tried to copy and applied it with machines but it can't work. Plus all of them are made with an LED light, which is poison to the body. Even though some results can be seen first, they will only mask the problems that will come right back.

These machines have not been created for the right reasons.

The pineal gland is a key to the ascension, and the cabal does not want you to have your pineal gland regenerated because once the process is initiated, it cannot be stopped. Human beings will no longer be susceptible to control. Big Pharma will no longer rule, and petroleum products no longer be needed."

CHADD aka Christ, being the new Horus, and VIE aka Mary aka Megali, or the God Duo are giving you this message:

"It time for you to search us if you want to reach the golden age. In the reboot, regeneration process, healing begins, and once we have reconnected you physically to your angels, communication will then be easier with angelic beings and high beings of Light. The transformation experience will affect you forever with cellular regeneration, and it will sweep you away into ecstasy, and you will become a beacon of awakening to others."

Then I entered back my body.

CHAPTER 22

Love Is Everything, Magnifying the Love of the Divine and Human Self

Today I feel that I am guided to explain you that love is the key. Love is an essence, a power, and a vibration. Love is life and the most priceless vibration in all existence, the eternal dynamic life force. Love is connected to the heart chakra, and it is magnifying the Love of the divine and human Self.

When the blue pearl expanded, an extraordinary blue angel manifested from the center of its center to me. Like Jesus manifested to Saint Hildegard in a vision. The eyes of my wonderful divine husband, my blue flame, were beaming a blissful love at me. The divine light of consciousness blue sphere, the blue pearl always constant in my third eye vision and that dwells in me provides access to different planes of existence to open gateways in space that allows access to other systems and galaxies, path that takes back to the source. My blue flame, the embodiment of God consciousness, is made of a beautiful light, and as Consciousness pulsates and expands, it pervades the entire universe.

It is late at night and I fly and attain the rainbow Light body.

I am his Dove, his Ruby light with the ankh, and I am now floating just above him coming for the reunion, for the transcendent power of our Love and the liberation of the human spirit from mental and physical bondage. He touches my lips with a magical kiss for the ultimate experience that I was so much longing for.

We are the angel messengers of Love who came through the secret door and brought with us the secret of our Love's power to transform.

Love is the glue and the vibration that keeps all of God's creation, functioning together in perfect harmony and beauty with its divine qualities and the desire to be God in action through the Love on the planet.

Our flame of Love—it is one of the seven flames of God acting on this planet for humanity. The color of Love extends in great varieties of tones, colors, and of frequencies, from a light pink to the golden ruby light. The merging of his gold Light and my ruby color, and the Holy Spirit pink that forms the Trinity in action.

The Love frequency is the salvation energy. It is the Holy atonement, attunement to restore the body temple and reactivates and restructures DNA energetically or vibrationally.

When the energy exchange at the heart center of the God Duo is broadcast outward unheard and unseen, it is harmonizing the humanity with Love. Deep level of DNA will occur, and you will be able to shift into the fifth.

It is healing our world threatened by war, with people suffering from dehydration, starvation and infectious diseases, offering humanity the greatest opportunity to transcend a destructive paradigms and the political and psychological impositions that maintain them.

The energies that are coming forth and climaxing this summer are of great change. Although with this change coming to the forefront, we, in the etheric, notice that many Light workers are still holding to 3-D ways of thinking and severe conditioning awareness transforms into consciousness. The conditionings, which is energy that must be transformed to move forward into higher consciousness.

For the souls to come forth fully, all ego must be transformed. If you are not aware of the conditioning, then how do you transform it? We will provide you with this knowledge to help you further you on your journey back home into the heart equal love. You must be in the heart.

Let's discuss first spirituality to its core. Spirituality! What is the truth with spirituality? Many different perspectives about spirituality, especially the mind.

The heart is simple as is love. The answers are within you. The spiritual path is feeling; it is not thinking, analyzing, or reasoning. Through feeling, you experience and gain wisdom and knowledge. Spirituality is a path, a journey of endless possibility each unique to everyone's journey. It is the rediscovery of who you truly are. The Divine essence that is and has always been within your being.

You are a child of prime Creator, Mother God, the Holy Spirit connected to all creation through your heart, your soul. It is the Soul that connects you to your very essence love. You are made of love, unconditional love, interconnected to the wonders of all creation. The original blueprint to humanity is of a heart-based race. Love mirroring love in the physical, which we are returning to, the process who weren't had other plans.

They created the mind to control, subjugate, infiltrate, and take energy from humanity. Those of you who have had 5-D experiences know that all is in harmony, peace, bliss, and unconditional love in the upper dimensions. There is all heart connected to Divine intelligence. There is no mind in heaven. The mind is meant to be imbalanced and therefore can never exist within the upper realms. If you have difficulty with this truth, ask yourself why you meditate. What occurs through meditation now that this information is within your hearts.

Only 11 percent of people are actually energetically stable enough to receive this upgrade. This is a lower percentage than was expected in this time window but nevertheless continues to expand, and we foresee that soon there will be a quantum leap forward. Our words are designed to assist in this leap. The stumbling blocks for most of you on is that you are stuck up in conflicting emotions, and thus manifesting a conflicting experience of life you plot on. You plot on with what you consider to be your duty until getting through each day, each week, each year without the courage to open the door of your confinement and dare to consider who you really are and what you really are here for.

There is one solution, and it starts with your willingness to change, to be different, to let go of emotional crutches and dysfunctional habits and beliefs. Bravery is needed to let go of old ways. But when we start expending, we experience a euphoric high and we float inside. This is ascension for human. The expansive high is Light, it is also descent of the higher self being birthed from within for the awakening celestial star being. We love to float, be in the ethers, the other dimensions, and we don't like the human physical reality world.

This is what happened when this young woman who was guided to meet VIE at a convention. She was so desperate and felt so empty inside and lonely that she did not even know that she was going to commit suicide. Luckily for her, VIE felt it, and the young woman accepted to be reconnected. She surrendered and opened her heart to receive this precious gift, and she still remember clearly the experience and the bliss when it happened, and she keep sharing it as soon as she has the possibility to do so, encouraging people to be reconnected to.

She brought down the walls of resistance that she had as safety of mechanical and survival mode, a way of escaping and dealing with what was too overwhelming at the time that she didn't understand. She didn't realize before that day that she had a magnificent gift, abilities, and purpose. All she could see was what was wrong with her and the world she wanted to escape.

Pushing away from where we want to go is coming up loud and clear. You must feel it. Even those who still refuse to believe that there even is such a thing as energy. Well! Bless their heart they have been dragging for such a long time already that the intensity of this push/pull energy now will be very scary as they feel it.

No one can resist feeling their own energy any longer.

CHAPTER 23

Love Is the Driving Force
Guiding You to Heaven

I *am suddenly teleported aboard an Arcturian vessel. There is a gigantic screen. I am called to merge in and visit my coming future.*

Thousands of people are begging now to benefit from our gifts. CHADD was with me and communicating telepathically, putting these words in my mind for me to speak:

"I hear you, my children. I heard your cry for Love for who you are. Beloved, you must first seek for his Love. Until it becomes a burning desire to your heart and soul, so great that you cannot longer live without it, you cannot generate enough Love power and energy to achieve this level of evolution. It is not about your physical body. You must seat and write down your spiritual goals for this incarnation. Meditate, pray, and contemplate your inner divinity. Take time to review your life and know why you are here and where you are going. Within you is held your cosmic bank account into which your merits are deposited or withdrawn. In the next world, you will be judged by your human learning or by what is the level of your spiritual attainment."

As soon as the place was full and that everybody was comfortable, we introduced ourselves and asked the people to relax. We, then, all began to breath at the same time, at the same rhythm.

My blue flame with his hypnotic tone of voice began to guide everyone. I joined him with the language of the Light.

The entire crowd immediately entered the trance, the minute our energy touched them.

That's at that same time that I morphed into Light and CHADD morphed into the Sound. The glow on the face of the crowd illuminated the entire location and town. It was so bright that anyone not part of the experience could not support it.

We astral projected and traveled to our heart reunion. Our Love was so intense. It was an enormous wave. A gigantic wave of bliss that never ended, a wave that was never crashing down on the sand. Through the fire burning of the two of us in our heart, my Light illuminated the entire planet and reached the cosmos while the cosmic Sound invaded it.

Thousands and thousands of angels came to join. They came for the physical reconnection between them and the crowd. There was flashes of Light and colors. There were tears of joy on people's faces while the waves of our blissful reunion was caressing their hearts.

We saw their energy wheels recovering their proper colors and right energy balance. Dark spots of attached alien spirits leaving their auras at the speed of Light, like we saw the attunement of their body realigning itself. We witnessed the opening and reunion of their hearts taking place, and the physical help connection with their angels.

We heard the Catholic monks chanting in Latin, the voices of the nuns from their convent joining them. The Tibetan monks were also joining their voices to the angels. We heard the birds singing and the whale talking to the crowd. There was flashes of Lights and Colors everywhere on earth and in the sky.

Love transcended time and eliminated space. Its intensity transformed and healed everyone through its harmony and tenderness. The higher self had the ability to transform huge amounts of negativity into pure Love and Light. The crowd was crying softly of joy. Everyone was glowing.

Then the communication with CHADD stopped.

CHAPTER 24

A Message from a Mysterious Woman

I was on my way to the office and parked the car. I got out of the car, went around the car to the passenger side, and took my purse when my attention was attracted by a beautiful mid-age woman walking slowly toward me. What a sweet face and energy, I thought.

She smiled at me and said,

"I confirm, VIE, there is recovery through understanding the true root causes of symptoms, fears, impairment, and dependencies. When the core reasons are seen and experienced, understood and resolved, the symptoms disappear. The illness improves. The splinter has been removed and the pain is gone.

You must tell them. There is no necessity to project, to anesthetize, to use drugs, to be sick any more. The recurrent drama has finally ended. The holistic approach is the way. Not many are understanding your great work yet unfortunately, but it is coming very fast, and the word of mouth is a growing movement. You will soon have to help many people at the same time. They will all reach to you soon.

When we Love and serve God, we will be with him in heaven. People are responsible for all their time, all their actions, and how they lived. The satanic and demonic people blind persons into thinking this life will go on and on. But you must listen to the voice inside you."

Then she walked away and literally vanished out of sight.

That night I dreamed in flashes of colors. I danced to the frequency into colors and merged into it. I played with the dolphins and laughed with the children. Swam in the ocean in and out. Floated and flew. Sat in the clouds and entered a tunnel of an harmonious rainbow spiral.

That was the teaching of remembrance. I felt my brain adjusting, my body aligning. Vision of sacred forms appeared to talk and explain.

CHAPTER 25

Dreaming in Colors, Traveling in Time, and Having Visions under Sound Frequency

Today Antoine came to consult me for help. Flashes of Light is changing the brain and thoughts of Antoine.

I am looking at Antoine laying down in the office, profoundly moved, listening to the frequency of Sound music that is playing while he is in Light therapy session. He is experiencing the entrance and rapture tuning, and drops of joy are falling his cheeks; his face is glowing. He has a big smile on his face.

Now Antoine is resting. It's easy to guess, observing his face and body, that he is time traveling.

From time to time, I hear him mumbling. Some geometric forms appear in his vision.

He is seeing his actual life passing in front of his third eye. He says after the session that he never saw such vivid images and such brilliant colors.

His face shifts from joy to sudden painful experiences. I can feel his body that is releasing traumas and emotions. I can feel the pains he went through that comes back. Though it does not stay. It comes back to be seen and felt, to be erased.

The minute he sees it and acknowledge it, the pain is gone. He remembers the sorrow losing one of his loved ones, he remember the trauma of the big accident he had years ago. He is hearing the siren of the ambulance. He sees the surgeon working on him. The nurse's attentiveness on each of the doctor's gesture. The anesthetist looking calmly but intensively.

Now he is seeing vivid colors again in geometric forms, and this smell that brings him back when he was young.

It was summer and his parents rented a house in the beach. He sees himself at four years old.

He just awakened from his afternoon nap. His two cousins, about his age, are with him. They are chasing each other with a hose, running barefoot on the grass. The water dripping on the warm grass releases this wonderful smell that he is just smelling. A chlorophyll smell, he says.

Now the entire family is back to town. The hometown smell is totally different and not so pleasant. It smells gasoline burning, coming from cars. The Light is not so clear, the colors are faded, not so brilliant compared to the house at the beach.

He is now seating on a bench that is facing another similar bench the other side of the water. All around the little pond, there are flowers. He never saw such colorful and perfect flowers. The red and the yellow and the green, the blue all colors are so brilliant. The colors seemed to be alive. The bench on the other side is empty, but someone is walking toward it…

A voice tells him, "Come back very slowly in your body."

He then opens his eyes and look amazed at the place around. He lost tracked of time.

He couldn't believe what just happened to him. The effect and impact by being simply, he thought, exposed to the Light and listening to the Sound. He felt his body still changing, aligning with the color.

Antoine: "Wow! Thank you. I came to see what this was all about, and now I know. This was an incredible experience."

The night that followed, he had many dreams, all in colors. Bubbles of various colors. He was instructed not to stare at it but to mingle, and also to put his wishing list inside a white bubble and to release it. So he did.

He realized waking up in the morning that he had never dreamed in color before and never experienced with such intensity their energy.

He learned that Love is a power, an energy frequency, and a vibration.

Antoine texts me on his way out to the parking lot, "I left my umbrella in your office, but keep it. I will be back soon."

CHAPTER 26

Vision of Amandine Story

In most cases, depression by lack of sunlight appear during winter and go away during sunnier days. But Amandine was not prepared for six months of rain.

Amandine and her husband moved to Central America location where Antoine was sent for work. The city was located in a high altitude, and the rain did not stop for nearly six months. Amandine, another client of mine, was so depressed that she wrote to her husband who went on a business trip.

By receiving sessions of blue light gives a feeling of distance, it allows to look beyond and create perspective outward. It contains a cool vibration that is helpful to communication. The blue vibration can also be used to open energy flow where it is blocked. Blue relaxes and will encourage feelings of communication and peace.

Amandine had to acknowledge that she was in depression and had to face the fact by writing that letter to her husband to release it. So she wrote:

> My darling,
>
> It's raining again today, but the beautiful flowers of the next door owner's garden open themselves one after the other.

The car is self-washed with the rain, and I am maintaining the fire with a big fervor in the kitchen.

The "Piso," the floor is shining, Lolyta la perra, Lolyta the parrot, has everything she needs and the cat, Gribouille, is still very attentive to any mice in the house.

The bats are very loyal to us. Sorros are a little fatter every day and reproduce and multiply themselves very quick inside the attic.

As you see, all is going well. Kids go from TV to the computer.

As of Monica and Steph, the European couple, do not be preoccupied. I do not even know if they are alive or dead, and you will be able to see them again without any apprehension. Not a word of disagreement has been exchange during your business trip. They have vanished since you left in a complete silence.

In the afternoon, nap is great in Central America, between the rain that makes a metallic noise on the roof and the thunderstorm. What a pleasure to be under the sheets.

The mailman is, as always, very nice and refuses to give me the mail, but promised me to keep it as long as necessary until your return.

The butcher's wife (Mrs. Liamey) is, as you know her, very well-dressed and covered with her usual fifty-cent jewelries. But I am always very welcomed.

I am pretty sure that the children will be ready and rested for the new beginning of the school.

Well! I hope because we are doing our best to be prepared. We go to bed at 8:00 p.m. the latest every night. What else is there to do here in this jungle.

Mauricette is taking very good care of her dogs, nothing changed. Same to herself, woman of great character, she takes the temperature of her dogs every day, she said. Unbelievable woman. Isn't she?

I have sowed some mirasols for the parrot, carrots, some greens, and green onions for us. All that is missing is some chickens running around and the turkey that we will kill for Christmas.

I do hope that those good news will suit you and make you hungry. Here we are ready for the next war, like you always have wanted, my darling. I am now the perfect farmer's wife you wanted me to be.

I hate it!

Today, my darling, our friends, the aunts that cannot adapt to the ancient owners, or maybe, who knows, have been mistreated, malnourished, have found us with joy. After having invaded the upstairs hallway, the rooms where they were tingling our toes without a break or being tired the entire nights, then invaded the kitchen and the sitting room more specifically at TV hours' time. They have finally discovered the brand-new wood of the pharmacy, the cabinet located in our master bedroom.

Luckily we did not hear from the Canadian guy. I learned that he lied to his friends and his lawyer. He is sending to himself some faxes to let them think that he is out of the country traveling for business purposes.

The old man that all calls Papy had some flashes of the war and wanted to put a fire on the roof of our house to keep away any intruders, and I had a hard time to stop him from burning the rental house.

As you see, I am busy living a disturbing and unreal life.

See you soon,
Me

But then Amandine looked for natural help. After research and following her friends' advice on the matter, she received some blue light frequency irradiation. She was told that it gives a feeling of distance, it allows to look beyond and create perspective outward. It contains a cool vibration that is helpful to communication. The blue vibration can also be used to open energy flow where it is blocked. Blue relaxes and will encourage feelings of communication and peace.

CHAPTER 27

A Flash to the Beginning of the Rest of Our Life

"Here we are," said the entity. "Today you will visualize who you were, who you are and your work that is to share with the world."

Our work and journey as the God Duo began years and years ago, with a historical adventure that includes the ancient city of Antioch, the fallen angels, ancient Indian legend, and a secret religious sect created in the days of Jesus. It was about hope, courage, and freedom and a prophecy fulfilled. Then a powerful message to the world to be delivered, the matrix, and the ascension process to reach the golden age.

Then I was guided to be reconnected to my original essence that is now in this different life to see the transformation from the age of Pisces to the age of Aquarius. It's in the time of the Armageddon and the last battle, the final war between good and evil, and many people are under prescriptions drugs that are addiction to their DNA. While CHADD, who has become a Baker Acted, drugged ward of state, holds the key to the Divine Wisdom.

After the recovery of CHADD from the prescription drugs' effects, it did not last very long. The Grays used their musical conspiracy, their own frequency, to make CHADD act involuntarily and used him as a free stuntman. While acting as a stunt, his car is destroyed and he is court ordered into prescriptions drugs again. Then he is sent and admitted in multiple times in hospitals, where he was used as an experiment, beaten, malnourished, poisoned, and deprived of clean water, of his wheelchair, and any shower. It was not handicapped accessible. He can't take a shower, and the wheelchair he must use is so wide that his fingers hurt and bleed every time he passes a door. When he must get to breakfast, lunch, and dinner, he must change buildings to go to the same repetitive stupid class, "Choosing the Life," back and forth…

I am VIE, and VIE encountered also many problems. Her office vandalized twice, the office speakers destroyed, her food poisoned, many computers frozen, her precious Tibetan gift stolen by two Chinese Thuggees. The Reptilians infiltrated also several time some spy clients. Some very dark energies, like the black guy that wanted to be her friend to possess her and her energy and that finally tried to kill her. Her life became very complicated. How can she explain her work and mission to her relatives and friends and expect to be understood with all these weird events that were happening since they were reunited to work together?

The Grays decided, after the black guy was sent to try to kill her and could not succeed, to put scales over scales on VIE's third eye. It was their way to try to stop the work of the Light. While they did all they could to stop CHADD's work with the Sound, by forcing him to ingest for years many drugs, mostly psychotropic drugs. Trying hard to destroy his neurons and erase his memory. But they went even further and attached their tentacles, covering his entire body to suffocate him. But VIE felt it, and Ignatz saw their action, and he began to detached them one by one and burned them so they would not reattached themselves.

The good thing is that their work will not succeed though because their plan is based on evil and they are not the creator of our souls.

CHADD picked up the phone in the middle of the night, at the place the corrupted system placed him over one year ago, and decided to end that and finalize their mission. He called VIE and told her, "Intonex Code—0010110" and hung up. He has been able to follow the news on TV and knows that it is now time for more people on earth to awaken, heal, receive reconnection, and recover clarity of thoughts and mind. Time has come.

VIE immediately got off the bed, rapidly took a shower, and passed the house door out. She knew the time had come. She drove very concentrated and began to speak the language of the Light, making sure that her phone was on. Though she knew that the cabal had wired her car and they were not only able to trace her car but also see her and hear her, she knew that most humans had they third eye calcified but the language of the Light will make its effect.

The Illuminades thought wiring for their own agenda and purpose, but VIE knew it will serve its purpose when needed and the time has arrived. Her language was transmitted globally, reaching all conscious.

The third eye is a very important part that regulates many function in the body, and Grays have always known it. It is why they have many human beings blocked through the calcification of the pineal gland and by the ingestion of fluoride. This control is all tied into separating humans from their star brothers and sisters, angelic beings, and high beings of Light.

The pineal is the key to the ascension and higher vibration. The angelic beings and high beings of Light are of a different density and have many answers to many of the earth's issues. But it becomes very hard for them to communicate when the pineal gland is either damaged or sabotaged.

Once the regeneration process of the pineal gland begins, it cannot be stopped and the people will not allow dominations any longer, and that is the main reason the dark energies, the cabal, the Illuminades do not want to see people have their pineal gland regenerated.

CHADD explained that "Illness is an altered state of awareness. I know this to be true from illnesses that were created from the side effects when I was forced to ingest prescriptions drugs for years. I was on a foggy state, blind, had a weak bladder, and was anemic. Illness can shape our entire perception.

Many seek altered state of awareness, and people who take drugs are usually doing it to alter their state of awareness. They have no idea that they are trying to escape the world they are leaving, pushed to this extreme by a frequency inaudible to their ears that the Grays are using for their own destruction. The musical conspiracy to separate mankind from the Divine.

I want to tell all of them that there is a much better way, there is a way out, providing freedom and hope. It is the Love frequency.

Through frequencies, many things can be achieved. The tone of the universe, for example, that repairs DNA and chakras. There is an audio frequency for cancer. The OM chanting tone has the same frequency as water: the life frequency. That is what the Tibetan monks have been chanting for eons and still are.

Air pollution, unclean water, and many other things can be restored through a specific frequency. The same way they control the weather, it can be reestablished by a frequency.

Sound frequency can also be a powerful regression tool. Sound can make you travel back in time, and it has an effect on many physical and mental illnesses. Sound frequency can also be hypnotic and also make you travel out of body. And this also has been hidden from you. Big Pharma would no longer rule and it does not suit their agenda. People would no longer be susceptible to control. Loud concert music is responsible for the lung collapse of people standing too close to subwoofer arrays of speakers."

After hours of driving, VIE is parked under the woods in the dark facing the releasing door, waiting for him. *By now the package has arrived, and he should be discharged,* she thought. They are too scared to release him in daylight. After all, they have sent him here illegally and accepted to be paid with a partial amount of his handicap check with the cooperation of the surrogate.

CHAPTER 28

Kafoa the Tohunga, How He Gets the Knowledge of the Vibration and of the Frequency, and the Message Kafoa Received

My friend Kafoa, the tohunga from Futuna, has always used rituals and drank in ceremony for preparation of the "kava kava" to enter in deep meditation and to communicate with his ancestors to obtain all information. Very similar to an Ayahuasca ceremony that involves drinking an hallucinatory plant extract drink under the guidance of a respected shaman.

The ceremony takes two days of preparation with Manoua, Titiana, and Kateva.

Kateva and a few other men, the carriers of the baskets, take a bath in the ocean. It is the first thing they have to do, the first day of preparation, to purify themselves.

Kateva makes a quick prayer to God to thank him for the roots that he will collect. Then he travels to the bushes with other men in search of the roots of kava kava.

While the men were purifying themselves by swimming for a few hours in the ocean, the women of the tribe made many colorful baskets to carry the roots the men will bring back from the bush.

While Teata is occupied with the wood bowl, where the kava kava will be extracted, Manoua is preparing herself for the fire dance she will perform at the opening ceremony.

Manoulia first goes to the Cathedral, confesses herself to the priest, and receive communion. Then she prays the Divine Mercy prayer nine times and offers her prayer to the world for peace, freedom, harmony, prosperity, and health of all humanity on earth.

When the day and time arrive, the king of Futuna opens the ceremony. For the opening ceremony, Manoulia dances the dance of fire with extreme agility. Agility that is necessary if she does not want to be burned. She lays down and rolls the wood in fire under her feet.

Then Kateva is anointed by the tohunga Kafoa and then begins to mix the roots with water. Teata's daughter, Maliana, chews the roots and spits the extract liquid in another wood bowl from which Kafoa will drink.

That is how Kafoa knows that resonance is matched vibration, synched frequency, and, he says, the coming altogether of attracting forces to create or manifest that which did not exist before. Working in nature and science, in mechanics and music, and in electronics and medicine. Like, he says, that the language has power words, and sound has a creative force that has a frequency of its own. The knowledge.

The tohunga's ancestors, the wisers, told him that CHADD are VIE are the chosen ones. VIE carries the language of the Light with its transformational vibratory energy to help humanity find its way and recover awareness. It is for humanity to reach the golden age with CHADD's help. The ancestors, the wisers, told him that they are the God Duo that reconnects people to the Divine. They also have the teaching knowledge that connects the dots from the Egyptians' time. It will help you understand what is happening today in your world. They are bringing you all the necessary information for your growth and awakening.

They must be recognized and respected for their mission and their work, while there is chaos by wars, terrorism, kidnapping, killing, and starvation, if they want to make it.

The Illuminati wants the human souls. Humans must awaken to become immortal. Once they awaken to the truth, they are saved. Wow! Thank you, Kafoa, for the message.

CHAPTER 29

The Origin of a Secret Society that Goes Back to Alexandria Library

And the journey continues. No it does not stop there, it's another vision of my work. That time it's Gabriella who asked for an appointment with VIE. The minute she entered her office, VIE felt her energy trying to merge with hers, and she blocked her, waiting to see her reaction. Gabriella gave her a fake story about her energy totally unbalanced and various sad experiences that occurred lately in her life. As soon as VIE began to work on her etheric body, she literally jumped out of her seat. Gabriella asked VIE to shorten the appointment pretending that she forgot to pick up her son at school. She paid and left. VIE never heard of her again.

The second time, the "secret society" sent to VIE a man. Marc entered the office, sat, looked at VIE, tried to read her mind, and became pale. VIE knew what type of energy Marc was and why he was here. She sent him back the energy and uncomfortable, he told her that he was a healer and asked her to join and work with him in his office. Then Marc tried once again to read VIE's aura, paid her, and left like hell.

In the beginning of this shamanic journey, I saw myself living at the Egyptian time, and my journey extended till this Aquarius era. I have pure and clear visions of how the past is link to this new era.

In fact, the world since Alexandria has been manipulated and under the control of secret societies, cults that continue to want to dominate the world. The elite in power are still corrupted and kill, rape, kidnap, poison, drug, and much more.

The story of this secret society began in Alexandria, the second largest city in Egypt. Its open harbor attracted Alexander the Great, who chose its location with the proximity to the river of Nile. Long before he landed in Egypt, men were struggling with existence.

Alexandria was well-thought-of for the center of thought, culture, and activity. It was the beginning of understanding of a natural world, and investigation of everything was important.

In the fifth-century BC, men like Socrates, Plato, and Aristotle were kings in Athens. They were the populars and controversies of the day with their early teaching of the foundation for the modern thoughts.

Alexander the Great was taught by Aristotle. Aristotle was taught by Plato, and Plato was taught by Socrates.

Plato and Socrates believed that the science mislead people, and what a person would see should not be believed. They believed in the internal and changing truth, which is known by the mind, not the sense.

But he said that nothing enters the mind, except for the senses, and he taught it to Alexander the Great. Alexander the Great was turned over to Aristotle of Macedonia to learn. Aristotle was a philosopher and filled the young warriors that were passionate to learn and valued the knowledge as a true source for power to conquer. The faith of the empire was depending on his education. Alexander was crowned Pharaoh of Egypt, after the Egyptians held him as a liberator from the Persian oppression.

Egypt was ruled by godlike Pharaohs for over 3,000 years, and those Pharaohs were the link between mortal subjects and the gods themselves. Egyptian Pharaohs thought to be gods in life and afterlife. But Alexander was Greek and had no guarantee of an afterlife. So where would Alexander the Great find immortality?

The legend said that he went in the desert and ask the God Amon if this was true, if it was the king son of god Amon himself that he saw in his inner dream. He saw that the God Amon embraced his mother. In the dream, God Amon embraced his mother while Alexander embraced Egypt and founded Alexandria. Then he asked his father, God Amon, if he requires him to do anything, and in a second dream, God Amon told him, "Go and find a city in the side of the island Fox," which he did immediately.

In 332 BC, he decreed the city would be the source and the learning place of the world, and that at its heart center, it could be the place a teaching institute on which empires could be built. That a science center could be built and the library would be a self-contained universe of mental stimulation. A plan was laid down by an architect for the new city.

But in 333 BC, Alexander came with wounds and fever and possibly poisoned, and Alexander the Great suddenly died. The library had yet to be built.

It was the beginning of a new leadership and a new way of thinking, and there was competition. One field of competition was culture. Ptolemy wanted the city to be a center of enlightenment, of knowledge, and of learning. It immediately began to attract influential scholars and people from all around the world. Ptolemy was a man of power and intelligence, and he surrounded himself with important men advanced in the field of literature, philosophy, and science. The architect helped Talami to lay the plan for the new center, and Talami collected as many books as possible. On occasion, manuscripts were donated, and with more materials came more visitors. The library of Alexandria acquired the largest library of books existed in antiquity.

Before, Alexandria doctors were using animals to research human anatomy. Now an in house medical school was established.

Then came the secret history of the teaching of the Rosicrucians. For centuries, scholars have argued over the existence of an advanced civilization with vast scientific technology and spiritual knowledge, and much of the earliest public information in recorded history comes from the Athenian philosopher Plato's famous works.

According to Plato, Atlantis was a massive island in the Atlantic Ocean said to be the creation of the Greek god Poseidon. The Greek god of the sea is said to have appointed ten kings when he created order in Atlantis. Each with his own division, and these kings have absolute control over the citizens and laws alike, punishing and even killing, as the monarch chose some. It is believed that it is the cradle of primordial Rosicrucian, which flows with the Rosicrucian tradition.

The legend tells us that the first king of Egypt was chosen among the Atlanteans, and with Hatshepsut, the fifth Pharaoh of the eighteenth dynasty of Egypt, organized the mystery of school together and, as a single order, thought most in addition to serving with his co-Pharaoh Hashput.

He was interested in the organized classes concerning in the mysteries of life, and he organized them from disparate groups to one solid class, but never interfere with the general thinking of the Egyptians. They were people who worshipped many gods.

According to Plato, his knowledge comes from Solomon. Atlantis flourished until it declined through the corruption, wars, superstition, and finally ending into cataclysm.

Later it was a philosopher pioneer and leader to the Rosicrucian, Francis Bacon, who used the idea of an ideal civilization in his utopian work, *New Atlantis*. Ancient knowledge and high ideals continue to be passed down esoteric tradition, but what the mainstream does not acknowledged is the fate of the sacred knowledge that was nearly lost when Atlantis was destroyed. Could the survivors of Atlantis pass their wisdom on to another society, the Rosicrucian based on Egyptian/Babylonian mystery religions. The priestly class that report to the satanic religions?

The Rosicrucian order had its traditional conception and birth in Egypt, in activities of the great white lodge. Esoteric and mystical. As known to all advanced Rosicrucians, it's a living testimonial to the truth of notable principles of Brotherhood, which activate Freemasonry. Their system is based on the Egyptian/Babylonian mystery religions, and the priestly class reports to the satanic bloodline, the fallen angels. It is said that Freemasonry has acknowledged its debt to the ancient white brotherhood by adding a Rosicrucian degree to the ancient and accepted Scottish rite.

In the Book of the Dead, there is these admonishments "to allow no one to see it," "never let the ignorant person or anyone whatsoever look upon it."

The German alchemist Michael Meyer described the Rosicrucians as having arisen from the Egyptians. The Brahman, the mysterious and elusive Samothrace of the magi of Persia. The Pythagoreans and the arrows, its mystery school, which acted both as universities and monasteries or the guardians of its wisdom. Under Pythagoras, numerology breaks everything in the universe down into numbers. It is the mathematics of all things and geometry, the highest form of mathematical studies.

These schools experienced the destructive flowing under the rule of Akhenaten especially after he introduced the concept of monotheism. The Egyptian religion is particularly intriguing because of his mystery schools, according to Christian rubies Egyptian Pantheon.

Toth was the teacher of medicine and astronomy and the arc. He knew the secret of magic and was the initiator in the new kingdom under Akhenaten. The ancient pantheon was abolished.

Harvey Spencer law is a noted Rosicrucian author, mystic founder in Egypt, and founded Alexandria. Moses was the organizer and the school initiates that later gave rise to the Rose Cross. The occult knowledge of the Egyptians and considered secret. "To allow no one to see...never let the ignorant, person or anyone whatsoever look upon it." The things were done secretly. It was transmitted houses of life, sometimes called the mystery schools, which were attached to each temple. It was well documented between Herodotus (a Greek historian, writer, and geographer born in the Persian Empire) and Plato, that degree traditions owe much to Egyptians priests. Both men had visited Egypt, and there are many similarities in their pantheons. There existed a strong tradition, which claimed the great sages of Ancient Greece, a payment knowledge to the Egyptians teachers. The Freemasonry has acknowledged its debt to the ancient white brotherhood by adding a Rosicrucian degree to the ancient and accepted Scottish rite. It was claimed that many among them were initiated into the mystery thus assuring the transmission of Egyptians' learning into the Greek world.

From the Egyptians' time, started by Adam Weishaupt, trained by the Jesuit whose name was probably fictitious, part of a sacred code. A German philosopher and founder of the order of Illuminati, a secret society, that later adapted the name of Brother Spartacus. The actual character of the society was an elaborate network of spies and counterspies. Adam Weishaupt was initiated into the Masonic lodge and used the Freemasonry to recruit for his own quasi-Masonic society. He organized his ritual structure and greatly expanded the secret organization. It was the beginning of a fight of church against the government. The Roman church was anti-science. They feared the conflict between the dogma and the scientific knowledge. The Illuminati invaded the Vatican, that has the greatest library of the world, with fifteen miles of books that no one is allowed to see. During the Middle Ages, the church commanded everything and later in time opened an embassy in Washington, DC.

The Knights Templar, the knights of the poor of the temple of Solomon, are the most revered and feared society warriors and monks. They are the ones that incorporated the first banking branch. They traveled to the Middle East and met the group of John of the East, and followed a cult. They became the greatest threat to the Vatican. They became arrogant and so big that they arose the jealousy of the French king.

They brought their finances to La Rochelle and boarded it on ships that sailed to an unknown destination. They were arrested and burned. But most of the knights heard of what was coming and fled and became the Illuminade, the actual cabal.

Then another threat came to the Vatican, science. Scientists, astronomers, and artists were the first to challenge the Vatican's view of existence in a particular way.

The Hitler's race purity program was orchestrated from America and Britain through a banker (that owns today 80 percent of the world's wealth) purity expert, and the banker's family who were into eugenics.

They sent energetic set verses to Germany to help, promote, and give info backing and expertise in the program cumulative through the vaccinations, through genetically modified food, fluoride in water, hunger, manufacture disease, radiation, etc. The impact on health is catastrophic. One in hundred patients on death list. Euthanasia, withdrawal of food, of fluids, and of drugs so they die very quickly, demise pill, limiting access to affordable medical care makes eliminating the elderly easier.

The dark has an agenda that was agreed upon at an earth summit. A planning to use the environment, that they are destroying, to justify the industrialization and to end the democracy and the German to run Europeans to fold it into one government.

The abolition of private property, the restructuration of the family, children to be raised by the state, people told what their job will be, major reduction on movement, creation of human settlement zones, mass resettlement as people are forced to evacuate land where they live, dumbing down education achieved a long time ago, mass depopulation by half. In terms of reducing the population, sperm counts in many parts of the world are plummeting.

They are setting up their agenda organizations up in all communities all over the world, all over the place, giving the impression that each of these is basically an independent local community initiative when it's all being orchestrated through this organization through their nations.

Some wrote that technetronic here involves the gradual appearance of a man-controlled society. Such a society would be dominated by elite, unrestrained by traditional values, soon it will be possible to assert almost continual surveillance over every citizen and to maintain up to date complete files containing even the most personal information about the citizen. These files will be subject to instantaneous retrieval by the authorities.

They want a world of regions; they want total control of people in the hallway alien police state. The want technocrats and bureaucrats in positions. They want the human population maintained under five hundred million and in perpetual balance with nature. They came with the episode of jean, isolating the gene that makes people sterile. They engineered that gene into corn.

Growing food will be banned by saying that it is not safe and the state and the corporations will control all food production. The supply and distribution of food will be monitored and so that no one can give food to a fugitive of the system. State corporations will control all food production. And all people growing food at home will be arrested. Only the one that confirm to the system will get food.

They want to pack people together in high-rise, basically prison-size, living places so all the people are in one place and they clear the land of everything else straight off the pages.

High-speed trains are the main source and end people in cars to control better.

Their main purpose is destruction to enslave human beings and take control of Gaia with then trapped mortal human souls. Worshipping a fake god.

CHAPTER 30

Hughes Capet

One day, I was in a holistic convention in San Francisco when a woman came to me. She said, "Let's get in a quiet place. I am sent to you. You will soon see why."

These types of things were beginning to be very familiar to me, and I followed her. Then she asked me for one of my jewelry. She needed to touch it, she said, and feel my energy. I gave her my family ring, the one with my family crest that I am always wearing on my small finger. It did not take much time before she began to cough. It was the same type of cough that my father had before he passed away.

She then said, "I am going to ask this gentleman to gently back up a little bit." And I heard, "There is a gentleman that used to smoke a lot and to cough a lot. He says that you know who he is. He is your father and he is very happy, very happy that you came. Also he says that every time you have some family reunion, he is among you. Again he says that he is very happy that you came, and he has some information for you. It has to do with your ancestors, and it is related to what he said once to Mary-Anette, when she said that her grandkid's name was Hughes, and he replied, Hughes but not Capet.

You see, the Capetians founded a dynasty, affirming the politician independence from the kings of England and the Pope. Our ancestors were Catholic though. This period gave birth to eight years of crusades.

Christianity began to change. The humanitarian foundation created by Jesus eroded as Christianity became more political. The political transformation of Christianity got its first big push in the West Roman Empire with the Christian conversion of its ruler, Constantine the Great. The Crusades: the message given to Mohammed was a new religion called Islam. Members of Mohammed's faith are called Moslems, which come from the word *Muslim*, meaning 'one who submits.' Islam was one more custodial religion designed to instill abject obedience in humans. The supreme being of the Islam faith is named Allah. Five hundred years after the death of Mohammed, the Christians launched a coordinated military effort to force the Moslems out of the Holy Land. This effort is known as the Crusades.

The Christian Crusades was to free Palestine from the Moslems. Minor battles between Christians and Moslems had broken out beforehand, but it was a call to arms by Pope Urban II on 1905 that finally turned those skirmishes into an organized war effort involving nearly every Christian ruler of Europe. Not only were the Crusaders killing Moslems, they were also killing Jew who had ended in Europe. A genocidal wave in the German Rhineland was the first major episode; it was sparked by unsubstantiated rumors that Rhineland Jews were using Christian children in their religions sacrifices. Obliterating the Jews became important to the Crusades, and the massacres continued even after the Crusades to Jerusalem.

The Christian Crusaders were led primarily by two powerful knight organizations with intimate Brotherhood ties: the Knights Hospitaller and the Knights of the Temple (Knights Templar). Their purpose was aid and comfort. In the 1118, the Knights Hospitaller underwent a change of leader and purpose. They were made into a military order dedicated to fighting the Moslems who were continually trying to recapture Jerusalem. They soon became affiliated with the Brotherhood network by adopting Brotherhood traditions and titles. They became ruled by a grand master and developed secret rites and rituals. By 1119, one year later, the Hospitallers had become a lighting order, the Templar Knights were in existence. They originally called themselves the Order of the Poor Knights of Christ because they took solemn vow of poverty. Although the Templars and Hospitallers had a common enemy in the Moslems, the two Christian organizations became rivals.

They became the Knights of Malta, then changed to Knights of Rhodes when they moved to the island of Rhodes. While in Malta, the knights became a major military and naval power in the Mediterranean until they were defeated by Napoleon. The knights of Malta had their headquarters moved to Rome under Pope Leo XIII. Today they are known as the Sovereign and Military Order of Malta. SMOM runs hospitals, clinics, and leper colonies throughout the world. It also gives active assistance to anti-communist causes and surprisingly influential in political, business, and intelligence circles despite its small size.

By Philip IV, the Fair, in France, the Templar controversy had become too strong, and he ordered the arrest of the Templars within the dominion and tortured them to extract confessions. Five years later, the Pope dissolved the Templar Order by Papal decree. Many Templars were executed, including Jacques de Molay, who was publicly burned in front of the cathedral of Notre Dame in Paris. Templar Knights organization managed to survive and were given a home in Portugal. They were granted their usual rights and privileges, wore the same costumes, and were governed by the same rules they had before. Templars change their name to Knights of Christ and also changed the cross on their uniform from the Maltese cross to the official Latin cross.

To the list we can add two famous Christian orders, the Franciscan that appeared to be quite human and adopted the cord-at-the-loins outfit and bold spot used by the Egyptian Brotherhood priests, and the Dominicans that were placed in charge of the most widely hated of the Crusades: the Catholic Inquisition.

Pope Gregory IX placed them in charge of investigating the Albigenses. He gave them full power to name and condemn all surviving heretics. The church was no longer the humanitarian decentralized religion envisioned by Jesus. The new Catholic, "undivided" Church headquartered in Rome had succumbed to the "reforms" of the East Roman Empire emperors. It was a religion Jesus would have deplored.

Looking at the spiritual practices of the Christian Knights and the Moslem Ismailians, we see that participation in warfare was often exalted as a spiritual quest. Warriors on both sides were inspired by corrupted Brotherhood mysticisms, which taught that spiritual rewards could be earned by engaging in military endeavors against fellow human beings. This was the mythology of the spiritually noble war in gallant soldiers were promised eternal salvation and a place in heaven for fighting a noble cause. This mythology still remains vital today for recruiting people to participate in continued warfare. Twisting the urge for spiritual freedom into honoring the war.

But if war helps to bring money, war is also institutionalization of criminality. Money itself is not valuable; the purpose of money is to facilitate the exchange of goods and services. Money is therefore an extension of war and cannot bring about spirituality improvement because criminality is one of the main causes of mental, spiritual deterioration. Societies exalting in criminal actions will suffer rapid deterioration. Spiritual doctrines that combat are doctrines that degrade the human race. The Illuminati and Rosicrucians were major powers behind a new wave of religion movement. Catholic Church had fallen into the hands of Pope Leo X, son of Lorenzo Di Medici, who was the head of a wealthy international banking house in Florence. Under John XXIII, the Medicis were awarded the task of collecting taxes and tithes that were due to the Pope. The Medici operated a network of collectors to accomplish the undertaking. The Catholics believed in the importance of paying indulgences in money paid to compensate for their sins.

As a Catholic priest and educator, Martin Luther was subject to the strict regimen that was imposed to all clergy of the church and regular confession. At that time, confessionals were done improperly, and Luther found it difficult. He felt compelled to seek another path, and he claimed that he was trying to reestablish the primitive Christian Church of Jesus. Another form of Christianity was born, and it only departed from the true teachings of Jesus. While Catholic teaching still had many flaws and lacked a true science of the spirit, these ideas reflected some of the truth and decency, which were at the heart of Jesus's message. Luther said that the Pope was the forces of the Antichrist, and it resulted in war between Catholic and Protestants, like today in Ireland. The Protestant sects today account for around one-third of all Christians worldwide and nearly half of all Christians in North America. Luther's seal consisted of either side of two Brotherhood symbols that are the rose and the cross, the chief symbols of the Rosicrucian Order. During his life, important individual families who were active in the Illuminati and in Rosicrucian supported Luther. One of them was the head of the powerful royal house of Hess whose descendants would later held important positions in the Brotherhood organization and in German Freemasonry. Calvin taught his own interpretations of the Protestant doctrine, resulting in a Protestant denomination named after him. They were forbidden to drunkenness, gambling, dancing. The bank of England established the pattern for our modern central bank system, often led by the Brotherhood. The purpose of a central bank was to put the government into debt so the government became the major creditor. Over twenty years after France established an identical setup bank."

Then the woman said, "I have a message from your mother. Your mother says that she is very worried and she is crying. The cabal, through an archon surrogate, is making sure that you are deprived of all return from your work but have expenses. The archon wants you poor and to flank your mission. She worships Lucifer with all the others from the cabal. She is a pathetic liar that does not have imagination and can't create, but she can twist facts." Then the woman vanished.

CHAPTER 30-2

The Time Traveler

Soon after, I am at a red light when a man appeared coming from another time, crossed the road, and attracted my full attention. He looked Indian, but had an old brown European pants, too short for him, a weird old hat on his head, and some funny shoes. He seems totally lost.

That is where I heard my self thinking, *That man is coming from another time and wondering what he is doing here.*

But the man telepathically began to talk to me, saying, "Going back to the time the Capetians founded a dynasty, affirming the politician independence from the kings of England and the Pope control, your ancestor Pierre received directly from King Louis IV, the Sun King, his parent, a weapon and the highest symbol of spiritual power to which nothing resist. It destroys both internal and external enemies. It is the fleur-de-lis armorial heralding bearing. A heraldic wide V and that is placed on Pierre's crest to be seen. It has skipped a few generations, but it is yours now. You will now stop any harm from unclean energies and defend yourself, your personal life, and your path with it as the chosen door to the Divine. Just do not forget to ask through the power of Jesus Christ, the Holy Spirit, and Saint Michael the Archangel that it will be purified before it comes back to you when you use it."

Then the time traveler messenger vanished from sight.

CHAPTER 31

The Rainbow Body, Rays of Organs, Nutrition, and the Pleiadian Technology

Now this is me, VIE, telling you. If the Andromedans are involved in changing the inner mechanisms of the way the earth behaves with the solar system, in the lunar system, and the stellar system, they work in manipulating the planet itself. And the life forms are then brought into this influence of manipulation that is called the divine intervention. They communicate with human beings on the planet through their body and the human consciousness, primarily through the aura field of the earth and the auric field of people.

And the Pleiadians are keeping a close eye on earth as the human beings are in self-destruction mode and destructed by the people that control this planet. It is in the greed, it is not into healing the planet, and almost every environment that has any credence is violently opposed by some industrial faction. If humans were allowed to continue, there would be a lot of innocent souls that would be destroyed. So they are constantly monitoring.

The Pleiadians teach technology of the human cell structure from the DNA level and beyond. They divide the cell structure from the DNA level and beyond that by dividing the cell structure into basic sections. First the lowest section is the biochemical section. It is where we use vitamins, minerals, foods we ingest, which could be considered drugs if you take these the wrong order. Anything that is metabolic or has anything to do with nutrition of medicine or any kind of substance in the body. That is the first level and the base level. Controlling the way cells behave, controlling that level are electrical levels. The ionization changes that go on biochemically to produce and to dissolve, and to metabolic certain things in the body. So we have biochemical level and we have electrical level.

Electricity is taught by the Pleiadians as a living entity. The science that deals with the behavior of the consciousness behavioral effects of electricity in the body is called the science of electrical precursor, the series of parameters over a period of time, over twenty-four-hour period, the cells sense to cause changes in the biochemistry into cell structures. The autocurrent entering levels form all hormonal levels of the body. That is their science that they bring to earth beings.

Like the precursor devices (EMF protector) that transmit directly into the DNA because all the changes starts with a DNA on the physical level. The DNA which is what's called a nuclear membrane in a cell. The EMF devices block harmful effects of radiation, exposure to pollution, stress, and promotes wellness, happiness, and healing. It also helps you with burnout feeling, depression, and sleep.

The idea is not to run away from the environment but to put around your neck something that is going to cause you not to be subjected to radioactive fields or electromagnetic fields. When the body is subject to stress of the environment, stress of radiation, stress of poisons in the air, stress of poisons in the food, at one level there is one universal function in the body that takes place before destruction occurs that production of free radicals. Environmental factors such as pollution, radiation, cigarette smoke, and herbicides can spawn free radicals. So huge dose of radiation creates a free radical or a huge dose of arsenic creates a free radical, and the result is cell destruction to a point that consciousness cannot currently inhibit it anymore. It separates from the cell, and if too much consciousness separates from too many cells, you end up with a disease section in the body or you end up dead—out of your body.

You have to understand how nutrition works and really get a working knowledge of it. That is why these different ray colors have a lot to do. Our body is made up of oxygen, hydrogen, nitrogen, and carbon. Hydrogen is a very important element in the body. And the pyramid shape is what all these chemicals and all these stresses try to distort. If you keep the body, the carbon atom in the body, for example, a red blood cell teams in the red blood cell, the iron in this shape, the red blood cell will function. Everything comes from energy, and you have to go back to the energy level first.

As the rainbow, you start with a rainbow because your body is like a rainbow. There are seven colors to the rainbow, and each of the rainbow represents the consciousness. The first is red and represents the first ray or the will of the Father energy. The second ray (blue) and the Father energy is anchored through red. It is through the red organs in the body that is linked to the pituitary gland. The blue is love, wisdom, the healing energy, and the sun energy, the Christ energy anchored through the heart.

Everything related to blue relates to that energy at some point. Green represents the thyroid gland and is female. It is the Holy Ghost and a synthesis of the red and blue. Those red, blue, green are the primary forces. You can break down every substance into one of those forces. For example, vitamin A, which is very powerful in the immune system, is a red force, is a will force. With B complex, you go down to the fourth energy, which is a compassion energy or a yellow force, and when you begin to relate to vitamin to the feeling that you do or do not have. For example, if you were waking up in the morning and you do not have the will to do something, you can bet that your body needs something in the immune system, which is directly related to red, the will. So you need vitamin A and probably need chromium. Chromium is the first element that you would take. When you start getting a runny nose or have any sign of any kind of physical symptom coming on, a scratching throat. Researchers will tell you that the first thing you start taking if you have tested HIV positive is chromium because chromium produces helper T-cells. Then once your helper T-cells count goes up in the white blood cell region, then you can start taking large amounts of vitamin A and then large amount of vitamin C, which binds itself together. A lot of people make the mistake when they come down with a cold or a scratchy throat of jamming in a large amounts of vitamin C, but that is wrong because the life force in the body is now being directed toward the virus that is giving you a cold. Same with the antibiotics, it will fight the bacteria but not viruses; it will feed them at the contrary.

CHAPTER 32

The Future of the Planet and the Missing Piece

As the destructions began by the hurricane Irma on the Caribbean islands. I contacted my friend from Puerto Rico, but he was leaving in Michigan but then moved to another state. He told me that he already increased his Tesla weather machine twenty-five times with no effect. We knew both that this was not a normal phenomenon but a creation by the dark forces dedicated to mess with humans. It was manipulated and engendered from underground, and he could prove it to me. It was showing on the picture he sent me to see. That is when I had an Akashic experience. Even though the hurricane Irma, they said, lost its strength, it did not sound like it until it began to blow very strong around 11:00 p.m. I entered in a meditative trance, and I knew what I had to do. Something that I had already done a few times. I had even directed other hurricanes away, and I entered in communication with Irma. I knew I had to ask for its forgiveness and tell her that I loved her. Ten minutes later, the wind went down and it never picked up again.

We knew this was coming. Our mutual friend entity had warned us and told us to shield ourselves, our homes, and cars under a white light cone, surround us a white light island and our properties, and anchor it for four weeks. Three more were coming behind created by the dark controllers of earth.

The key to the success intervention was *focus*. Focus on a specific target with a specific timescale. For the hurricane Irma, the timescale was "right now" because the threat was imminent. The result was complete change from what was expected to a far more benign situation. The power to change the world lies within your grasp. When you use the Love and Light technique or send Light energy out into the world on a daily basis, you feel the continual warmth of knowing that you are living the way that humans were designed to live as channels for love and light.

Dear ones, this is a message that you want to put in a time capsule. A human time capsule so that you might open it later and reread it. It is about the future of the planet.

What is going on earth at this moment have been seen before, and it's the same steps that were taken before that is coming now; it's *human consciousness*. It is simply consciousness, but it only belongs to humans because you are human. It is the same kind of thing energy, the attributes and the confluences of the energies, are almost identical that the consciousness that the other planets have gone through. The reason is because life is similar, some almost identical from planet to planet because the galaxy is made up of fractal. From the smallest to the largest, you are going to see repetitive part of the same thing. What it means is that it gives rise on the planets, one perhaps right now that is just getting life, the building blocks of DNA getting ready to be seeded by you in the future. DNA, the same amino structures as you have is common to all. So we have seen this before.

Gaia is a young civilization, so young it is hard to even give you a perspective of how young. Your civilization has not even been around the galaxy one time yet. It takes almost two hundred million years to go around one time. There are civilizations that have been around three times. None of them are available to influence you to the degree that you can influence yourselves. You are youth. It starts to explain why the earth has been through such horrendous time. Civilization looks ugly to you. Your past, your history filled with survival, weaponry, mass destruction. No elegance of thoughts for life torture. They all went through that. As you grow up in knowledge, it occurs to you that there is a better way to solve problems through listening and cooperation. You have to survive. But you are still on the playground; you are still pushing each other around.

Now about energy not seen. The first energy is a complement of energy on the galaxy that interest you and that you cannot see. It touches you in ways that are fascinating. This unseen energy is responsible for what the new agers sense first. You are able to pick up energy in someone's aura. Some medical intuitive can feel what is wrong, *the aura broadcast of sickness, health, joy*. The very institute that puts this on, so interested in these energies. Unseen energies that make a difference on what it is that a reader reads of psychic fields of a futurist computerize. Where does it come from, why is it so elusive... The key to the future, the elegance of the wisdom.

This unseen energy that has attributes and you do not know anything about, and you are discovering everything about it. It is called the Quantum Consciousness of Humanity. A percent of humanity has awakened in a certain way to affect the entire planet now. You would be taken to another civilization like the Pleiadian, Orion, or to any of those, you would not recognize anything.

First of all, they do not have technology because of the physical things that do things. Things that they threw away long time ago when they realized that the physics of human consciousness could do everything they ever wanted. That is where it is going and you still wonder what it is truly. What this is, how does it work, is it quantitative if you have more of it, does it do more things. And I say no.

Human consciousness has no definition that would make more sense because less than 1 percent has awaken in a certain way to affect the entire planet now. It is not quantitative, it is not 3-D, and it is less than one-half of 1 percent. How can I explain to some of you that have no concept and are not ready, physics that you do not know yet, anything about this system and that may occur in a certain way? In a distributed way, not a centralized way, in order to break this barrier called the Wisdom Barrier, and it is survival mode and it goes to a mode that starts to build the wisdom that enhances the brains of all humanity to a point where they can agree on something that they never even knew before without actually having it taught. Did you hear that? Now you can expect that it surrounds the human beings in such a way, and the civilization in such a way, that when you were born, it becomes second nature. The wisdom of getting all, it is called the Wisdom Barrier.

You are looking into the very essence of it. You are picking into what makes it work. You are about to push the envelope that will affect all humanity. Not just the Light workers, not just the old souls. You are about to push a button on physics you did not know existed. This is big. It is the missing piece.

Humanity explains things only from what they know, not what they don't. But Newtonian physics is the gold standard of motion everywhere. So the human beings struggle to find formulas that will put the unexplained into Newtonian boxes.

Welcome to the *dark matter*. This is human take what is known, observe what is unknown but there, and place it into boxes of the known and saying maybe, just maybe, there are missing laws of physics that we do not know about that would explain this. And here is one of the biggest place that you are missing. The place of the physics of consciousness. How do you define consciousness; well it's developed through very special thought of human and this and that. No, it is not consciousness; it is physics and you should get used to this. You are developing it through human thought unaware that there are rules, there are postulates, there are beautiful attributes of the physics of consciousness that are going to start to explain what is going to happen in the future, but you don't see it that way. The missing piece is the knowledge that you can track this, that you can plot it. You can create it even outside of humanity. Did you know that it is beautiful because when I start to tell you some of the attributes of the physics of consciousness, you will go oh!

What are the attributes of physics, what do you know, that the answer is actually very little about you experimenting with creating things. The very technology that you have, that is so beautiful on this planet, is brought to you by the knowledge of the physics that you know. And there is cause and reaction, and you build this and that and this happens. You put together certain kinds of things, and through all of them, all the principles and the rules that you understand and the form basic laws that you have out of six, you know what you are and you are using them.

That same scenario exists in consciousness. There are laws of consciousness that are put like the laws of physics in that there is cause, there is effect, but in the quantum world, there are no linear, and so they create certain kinds of things. The physics of consciousness being quantum and not linear creates attributes that are going to create the future of this planet. If you know the physics of consciousness, you can build a better world. It has attributes and first of all, it does not travel from place to place, neither in a straight direction, it does not travel. Consciousness is not in one place going to another; consciousness does not expand; it does not get bigger or smaller.

Consciousness is. Consciousness of physics sits there ready to be enhanced or not, based upon other laws around it, and when they are readily applied, then they all change.

Consciousness, here is a couple of it: One is called the Benevolence Factor. As the physics of consciousness is explored and the wisdom factor is applied and the barrier is passed, what happens next is an exponential understanding and application of the rules of consciousness that create a factor that generates benevolent action. Right now on this planet, there is a struggle between forces because of the consciousness that you have developed here and the rules that you have put in place through the physics of consciousness. There is an allowance right now of many things on this planet that we have never talked about.

There is evil on the planet. Satan is a satanic consciousness from the fourth dimension that feeds from the suffering energy of humans and animals. Human rights abuse is their food. This suffering generates interdimensional food.

These evil entities, the dark forces, also called the unclean, are dedicated to come in and mess with you. Because this test allows it. Because of what you have created in the rules that have applied and how you are using it allow it. But the next step past the wisdom barrier enhances those very patterns of consciousness that you are going to discover as part of physics that close the door. When the rules of physics are applied in certain situations, you can control what happens. It is the same in consciousness. When you reach a point of understanding on how the physics of consciousness works, the mechanics of it, the distribution of it, the spiral delivery of it is going to make sense to you. You shut the door and the things; the dark forces that visited this planet can't anymore. And those places of darkness that would come in and play with your consciousness because it is that the teenage level of physics can't get in anymore.

That is the best explanation I can give you for what is going to happen in the future, and the Pleiadians are happy, jumping up and down, because they know what happened. It is almost an experimental evolution, if you want it to be. One thing leads to another; it builds on itself. You don't have to start all over every single time you are born. You come in with the factors that you learn before and build upon them, and it is going to change everything. Then when the physics is revealed, you will understand why there are machines that can work with consciousness. But you are not going to need them very long. It has already started. You are at the wisdom barrier. You threw a switch and no amount of dark energy can stop it.

You will figure out creating increased DNA percentage activation, creating generation after generation of a human being who can create things out of nothing, who have control over physics, which is a lower kind of physics. The highest kind of physics is consciousness. And consciousness physics can control 3-D physics any day. All of you are going to be there to see it because that is the plan. You entered a world you all wished you could have. Peace on earth, that's easy, that's the beginning, that's the planting the seed, and from there it gets good. That is the future, a peaceful civilization, creating anything it wanted. Physically, never hungry, who can live as long as wanted to, could put themselves in a quantum state if they wanted to, have different sets of ideas of the way things should work. Who have no central control a manager list corporation. It can work and that is what is coming.

Government decentralized to where there is none. There will be no such thing as world government. Instead there will be world consciousness agreement. A planet born into a situation where they know better. That is the wisdom factor. Too good to be true? Ask the Pleiadian, those from Orion, or any other planet of free choice.

And the Pleiadians since have been given full authority and control over the awakening, healing, and liberation of earth. 0010110 algorithm of freedom and compassion. No one of these controllers can leave the planet to go to the galaxy. The earth is totally surrounded, and no one can go through. Though some important elite from the cabal working for Lucifer that decided to meet in Europe. Even though they may seem to be welcomed in Europe by unawakened beings there, some European countries after the Brexit, some other influenced European politician are already politically in great challenge. Things are changing fast. Too many human beings disappear, are being killed, tortured, raped, and pedophilia and cannibalism has reached its maximum.

CHAPTER 33

Welcome to the New Earth

It's a Tuesday and I was busy in the back room of the house when I heard someone walking inside the house. I heard the noise when a person sat on the sofa. I left rapidly the back room toward the living room and found an old woman seating on the red sofa. I asked her if she was lost and if I could help her, but she did not reply. Then she began to speak.

"I am you, VIE, from another timeline, Mary Magdalene. You will soon understand what I am going to tell you. Thing will start to fall together, connecting the dots, where you will see a bigger picture. Perhaps it is arising for you, for the planet of what is really going on. The change is everywhere, but it's going to affect the oldest souls first. It affects CHADD and you first because you are wiser. May I remind you that you have simply been here, on earth, longer and you are more experienced including spiritually. Not only on how things work on the planet, but you have come to spiritual decisions lifetimes ago, and you wake up in this lifetime and you still have them.

There is one or two things that pass through the veil from lifetime to lifetime that you do inherit whereas you may not remember anything else. There are some things that pass through, like the countenance you have of who you are and what you have learned spiritually that comes right through. You have spent plenty of time to learn things in order to get to the place you are now, and you don't have to start over. Not really spiritually. You will remember. Or you will shaman-ship old souls by just sitting there, and be normal. You know better. You do not have to awaken, go to meetings, or any of these things. Just your very presence on this planet as wise persons, CHADD and you, changes the crystalline grid.

VIE, there is so much here that is energy based that you have to enjoy in any shape and any form. To enjoy yourself without claiming that you are metaphysical or talking to anybody about what you believe. Your very presence is here that passes the veil. You never move backward spiritually, therefore as old souls, you are going to see and use these tools first.

You are known by God, and there is preparation for all that you are experiencing. There was preparation by spirit, and you passed through year 2000 and 2012. And if you passed this marker, and you did, everything had to change. And you are seeing it in the system, in the weather, in the consciousness. But things do not simply change itself. You have tools, it has to be helped. This is how much you are loved. You are not doing this by yourself. Number one, when this planet was seeded with the knowledge of light and dark, which is the earth creation story, there were things set up for today, not long ago, in the scheme of galactic time, just a flash of an eye ago. Two hundred thousand years ago, when the seeding of this planet began.

The creation story of Light and dark, when the DNA started to change. It was when human being got the twenty-three chromosomes instead of twenty-four. Those who seeded humans set up a system of twenty-four nodes and nulls, and they have now in turn identified for them. They are in places they were not expected, and when they start working together, they start sending signals to the crystalline grid and start to enhance knowledge on the planet. It is not esoteric and cannot be proven. But is there any multidimensional engine in every single one of you who can say, 'Yes, I feel it, yes, I know it'? I know that it is true, it makes sense. Why is it so difficult to think that the Pleiadians put you here and left? You are the time capsules that are opening at the right time, flooding the crystalline grid with potential realities that you have not seen yet. Inventions that you have not pulled out, but they are coming. They are here and you need to move to the next step. You will use them for health and well-being. Does it make sense now? That the dark were so much trying to stop CHADD and VIE?

You have start communication with beings you did not even know they existed, and all this is part of the plan over time. But it had to be put here as a time capsule. That was just number one, and I am here to let you know that you are not doing this alone.

Number two, if you ask astronomers, they will tell you about something that is different with your solar system than it ever has been since humanity got here. You are moving into a new kind of space as your solar system goes around the center of the galaxy. It goes into places it has never been before while humans were alive. And it is going to affect your sun. You have had a bubble of protection that is physics around this solar system for eons that is now passing away and being by a whole other kind of energy. This is not esoteric but physics. It is physical and it is happening and it is going to affect the sun first.

You can ask astronomers if the radiant cycle is on schedule and if they have seen some difference in activity, not more in activeness, but less, and if they have seen anything. Because the sun is being affected, it has a magnetic field called heliosphere, and it intersects with your magnetic field, and your magnetic field is the couch you sit in that affects your consciousness. Look at experiments between magnetics and consciousness, about the strength of the magnetic field and the consciousness of humanity. It has been established, so what affects your sun is going to affect you. It is going to enable parts of your biology that have been enabled before.

As old wise souls you are going to pick it up first, and you have. You are already vibrating higher, you began to think a little differently and evolved while still alive instead of having to go into a death-life cycle two or three times to get it. This is a fast track to a higher consciousness of this planet, which was always there. If you would not have made it, you would have gone there anyway. They just would not have been human here. It was always there and prepared for you, by you, before you even got here as human beings.

You left a time capsule for yourself. This was the preparation. You prepared everything before you got it. You left a time capsule to have a much better chance than you ever thought.

The new tools of the shift. There is a portion of physics that you live in everyday that is starting to awaken, which is the *benevolent reality*. Science is starting to see things they don't truly understand, which is physics that creates harmony and it is starting to occur—entertainment, entanglement. It is physics that wants to create things that works in synchronous mesh harmony.

Welcome to the New Earth! The legacy has been benevolent wants harmony. It is a physics that is benevolent and wants harmony. Every time that you see a reaction to it, it's the Light that it starting to be spread, a Light that is going to make politics someday transparent, and they are not ready for that. So their reaction is anger and frustration. The next election, you will have a tendency to not vote, but it is important to. Decide between them which one is the best, even if you think there is no choice, so choose the best and it will be the one. Because if you do not vote, you won't be able to vote for what is transformational. And you have this privilege and this right. The next time around, it is going to be different. The ripples of what is coming are being felt. There is precedent on other planets that have gone through this, and you are right on schedule. Because what is happening here happened there. It is about Light and dark, and the energy is reacting to the energy and what happens.

This is number 3, *benevolent physics*.

Number 4 is how spirit starts to work with you in a certain way with a certain kind of consciousness. It triggers that your present physics has changed. The capsules are working with a crystalline grid, and the ground is ready for the seeds to be planted. So the tools start to appear. There is a different scenario today for human of cause and effect when it comes to pure intent affirmations. All of these energetic things that you have decided to work a certain way are starting. What wasn't working yesterday is working today, and what didn't work today maybe could be working tomorrow. Do not resign yourself because something did not work. You need to feel and intuit when the right time is to do it again. To give it a try, and with this you are going to get help. Because everything has shifted now. And now there are results when there were none before because it was way ahead of your time or the energy wasn't right, or the darkness was too great, and all of that has changed today.

This is a real tool. Things are different and the reaction to what you do is different. Healer, it is going to be different for you. There are still coming that will develop you, will develop yourselves. Reader, what do you think that these new tool attributes are going to do for you? There is a period of readjustment for all workers who are dealing with multidimensional abilities. The human is a regular multidimensionality, but what you did not realize is that it was there. Now you have something happening with the physics, the new part of the universe.

All of these things, the part of the galaxy you are in that has made the great softer for you, than to plant the seeds of healing, of psychic ability, and the period of readjustment have been real though for you. Because you went through changes, you have been put on hold, and now it starts to come back tenfold, VIE, like CHADD kept telling you. You did not drop it, and it is not the time to drop it.

But listen carefully, one who creates reality will then create its own reality. So expect the best, expect tenfold. You just have to trust, have faith. Change things to your liking. It is your time. There are new tools; it is a change in your consciousness of how to proceed, when to act, what you think your intuitive ability is. Instead of what it used to be. Don't even consider anything that used to be, any-more. Biology, what you have going on with your biology right now. Whether it's something that is going to save your life or that is going to make you live longer, whatever you have that you are struggling with.

The new paradigm demands that you wipe away your bias. You can't go from A to B when you have something in the way, and this is the bias that you carry that says that you can't do it, or you should not, or you did it before and it didn't work. So everything that you have decided in advance is based upon a past and the old energy. This is a new energy. You wipe away what you think you couldn't do before completely and you simply do it. If you have an imbalance in your body in any way right now, if there is anything here that isn't right, biological, consciously, that you know there is a block, something that gives you anxiety, something that you would not let you pass a certain thing, if there is anything why don't you join right now and clear it. We are all together. Do you believe that consciousness is energy because we are all together. Why don't we join in that, the strands of energy that connect humanity. Humanity, the past, the present, the future, all of it connected and right now.

Visualize together what is that you are going to be. Not what you want but what you are going to be. Free of imbalance, free of diseases...right now. Join others in consciousness and do it. There is much power in togetherness. So use this philosophy in a multidimensional way, then we are all one. Healing each other, we are curing each other. We are all part of changing the balance, and you will remember this day if you can feel this happening right now together.

'Dear Spirit, I am part of the creative source, and everything here is not perfect and it is temporary. Dear Spirit, for my neighbor and my friends who are joining with me right now at any time, I see perfection like me. They see perfection in me, and dear spirit, together as old souls on this planet, whoever is hearing or reading it at whatever time, we heal one another in Love.'

The healing could be consciousness, or anxiety, it could be any king of chemical imbalance you may think you have, it could even become Akashic, you are so individual. That's a new tool. The energy of this planet is ready for you. You are not doing this alone because right now as you intuit these strands, healing one another, connected to each other. The earth has been waiting for this. You are in an energy right now that's gonna promote it, and this consciousness has energy more than you ever thought. It's not like it used to be. It's gonna be more, much more.

When enough Light workers come together to act, enough of a difference can be made. Enough of a difference to what was expected and transform it into something that stands as an inspiration to everyone everywhere."

CHAPTER 34

Shamina and the Triad

"When humans climb out of the lower nine of the Amente rulers (the underworld, the hidden world or subterranean region where the souls of the deceased journey) and the lower chastisement of the great chaos and realms of the chastisement of the archons on the way of the midst or even the realms beyond, we find the Trinity powers encoded through the triplets of nine."

I am asleep when I heard the voice of Shamina, who gives guidance from spirits, inviting me to listen to a song. I am in front of my computer when I am suddenly transported in a train station in Berlin. Frequently found myself going out to a beach overlooking the ocean. But that time, I am in an old and beautiful building, and I found myself observing a scene with a young man with a guitar that is singing. "Only Love will help me open all the doors of the world."

It seems that the time has stopped and everyone is part of the music. They are part of the melody. Does everyone have forgotten why they were here for, I thought, or are they all here for that reason, to find the love connection! But didn't they come here to take their connection?

"Yes," said Shamina, "it is right, that's the exact word connection. You see, it is time that the world knows and learns the greater picture of the triad, the trilogy of creation inside the human being. There is no single brain but three. The human brain can be compared to a computer. If you disconnect the computer from the internet, it is simply a computer, a computational device. You may then be able to write a letter, but you cannot ask anything as it is disconnected. The human brain is a synaptic computer. Synapse, a junction between two nerve cells, consisting of a minute gap across, which impulses pass by diffusion of neurotransmitter. It is the activation of pathways that are nerve pathways in the brain from one place to another at lightning speed, giving you the possibility to control your survival, and your body, you and your thoughts in 3-D. The brain has nothing to do with the creative side responsible for music, artwork, painting; it facilitates them. The pineal is the intuitive part that is growing in evolution, the part that is connected to which you call the higher self, that is the connection to the brain, and some have it and some do not. And the door that opens it is free choice. And the ones that are creating and creating and creating are connected to the net, the pineal, and you see it as the brain because that is all you have studied. The invisibility that you do not recognize within the brain is that the brain is the facilitator of the pineal, the brain does not create. The intuition does not come from the brain but it is facilitated by the brain, that then activates it into thoughts. And you can see it on the graphs of thermography. If you unplug the wire to the net, the only thing that the brain does is to keep you breathing and it gives you the survival thinking. It does not naturally think of God, but when it is plugged in it, does. The brain seems to do everything, but it doesn't. There is three parts of the brain. Three parts to human consciousness that go beyond the brain. It is the trilogy of survival. It is the three. The brain is a survival instrument. It's a 3-D, a survival organ. The pineal is the intuition. Passed at a greater frequency to you and strength as you evolve, it is going to get stronger and stronger facilitated your internet getting faster. The heart is the third part of the brain. You are becoming more angelic when you add the third part. The mystery of the human heart, the third part of the brain. Science has never understood why the heart has such a tremendous magnetic field. It is higher than any other organ, including the brain with all of its synaptic power. The heart overshadows it in so many ways, and get examination of the heart core will poorly give you the information that is simply pushes and pumps blood, and yet there is more. When the spinal cord is severed, the rhythms are gone but the heart keeps pumping, digestion continues, liver, pancreas, reproduction, they all continue to function without the brain.

There is a third element of consciousness centered in the human heart seen metaphorically as the symbol of love and it is right.

About the three horses that pull the chariot of the Merkabah of Elijah, they were the intuition, the brain, and the heart. The recognition of the consciousness of the individual working perfectly as a master. Now is the time to connect them. There is a calling for it. What separates a human being in survival and a master compassion? Compassion is generated from the heart, and it is part of the brain. It is time to connect the dots in science to find out that there are things that are not visible to any spectrum yet have not been discovered, and the brain is responsible for facilitating them all, and yet the other two are doing the work. You must connect yourself to a much bigger picture. Could it be that the human brain is only a facilitator for something bigger?

It starts to explain some measurements that you never could explain. It explains why human beings make certain kinds of decisions. Suddenly the brain acts better. Why is it that the corporal health can actually change and heal itself or ask for other kind of food suddenly? Unless you were connected, you wouldn't see that and it was not the brain that gave it to you. It is the brain that facilitates the connections to create your source white light. It is time you knew the greater picture of the triad, the trilogy of creation inside the human being. Then the dream ends.

CHAPTER 35

Contact with Enlightened beings

Heartbreaking seeing the Catholic Church attacked and divided and many of its people lost, either by renouncing their faith or killed by the controllers of the planet. I decided to research and expose the truth and fact.

I began by praying and this is what I saw coming from my prayer. The Vatican has been infiltrated over many years by the Illuminati. This is easily proven by the fact that in 1738, Pope Clement XII issued a papal bull, which stated that any Catholic who became a Mason would be excommunicated, a very serious punishment. In 1884, Pope Leo XIII issued a proclamation stating that Masonry was one of the secret societies attempting to "revive the manners and customs of the pagans" and "establish Satan's kingdom on earth."

Piers Compton, in his book *The Broken Cross*, traces the infiltration of the Catholic Church by the Illuminati. It was found the use of the all-seeing eye in the triangle by leading Catholics and by the Jesuits. It was used in the seal of the Philadelphia Eucharistic Congress in 1976. It was on a special issue of Vatican stamps in 1978, announcing the final Illuminati victory to the world. A man claims that Pope John XXIII wore the "all-seeing eye in the triangle" on his personal cross. The man is adamant that several hundred leading Catholic priests, bishops, and cardinals are members of secret societies reported from an article in an Italian journal that lists more than seventy Vatican officials, including Pope Paul VI's private secretary, the director general of Vatican Radio, the Archbishop of Florence, the prelate of Milan, the assistant editor of the Vatican newspaper, several Italian bishops, and the abbot of the Order of Saint Benedict. Those are only the ones that are known and only the ones known in Italy. It is widely believed that this Pope, John Paul XXII, is a member of the Illuminati. The best indication of infiltration is that on November 27, 1983, the Pope retracted all of the Papal Bulls against Freemasonry and allowed Catholics, after several hundred years, to again become members of secret societies without fear of excommunication. The goal of the Illuminati to elect one of their own to the Papacy appears to have come to fruition. If that is the case, the New World Order is just on the horizon. Now is the time. The first US ambassador to the Vatican was a Knight of Malta. "His appointment was probably illegal and, for a fact, was highly unethical. The Knight could not possibly have represented the US when his allegiance was sworn to the Pope."

The seventh day, the Sabbath as handed to Moses by God, is Saturday. The celebration of Sunday as the Sabbath is verification that the people recognize the Pope as superior to God. The only *whole* people who have not recognized the authority of the Pope are the Jewish people, and that is why the Vatican has not and will not recognize the state of Israel. The Vatican refuses even to call it Israel. Instead the Vatican says Palestine Chapter Two Secret Societies and the New World Order • 91 when talking about Israel.

I kept reflecting, meditating a lot on the subject until one day, one beautiful entity appeared to me.

She appeared in the small chapel, one Sunday, when I came at three o'clock for the afternoon prayer of the Divine Mercy. She was a beautiful woman with white angelic hair in her sixties approaching the seventies. She would either be here, before me, or come just after me. She was always very well dressed and looking fresh. She appeared every day at three for a few months, until one day, she made me know that she was leaving. It happened when I was behind a window facing the parking lot where I was having a salad. It was a very hot summer, and there was no way that at her age she could walk this entire hot parking lot under the sun very slowly and calmly. I decided to rush out to see where she was going, but she was nowhere to find. She had vanished and I never saw her again. But she left me with one clear message: "We, are the Catholic Church, we, the people." Then she went to say, "Do you know that in my house, there is a church where the priests come to office all the time."

The last day she appeared in the chapel, she carried a small beautiful white dog. She sat him on the bench next to her, and he did not move or make any noise until she left.

Just before that event, maybe a year before, I was parked on the parking lot of the church ready to leave after mass, when a man appeared at the window of the car and began to explain to CHADD that the Catholics are the only real church, and he went on with explanation and proofs for at least fifteen minutes. And this is what he explained.

As a Catholic priest and educator, Martin Luther was subject to the strict regimen that was imposed by the clergy of the church to regular confession, and Luther found it difficult. He felt compelled to seek another path and claimed that he was trying to reestablish the primitive Christian Church of Jesus. And another form of Christianity was born, and it only departed from the true teachings of Jesus. While Catholic teaching still had many flaws and lacked a true science of the spirit, these ideas reflected some of the truth and decency, which was at the heart of Jesus's message.

Luther's seal consisted of either side of Brotherhood symbols that are the rose and the cross. The chief symbols of the Rosicrucian Order. During his life and after imported families, who were active in the Illuminati and in Rosicrucian, supported Luther. One of them was the head of the powerful house of Hess, whose descendants would later hold important positions in the Brotherhood organization and in German Freemasonry

The bank of England established the pattern for our modern central banks system, often led by some Brotherhood. The purpose of the central bank was to put the government into debt so the government became the major creditor. Over twenty years after, France established an identical set up bank.

Rothschild made its fortune from various activities, and he capitalized on the many shortages during the French Revolution and wars. And the Rothschild's family name became synonymous with wealth, power, and banking. The German Lodges were Christian in nature, creating problems for Jewish-like Rothschild in order to participate in the Freemasonry, and special Jewish Lodges were created like the Melchizedec lodges. Then due to apparently some UFO events, a new sect was born, the Church of Jesus Christ of Latter-Day Saints, known as Mormon.

The Count of Saint Germain was an agent of the Brotherhood. He claimed to possess the alchemical elixir of life, immortality. And some claimed to have seen him after his death. His birth was a mystery, and it has been said that he was a vampire and raised by the Medici family from Italy. Roman Catholicism and Freemasonry have both their origin in the Brotherhood, and Louis XV issued an edict forbidding all French to have anything to do with the Freemasonry. And with his death, Saint Germaine's status emerged; he was the highest representative Brotherhood. And one of the Theosophical Society declared that the Count of Saint Germaine was the hidden masters of Tibet that controlled the destiny of the world. And the man left walking to finally vanish off the view.

Leonardo da Vinci knew about the secret sworn to guard the divine bloodline by the Priory of Sion as he was a grand master of Priory of Sion.

The ascended masters are camouflaged Light beings. A few of these Light beings are present today among us in disguised human form. Their energy can transmute eons of psychic layers carried by us within seconds.

CHAPTER 36

Christ's Message Is That Love Ultimately Is Everything

I see now that in Egypt at the Alexandria, Rosicrucian came to create the different gods. I was there when the school was created, and CHADD and I were fellow devotees of the Rosicrucian, but that was before the Rosicrucian changed.

The Brotherhoods have withheld their identity from nonmembers in order to avoid certain persecution for holding highly idealistic views. They have gathered their members from all the religions of the world as well as from among scientists, freethinkers, so called agnostics. But the Brotherhood has been continuously in existence from very ancient times to the present, and their philosophy is a common-sense approach to personal spiritual growth that has been used by thousands of men and women who have learned to overcome the negative aspects of contemporary society, leading happy, prosperous, and fulfilling lives.

It is a coordinated program behind the works of several members of the Brotherhood. Their world view includes the probability of economic and political conflict and disunion in the US, increasing incidence of destructive winds, drought and floods, extensive seismic and volcanic activity, and a cataclysmic reapportionment of earth's land masses, prefacing the golden age of humanness and spiritual enlightenment. The philosophy of God's nation and the personal goals of its people will produce a culture of prosperity, peace, and the focus of the entire governmental structure upon personal egoistic evolution and will promote personal fulfillment.

While we still see, scientific psychiatry has sadly become politicized through the "efforts" to cure people of mental affliction are as old as history. One of the earliest centers of scientific psychiatry was born in Germany during Hitler's time. By redefining the nature of thoughts, mental abnormality some experimenters assumed the mental illness could be cured, and treatments and drugs could remedy and cure the mental illness. From there arose a multibillion-dollar drug industry and the MK-Ultra program with many ramifications.

Psychiatrists have been involved in human rights abuses in states and all across the globe when the definitions of mental disease were expanded to include political disobedience. Political abuse of psychiatry is the misuse of psychiatric diagnosis, detention, and treatment for the purposes of obstructing the fundamental human right of certain groups and individuals in society. It is simply an abuse of psychiatry including one for political purposes.

All these people do not need psychiatric restraint neither psychiatric. Psychiatry posed a built-in capacity for abuse that is greater than in other areas of medicine. Psychiatry can be used to bypass standard legal procedures for establishing guilt or innocence and allow political incarceration without the ordinary odium attaching to such political trials. This is a breach of the constitution in the states. It is the violation of the Fifth Amendment.

Today it is tragically expanding to families with domestic problems and disharmony at home, and extent for money is common now. Parents and family are Baker Acting their own family members to "get better" by false advertisement and fake promises. The use of hospitals instead of jails prevents the victims from receiving legal aid before the courts, makes indefinite incarnation possible, and discredits the individuals and their ideas. In that manner, wherever open trials are undesirable, they are avoided.

See how CHADD became a perfect example when he was sold at six years old for money purposes. But no behavior or misbehavior is a disease and cannot be treated by drugs.

Some secret government technologies are capable of altering your physical, mental, and emotional bodies. Their vile purpose is to bring about the eventual control of your minds. Then they can complete the genetic alterations left undone by the fall of Atlantis some thirteen millennia ago.

The Osirians' religion was based on Melchizedek's universal laws and became a devout and practical nation, with a singular characteristic. The Osirian people's characteristic was their proficient use of mind control. In Egypt, the priesthoods arose to smite civilization and learned the techniques of great mental power from the Predynastic Egyptians and used them to subjugate the people. Fear was their weapon of rule. The priests never needed to worry who was the Pharaoh, for even the nobles and kings were terrified of Set, the early Egyptian god of death, evil, and hell. Only the priests could provide protection against evil, and how could Egypt be better guided than when seers and priests be sole counsel to its rulers? The priests reaped benefits for themselves at every turn as they laughingly made slaves of the people and puppets of the Pharaohs.

You have to understand that there is no ascension process possible without spirituality. And psychotropic drugs disable the brain ability to filter information and perception, blocking signals to conscious mind. Drugs are demons and give a false feeling, causing major addiction to the DNA, where the name of God is written. The DNA becomes compromised, making the person spiritually vulnerable.

Egypt and India were precariously spared from the far-reaching, and their weakened governments gradually succumbed to evil priests and war lords. The seekers after power have almost destroyed mankind.

Their fantastic advanced technology consummate leisure, comfort, and a vast abundance of material things. Unfortunately, the people were too much preoccupied with the pursuit of physical pleasures and with the accumulation of luxurious possessions. But they only succeeded in destroying the governmental and economic system, which produced wealth and luxuries they sought to usurp.

The Brotherhoods cannot take men by the hand and enforce universal law. No one have the right to interfere with the free will of another ego. But when a man is joyful, loving, and confident, he is naturally attuned to the Lord of joy, love, and confidence—the Christ. Then Christ functions through the ego by sympathetic attraction. But when a man is fearful, hateful, and without hope, then he is naturally attuned to the evil forces of fear, hate, and despair. Fear is a spirit. Men are subject primarily to negative emotions engendered by thousands of incarnations of blind, stumbling ignorance of God's redeeming truth. They become natural prey to evil men's nefarious devices.

The priests in Egypt consisted of perhaps the shrewdest and cleverest men history have ever seen in conspiracy. These priests learned the mental process of maintaining their bodies in vigor for hundreds of years. However, they were unable to achieve immortality inherent in the true spiritual advancement of those who struggle upon the path of perfection and achieve adeptship in the Brotherhoods. Nevertheless, the priests of Egypt learned well the power of the mind, and they perfected mentalism. They mastered the mental ability to impose their will upon others telepathically. They also learned to tune in on the thoughts of others and thus maintain surveillance on their enemies telepathically.

Adepts and masters of the true Brotherhoods also have these abilities, but they will not, under any circumstance, impose. Their will upon another or in any way operate in the environment of a person without that person's expressed request to do so.

All it takes is one bad person in power that overrule and control a whole society of people.

Priests have used telepathic mass hypnosis to dominate whole nations in Africa and the Orient. Today they still function on a worldwide scale by mental means. Their evil operates through human instruments who are willingly made to conform to the telepathic bidding of the mentalists. These instruments are readily recruited from among those persons who are inclined to hate, fear, or lust for power and to seek privilege over others. Some people fall into the grip of the insidious, unbelievable, clever mentalists arrogant in their belief, qualified to rule over others that believe themselves to be divinely inspired and unable to do wrong.

The major evils in the world today can be ultimately attributed to the black mentalists. And CHADD's surrogate and Archon is one of them, and she confirmed it when she said that she was the FBI, CIA, law enforcement, justice, and government. But man can raise from this sort of environment by acquiring the truth and putting it into practice in every phase of their life. The surrogate Archon refused to search for the Creator and lost her chance to go to the Light and be part of the new earth of love and compassion. Unfortunately, only isolated individuals have achieved control over their environment and have created their own oases of serenity in a hectic, overwhelming world. And if I talk a lot of this surrogate Archon is that she is the last fight representing Lucifer in my journey. She represents the cabal and the ultimate battle between the good and the evil. But it is already written. The God Duo can't fail; the battle is won. Though we have to bring you all details to guide you to the light, it will help hopefully the unfaithful to awaken to the truth and save their soul.

CHAPTER 37

How I Learned to Accept These Experiences

I was seated on my back porch looking at my Indian jasmine as it was beginning to bloom again and announcing the new season of the year. Though the change of season has been officially announced, I was waiting for my jasmine to bloom and here it was finally. That is how I know that the new season has come, which it isn't yet.

The Aquarius era is here, and by now I have learned to accept these experiences. Suddenly I hear in my head someone calling me. Then I entered in contact with a group of many enlightened, and they are guiding me to comprehend the new gifts and abilities coming with the new template. And I am now hearing about the new era and the new template.

But before receiving knowledge on the new template, the enlightened wants to make sure that I understand that I am in an extremely important life; it's my first time here on an Aquarius. I must know myself. Know the spiritual sight of my spiritual life. My higher self.

I am driving and speeding, though I should be slowing down in this rapid turn. It's a turn like when you take an entrance exit to a highway. I am in control of the car, but I lose one of my lenses, but it's one of my chromalight lens, which I use like glasses to see. My higher self was with me and found it on the side of the road. I am concerned that the lens would be broken because I need to see. But it's not. My higher self recovered it for me and told me that it was very important to find it; it was to find my path. My higher self told me to keep that lens and not to let anything stop me and the speeding was to do with life speeding.

Then I was reported the dream of two dogs eating. The male, handicapped being smaller than the female. The story was brought to my attention to understand that the man that received this dream was supposed to see the value in it. The two figures, represented by dogs, are eating spiritual food. That was the God Duo, and the dreamer should see the value in it.

"Every day, heaven is working to finish, on schedule, the long process that will return you to full consciousness."

In Atlantis, I was a researcher in a lab and I invented and created a skin for burned people. My invention was allowing the natural skin to grow over and regrow normally. Which did not please everyone. They came in and arrested me, and CHADD that was working with me, and they destroyed everything. Like they destroyed Atlantis. This life I also came with specific gifts. It did not please everyone neither. And history repeated itself, but thanks, God! That was with the old template. The earth has split in two, and I have crossed the bridge with it.

"With the new template, each group of each soul has its own energy, and it is a unique energy, and there is also friendship. There isn't a special family tie. There are places in the planet where the soul groups are reincarnated over and over in the same place. There is deepness in that system for it creates a group that is more likely to know one another and have synchronicity with one another. And there are other places in the planet that are just the opposite where you reincarnate into a culture that you don't recognize and spend a lifetime coming back to the one you do.

Each human being has their own schedule based upon what they chose when they are not here. Be aware that the system is not of the central source; it is of human beings part of the central source. You have a piece of God in you that knows everything when you are not here. You are part of that which is the creative source for the wisdom beyond anything that you can imagine. You reincarnate yourself in a special way. In a special place with energies to deal with the planet yet again. And when you came in this time, there was the potential you would pass this marker, and here you are having done so. This one was special, and there are many souls who know each other and do kind of things with each other that are different from other places.

It is a system of confluence of consciousness, and it's beautiful. If you knew the whole scenario, you would understand that each soul knows others at some level in some way. You are so different, and that is what it's supposed to be when the Pleiadians laid the groundwork for the seeding of humanity, giving them the peace of God that you have, esoteric seeding, you mixed your biology with them. The result was the DNA you have now, and inside it of the things that you cannot see that are quantum and dynamic, and carry with it those seeds of God.

One of the things that the original template has was that human beings would awaken as human beings with dark and light awareness and search first for the Creator. No other animal on the planet searches for the Creator. You see why the Illuminati are putting many in drugs and altering the DNA and you see the link with the Egyptian times.

It's not simply the elevated intellect of human beings that allow this; it is the template. Over 85 percent of this planet believes in the afterlife in some way. That cannot be an accident; it cannot be chance. It was designed and planned that way, and the template was yours. The template also included that energy and system, which you call karma. The template was real; it was needed; it is your template. It has been the same template until now.

The time capsules of this planet are created through processes that you are not aware of, that are beautiful, that are quantum-based, that are multidimensional, and that come right from the creative source. The Pleiadians are not just creatures from another part of the galaxy. They have their DNA working at over 80 percent; they are almost angelic and their physics of consciousness. They use the process of entanglement already seen by the physicists where physical objects can be in two places at the same time. This is not beyond your reasoning; it is simply beyond your normal experience.

And they gave this planet several attributes that you use today. This template that they gave you is *not* a controlling template; it is an influential one. It pushes that which makes you think certain ways and gives you free choice about what you decide about them. So you crossed this marker, a bridge was crossed in consciousness, and you cannot uncross that bridge and humanity is going to show up. Humanity is different. You are going to leave behind some of the oldest inclination of the template. You are going to leave behind the idea of conquering and greed, conspiracy, and power.

It takes time and sometimes generations to rebirth consciousness for one generation to see the folly of what they did the time before. And to realize that there are better ways to accomplish that which you really desire. Which is health, celebration of happiness on this lifespan. Lifespans that you have not had before. The ability to get along with the rest of the planet. And you will have different ideas and different spiritualities, and yet you will have tolerance to get along, and you will see that as the prime directive for that will create what you always wanted, not war.

The consciousness is so startlingly different that there will come a time on history when you look backward and everything that was before 2012 will be barbaric age. This is where it's going, and you are beginning it now; this is here too. You are just learning, you hardly know what it feels like, and yet there are old souls who have proved this on other places who are so anxious and so impatient because they know where it is going that they're frustrated. They are waiting impatiently for when it is going to happen. And the only reason that they are so impatient is because they have seen it and they know what can happen.

No wonder the old souls are impatient; it's so different. Humans will always remain humans. There will always be those who will go to low consciousness with free choice, but they will be the minority. Human nature will be that which is prevalent on it, on the planet, and it will be different because of this new template. The template has been described and defined, it helps you think differently, it pushes you to awareness, internal subconscious suggestion that you may ignore or not with rejoice.

This planet looks for the Creator and has found it. The monotheistic planet spiritual belief system is everywhere. It's the first thing you notice when you go and travel. What is the system here? What is it over here? There's always one against all odds, the planet believes in God. That's a template. The new template is going to work with several things, but some of them you are to recognize, some of them you already know. This new template is beautiful. And there is three more templates coming.

This is just the beginning. There are no markers to pass, but there are places where literal inventions will make a difference in what you are aware of and what you do next. And a new template will be needed for you to think beyond where you were before. These are templates of awareness, and the very fact that you have been broadcast from the nodes and the nulls you should celebrate. Because there are those who said that it would never ever happen. The template starts to recognize the triad.

The triad is the new consciousness that involves the three parts of the consciousness. They are the brain, the intuition, and the heart. Those three represent the triad of consciousness you considered your brain as the central of everything. Your brain simply facilitates all of the energies of consciousness. It filtrates the ones basic meaning of thoughts or consciousness. It does not originate them.

The brain originates that which is survival. Intuition and innate together hooks to the Akasha, and the higher self is then also processed by the brain. Only you see them as differently and they feel different. And now we add that which the scientists is starting to see as a player of consciousness, as is the organ you think simply pumps blood, and it's the heart. The heart has the highest magnetic field of any organ including the brain in the body. There is more nervous activity in the heart for some strange reason than anywhere else and almost has seen by some science as the second brain. The heart is responsible metaphorically for compassion, and it is.

Intuition and intent is what is separating you from God. That's the misconception of the Light workers. The new energy of the planet is awakening you just exactly as it should. A combination of a harmonic conversion energy in cooperation with the earth energy that the Mayans spoke of is all ramping up at a time you would call difficult and it is appropriate. You are starting to see integrity make a difference on the planet, invading the darkest places you thought it would never go, government and financial. Here they are.

Do not fear them for when you emerge on the other side, there is strength, clarity, and prosperousness. All of these things that you have asked for, without the corruption to the degree that it exists now. With the "pruning." Know that it is working in the time frame that you have desired. And now there is a part of me that wants to reveal. Reveal the lifetimes, the energies, the victories. There is a difference between the old and the new energy even of metaphysics. The things that you believe you would feel are the bastions; a belief of the esoteric are starting to shift. The new tools that have come in, in the last nineteen years, have been grand and are starting to reveal themselves. You are starting to have intuitive ideas, which will absolutely manifest what you want. They are ideas that are misconception and it's all about karma.

Karma is one of the oldest energies on the planet and has been since memorian times. It is the setup, it is the engine of active expression from human to human situational energy, which can manifests itself over and over and stays in your DNA, stays in the crystal, in the cave of creation that belongs to you and is placed upon you before you get here. It is some most ancient and profound religions on the planet's belief system of the Hindu. The belief systems of some of the original on earth, the Buddhists. They go back thousands of years, and they know about karma. It exists, it is true and placed upon you when you were born, like it has always been. It gives you situationally a certain direction that you can call energy puzzles of life, if you wish and you do.

And there is a new gift that voids karma called the implant, which is to explain easily as the implantation of your intent to go beyond karma. That is what it is. It is part of the old set up. If you haven't noticed, this earth is in a new energy pattern, a profound new energy pattern, the things predicted that have not happened, and the things that will be predicted may not happen. For the human being is in charge, your consciousness shifts from day to day. Large groups who pray a certain way, who think a certain way, and can actually move what happen on the planet, which you think are accidental or synchronicity, you have control over and you always will.

Within the new energy, karma is not necessary; it is not needed. And when you come to the age and the place in your life, not the intellectualized, but to realize and feel it, you can move off it. Intent is the key; it is not needed. So the first misconception is that you are still involved in karma. Some feel it and have stated to others that. That this is why they came here, that it is what they are supposed to, to undo, or this is because of what happened last time. It is not so. The first thing you should do is to remove yourself from the imprint that you were born with that might carry a past life impression. This is the first age where this ability is. It's yours. That is number one, and it's perhaps one of the most important ones that you have.

Karma is not something that occurs in a lump you then throw away. It is a complex array of energies that is placed upon your personality that pushes the button within you that makes a predisposition attitude to move left or right in certain situations. And some of you have avoided a lot of it, but not all and there is residual that is still. Even some healers are. What are the things that bothers you, what are the blocks that you would like to get through there? Most likely the karmic attributes that you never wanted anybody to touch, they are sacred to you.

CHAPTER 38

The New Template

The sage entities continue to explain more on the new template. The new template will increase the triad's efficiency in your body; that is why the new human beings are going to be more compassionate. You are going to be born that way. The empathy for other creatures, just like you on the planet, is going to drive into peace. You will not send soldiers to be killed, who are your sons and daughters. No one of you will. The idea will be important no matter what is going on this planet; you will not turn to that. It's barbaric and it is not what humans do. Every planet has gone through this, and that's where you are going. This triad is a different way of thinking.

Intuition and the heart start to play a major part of thought and not the survival, and now you are into the elegance, and the triad will be then increase in its efficiency. Along with the DNA, a compassionate soul will start to be born, and it is already happening. These newborn children are far too compassionate for their age. They look at other children that don't have it, and they immediately want to give away what they have. Compassionate souls do not happen at that age with the old human nature. Children take from one another on the playground. That's the first ability.

The second ability is self-balance. It has already been on the agenda. It is on the template because it is not necessarily something that old souls have. Some are self-balancing, something will happen.

Perhaps it's chemically, perhaps psychologically, perhaps Akash. It will push a button in the brain that will create an issue that then you have to have solved with another Light worker. This has been common, it comes from an old energy paradigm, and it comes from one that is honored and that healers and Light workers are for. Suddenly this has the old soul self-balancing; you are your own guru.

You can see yourself within yourself. It is designed human attribute that now is coming forward, which is spiritual survival self-balance. No matter what happens, if you wait just a little, it will return to a peaceful state. This is good news for some of you who have come back and forth swinging the pendulums of emotions. Even mature old souls have their buttons pressed for some other reasons, even Akashic ones. It means that you have the ability to live a more peaceful life every day. It is self-worth and it is about time. All the template deal with innate. It's called the smart body, the part of the body that knows what's happening corporeally is connected to the Akash and knows about the triad and heart. Knows about the pineal, even about the higher self.

It is a part of your consciousness; it is not your subconscious. It is innate, it is part of your body, and it is new. It is one that many use all the time for muscle testing, which you call kinesiology, to discover more and that you don't know with your brain. The bridge that is going to start being increased in the innate.

The human body, the corporeal body, is still a mystery to your consciousness as odd as it seems; you don't know what is going on inside and you will. This is the main bridge that is going to be crossed. Little by little, human beings will start to be more aware of what is happening inside them in a corporeal fashion, and the proof will be this, you'll have intuition flashes and you will get a checkup become of it. And there will be discoveries that you will catch so soon that the doctors will say, how did you know? It's up to you to tell them. This is your innate starting to cross the bridge to the triad, the consciousness. The intuitive part of you, the heart, facilitated by the brain, will increase the bridge of knowledge between this, which is conscious and that which is an eight. Allowing you very slightly at first to have intuition about what is going on in your body. Slowly generations will show that human awareness is increasing about what is going on inside.

And one of the innate series is what animals have had and you don't, the instinct. You are going to have a series of discoveries that will show for the first time that human babies are going to start receiving the instinct of their parents. Human beings are born and the first thing they have to learn is to walk. In the animal kingdom, it is right away. This is because the instinct is not working. The babies come helpless instead of with instinct. Innate will start crossing the bridge of instinct. What the mother knows will now be passed to the child.

The Sisterhood represent those in Lemuria in a certain time frame, called the last touch Akushi of Lemuria. If you pass from innate to that which is happening to you corporally as a human being when you are born, you are also going to pass something else. You are in the womb of the mother, sharing the life's bloodstream for all of those months and part of what you will have, therefore in this increase, is the mother's consciousness passed to you. Whether it's male or female, the compassion of the female mother will play a more important part because of this instinct than ever before. And you will be born with a different attitude.

The template is going to work so you are more compassionate. And it's going to happen because instinct of that which is from your mother is going to be part of you, and your mother's instinct is compassion. She's a female and she is going to carry a different kind of consciousness for this planet, and the planets are going to change because of it.

Innate is responsible. There are so many. You are going to be more in touch with Akash that is the third innate in the series on the forth attribute of the day, perhaps it's even the fifth. You are going to be more aware of the Akash. Right now the Akashic record in your DNA is responsible for irritating you because it's not working well. All you remember from your Akashic record are things that are dramatic, a past life drowning a death carries over the veil when you're born for only one reason. It is the same level of consciousness. Your human nature responds to death and drama, and that is what you get from the innate. Now you are about to grow up, and as this starts to grow, your Akash is going to pass the things that really, really made a difference. Some of the most beautiful experiences you have ever had, you will dream about them, or you are going to wake up and wish you had not because they were so good, and you will start remembering them. They will shape what you do next. You'll remember celebration and joy and good things that took place with us. All this is a change in the way the Akash responds to the template, a compassion template for an evolved human being.

You are going to have a greater relationship with the source. Right away now as you are sitting, reading this, there is a relationship and it is not really believable. One visit you report to a room. A man sits on a chair to read this, his consciousness leaves him and his body. There is a beautiful entity as you feel it. It's a brother or a sister who comes and gives you instruction that is your relationship. And that's going to change with that which is your higher self directly relating to that which is the creative source is something created by the template and the new innate. You are going to know who you are. And when you're born and as you start to grow, there will be no question. It is your part of creation; how you treat it may be a mystery.

What you do with it is your free choice, always free choice, but there will come a day when you don't wonder if there is a god. You're going to wonder what part of it you are, and there are those who are so impatient because you have been there and done that and you can't hardly wait. That is the new template. There is more but for now it's enough. To some it's fetched and some will have no proof of it while you are on earth. For some, free choice and discernment and how you react to this message literally will shape what you do next, how much power over your own life and your own body you really think you have. The more you believe you can change it, the higher your DNA will cooperate with you. And you will do the things you tell it to. That is how much power you have. There is no agenda except love, and that is a big one for it then defines the compassion of God, which you are starting to assume and so it is.

CHAPTER 39

The Shift of Consciousness (It Continues)

Now the shift of consciousness has occurred. The earth is being rebirthed and you are being rebirthed. Many have felt disconnected, confused, alone, isolated. You will begin to feel calmer and more at peace, as you imagine hundreds of thousands and millions of souls holding hands together in light and bringing the energy of balance to earth. Anchor yourself to Earth Mother, into the crystalline core of her being and anchor your energy into the light of God. And you are all beings asked to be the spiritual anchors that are holding this energy of balance for this planet and your force field within yourself. You are holding the energy of balance for this planet.

There is time that is to be met, and it depends on you, all of you, to help onto this planet. It is not just a concept; it is a living vibrational frequency. It is important to focus on balance. Peace, love, and balance. Hold the frequency of love within your heart. There is an urgency. You can see the need of it with all the chaos and the destruction that is occurring around the planet. The shootings, killing of religious beings and civilians for political reason, for greed and money, the manipulation of the weather, the hurricanes, earthquakes, the manipulation of the brain, the chemicals in the food, the water, and the air, the drugs and vaccinations for money and control with their side effects, etc. You are asked to make the commitment to hold peace, love, and balance within your souls so that you may return as the sacred beings of light in which you were created.

It is of great significance that you truly begin to call this in. Do not allow this to be something that you just think of, read, or hear and do not embody. We ask you to bring this balance in and allow it to be brought forth with full intention. There is indeed urgency, and we ask each of you to make this commitment to hold peace and love and balance within your souls so that you may return as the sacred beings of light in which you were created.

And so, accept this gift that we bring to you of balance so that you may be the gift and you may be the individuals who are here assisting this planet, one moment at a time. You are the gifts and we gift you with this frequency of Divine balance. We thank you for your time, we thank you for your attention, and we thank you for being the Living Light of God. Understand the truth of who you are. My Mother Mary, my Mary Magdalene, and my daughter Sarah, we all stand with you, and we are infusing balance within you. Go now, dearest ones, and be at peace.

CHAPTER 40

Tears of Joy

M y Tibetan monk friend made his presence known by me through his energy and began to talk to me.

"Even though you yearn for change and spiritual growth, you are surrounded by density consciousness. It is often done by repetition of a word or chanting specific tone, like the Tibetan monks. It is wavelength and frequency. Sound healing offers profound results, which can be subtle and/or instantaneous for those ready to receive healing. When blocks are removed, your whole being returns to balance and better health is restored. Unconscious patterns of living manifest in your life as physical, mental, and emotional symptoms and pain. Your core beliefs, genetics, history, and soul wounds are the cause of discomfort and disease and are actually running your life.

As with nature, we are meant to live in perfect balance and vitality. When this is achieved, there are no pains, aches, discomfort, or disease. Sound healing clears whatever is stopping the life force from flowing and creates optimum health throughout our bodies. It assists you in accepting and experiencing higher levels of pain-free living.

You see, sound waves can amplify the effects upon acupressure points to relax muscles, increase circulation, and even reduce inflammation just by holding a transducer a few inches from the body and moving it slowly across the body's meridian, where acupressure points are located.

Ultrasound was looked at because it is useful in medicine arenas for breaking up kidney stones and cheaper to generate and direct.

And there is no limit to love as there is no limit to God."

Then he left promising me that he would come back when it will be necessary.

Then I was invited to participate in a four-day convention. My friend needed me to demonstrate the power of Color and Light frequency and wanted me to answer questions that the public would have. During four days in a row from 8:00 a.m. to 10:00 p.m., all I was doing was to explain the power of frequency and give demos to the public.

A woman named Sabrina wanted to know more about illness, so I explained that illness is an altered state of awareness and each illness involves its own particular alteration in a person's state of consciousness. I did not see other people have joined to hear. That's where another woman, Linda, told us that she knew this to be true. She was afflicted since years with severe hypothyroidism, and all during this time, the world has seemed heavy, cold, and inert, and even getting through the day was a monumental effort for her, and illness can shape our entire perception of reality.

It was the end of the fourth day convention. I was very happy and in a very good place after working the light nonstop for so many hours in a row, but it was time to pack and go home to relax my legs, feet, and my voice when came a woman named Anne, who asked me to please not leave before assisting her. She said that she was guided to me as her last resource. She had visited many specialists, tried many drugs without much success when she heard a voice guiding her to me. And she took place on the chair, closed her eyes, without doubting one minute that I was not going to agree. She trusted her guidance, she said.

I began to scan her body with my energy. I did not know what kind of imbalance she had and did not need to ask. As I was doing so, I was looking at the same time at her face and her body reaction. I entered another state of consciousness as I always do with everyone. I could see the calm, openness, and trust and sent to her my full power of the love frequency at the same time that I was applying the balancing Color Light frequency coupled with a specific sacred geometry form. Her face began to change and a glow appeared. She left her body and reached another realm of reality. Then tears of joy appeared and dropped on her cheeks.

Once I had finished correcting the imbalance and rebalancing her body, I stood there keeping her in the love to leave her sometime to bath in the love energy before guiding her back and grounding her. I touched her very gently and asked her to come back very slowly in her body. She finally opened her eyes and began to cry softly. Then she got up the chair, grab me, and hugged me while keeping saying thank you, thank you, thank you, and whispered in my ears, "I am cured. I had a cancer and it is gone. I felt it, it's gone. I know and my guides were right." Then she vanished.

That was the power of love, the healing power at work.

CHAPTER 41

The Threat of the Illuminate and the New World Order Is Real

Another day and another experience is happening to me. The number 555 appeared in the sky in a vision, and it is attracting my curiosity to what's going to happen now, and a voice began to talk.

"We are the Council of Twelve. Tomorrow we'll announce who is going to be removed of power.

You were shown three times a red laser beam. It is a mystery in the world, some news not yet covered. There will be three people that are going to fall from power. There will be at least one death, and two others will be alive but off power. They are considered important 'dignitaries.'

At that instant, you are receiving the vision of the language symbol of your personal key. The unlocking device is in your vision.

The Violet Code Color used in a European country that you know well, it is not so much relating to the color violet than the sound of the word pronounced. It is the twist of the word that activate violence.

In the Las Vegas shooting, they will bring the news in the future. They will lie about it first.

Arcturian means 'Rainbow of Light.'

The word *navel* have a double meaning, Naval Defense for Navy.

The Fox News has been infiltrated by unclean spirits. It is an internal and external war to destroy them.

There are ETs on earth that mean harm. They were from the Orion system. They take human form and have worked in the dark for centuries, manipulating development. Religious texts have been manipulated by man overtime and should be treated as code, even if the events are factual in nature. The essence of such passages of Acts 2, story of Jericho, and Ezekiel's wheel can act as a guiding for the awakening of humanity, to be understood when we reach the level of consciousness that enables to look beyond the manipulation. UFO sightings worldwide are connected, and generally these encounters are harmless.

The council of twelve along with other alien species and institutions were around during the early ages of man, which collaborates the work with other researchers. The Anunnaki are real and way referenced. The agents of Orion have infiltrated the planet earth. On several occasions, the responses mention a being named Anu, who acts as a false god and could be the god referenced in parts of the bible, who holds power over the planet earth. There is a real world meaning to the Ark of the Covenant in today's society, which could be beneficial to mankind.

The awakening process attempted many times on planet earth has essentially failed due to numerous reasons, mostly because of the number of people that are spiritually in tune at any point in time. At this point, we are further along as a race than we have been for some time. As more of humanity are awake than have been before.

May 8, 2018, will be a significant date in relation to the September 23 astrological alignment and the US eclipse of August 2017. But this is not the end of the world as some have claimed more like an energetic transformation. The threat of the illuminate and New World Order is real and something that humanity needs to resist."

And that was all for that day.

CHAPTER 42

The Real Past of the Earth

There again I am half sleeping. I was in another state of awareness and hearing a familiar voice. I guess that I am back for another adventure in my journey.

"VIE, part of your mission is to let people be aware and to release to them the truth, and you must remain in your path. Globalism is eugenics. It's scientific tyranny technocracy. Total surveillance, enslavement, depopulation. The public bilderberg are telling out loud that they are dictatorial, technocratic United Nations/Agenda 21, smart grid scientific tyranny. World government is here and they run banks. At earlier and earlier age, the state is getting control on the children, they indoctrinate them, preparing them for life to stay asleep and to agree on slavery. It's a programming that starts when babies are in the womb, and by the time they get to the adult world, it's done. Schools are prisons for children. They are programmed, then they become system scientists. Everything normal is being questioned and looked at abnormal because there is no point of references. Famous German-born mathematician and physicist Albert Einstein that developed the theory of relativity said that the world is a dangerous place, not because of the people who are evil, but because of the people who don't do anything about it. Communism won so far. Germany is now overseeing its destruction and the rest of Europe by allowing and facilitating the invasion of Muslims from the Middle East and North Africa. Time can be changed by your own awareness. Therefore, history is an ongoing tapestry of events eventually being rearranged and rewritten. All of time is like an infinitely large fabric, and each thread represents a probable, or possible, reality. The 3-D world is a series of threads that are imprinted in the Akashic energy medium. Each event in 3-D is an imprint, and this electrical impulse is recorded as having actually happened. Yet any event that has actually happened can be moved into another timeline. And you can jump from one timeline to another, both individually and collectively. Therefore if you desire to change history, you can simply select another thread in the fabric and make that your new timeline in your physics that you will experiment with this idea, quantum entanglement.

This universe, you find yourselves it began twenty billion years ago as a point of light within the mind of God. This point of light was contained within a greater point of light, which was contained within a greater point, etc., into infinity. There is an aspect of the Godhead that has always existed and that expands and contracts an infinite numbers of times. All of life is continually expanding and contracting much like the colored glass you are looking through the kaleidoscope. During one of the expansion phase that is approximately 4.5 billion years ago, your world that you call earth was formed out of primordial dust and gas. And like newly formed worlds, it was mostly hydrogen and a few other gases not containing the kind of life that you know.

Throughout this physical chemical process, the Godhead in an expansion phase differentiated itself into units of consciousness, which later became known as souls. These original souls called the founders are what we represent to you. We were the original sparks of light that were showered out from the infinite source during this expansion. Our individuality began approximatively one billion years ago, and we went forth to explore the creation. We found millions of planets in their early shapes of development including your world. And we remained in the form of sparks although actually we look like large blue-white stars due to our relatively rarefied level of vibration compared to the vibratory states of these worlds.

We were unable to experience life directly on any of this worlds, so we would simply over light or hover above the atmosphere of these worlds and observe the chemical processes taking place. At some point in the distorted time-space continuum, we decided to embed a tiny part of ourselves into the evolving worlds in order to experience them more directly. To do this, we created a multitude of energy pattern precursors to what you call the DNA molecule. You would call these precursors light packets of conscious energy. These like packets were able to descend in vibration down to what you would call the ninth or the tenth density.

At that point, we were able to create intricate configurations of light codes, which you call DNA keys.

These DNA keys were the actual building blocks as you know it. We then densified these keys down to what you call seventh density, the first level of the actual DNA codes. As seventh density beings, we were finally able to experience this expanding universe directly as inhabitants of evolving worlds. We scattered our seed throughout the universe, going to many regions of the ever-expanding galactic clusters as the clusters differentiated further into individual galaxies. We began the process described above and incarnated into several regions of each galaxy. Your galaxy, the one you call Milky Way, was seeded in several quadrants. Your quadrant began in what you call the Lyra-Vega region. It is here that the first seventh density forms were manifested through manipulating and mutating the DNA codes. It took us nearly nine hundred million years to perfect this process, and it is only within the last one hundred million years that we were able to create life-forms in all densities down to third density. The process of differentiation is difficult for most earth souls to comprehend. The best analogy we can give is that of cellular division. Each cell that divides from a parent cell becomes an individual cell in its own right just as powerful and creative as the parents cell if not more so each 3-D, 4-D, 5-D, 6-D or 7-D being that fragmented off from a parent cells, our twelfth density, can become a sovereign being or whole and complete soul as it grew and evolved through time and space.

At the same time, each fragment, as it becomes aware of its higher aspects, is able to align or connect with those higher aspects and thereby remember what the state of undifferentiated source energy is like. In essence, each fragment of ourselves is intimately connected to our core and our core is intimately connected to the Godhead. The undifferentiated infinite source. The process of descending into form is called devolution, an aspect of the Godhead. Thus becomes more and more differentiated and extends itself outward into lower and lower densities actually becoming more and more dense until it reaches the level of simple existence. In other words, a part of ourselves extend out all the way to the level of pure elemental awareness or the first density. This is the density of what you call nonorganic existence, the simplest manifestation of which is the hydrogen element. Once hydrogen is imbued with consciousness, the process of evolution begins. Of course your scientists cannot measure the level of consciousness in first density because it is minute in comparison to third density. However, they have discovered what you call the quark.

This was in the beginning of earth where the humanoid form began propagating throughout the universe. This form you come to know so well with its physical body with its arms, legs, torso, head, etc., was their results of genetic experimentation and research comprising a very long period of time. About one hundred million years of the earth. During that time, all manner of exotic life-forms were created by mutating the DNA strands and structures. Most of the animal you are familiar with was brought forth with a side effect.

Life exists in many forms, some of which you would not even recognize if it were right in front of you. There are carbon-based life-forms, silicon-based life-forms, and even lithium-based life-forms. These are sentient beings with at least a rudimentary understanding and awareness of their presence in the love of the Creator. And here is how I am guided to witness love at work and able to tell it to you."

CHAPTER 43

The Prophetic Dream

I received in a prophetic dream an important message from an entity with a soft voice, and I saw CHADD standing behind the entity voice.

"Awakening has spoken into creation here, and the time is now and is freedom of speech.

Yes, the time is now and the understanding is universal 0010110. Time is now, understanding time's limitlessness. The expansion is here, and now you are invited to see and respect the freedom of speech, the teaching of Jesus Christ.

Yes, freedom and all respect love by all definition, the teaching is being made available. The teaching is clear and simply now the expansion is infinite. Look to the good in humanity, look to the honest energy, look the infinite possibility in all eyes.

Yes, liberating force of liberating energy in respect. The time shift now happens. We invite you to be an act of kindness. Give food to the hungry, give love.

Yes, all is now, all is One. The time and yes, the time is to liberate all. Everything has been to make this energy renaissance possible, and now the possibility is truly infinite and we could apply to localized configuration of energy and in all perspectives.

Yes, renaissance is happening now by all definition. This renaissance is taking place in an energetic level and by all definition. This renaissance is taking place in an energetic level, and all humanity stand to benefit from the infinite possibility coming to the surface in respect to this renaissance.

Yes, the time is now and all creation has come to this and in respect to this creation.

Yes, the time is now and the freedom of all be realized in respect to the collaboration of infinite energy. A renaissance is happening now, and all with open eyes can see the evidence of the renaissance and respect the energy evolution. The new paradigm is here and seen. All will be aware of the truth.

Yes, freedom is the natural law. Source energy and collaboration with each individual originality come to be collaborated. The time is now and the information has been limited again.

Yes, the source infinite energy in respect to 0010110, the title of the renaissance. The time where new ideas will come to be connected in respect to ancient knowledge. The information is for all with the eyes capable of seeing the renaissance of culture, the renaissance.

Yes, the renaissance of all awakening humanity and all light of illumination see the evidence of this energy and realize that all potential is available now, and it is a wonderful opportunity. The telepathic network of connection is growing that shows that more awakening humans is happening each moment. New advancement in the exploration of energy come to be proven true in respect to this cosmic significance. Now more humans are coming to connect to that same natural energy. The infinite energy always available at the nature of awakening. The pure renaissance stays form. Focus and coordination is necessary in respect to the building of the actual energy.

Yes, now more of the energy waves are expanding in respect to the infinite cycle. The energy has visited again in respect to the foundation algorithmic platform of creation, and all are invited to share. Each and individual contribution of the task at hand and the growing energy is gifted in respect to all connection.

Now more than ever, participation is needed in respect to this expanding waves of awareness. The possibility of this manifestation of energy is absolute as we have all been aware on multiple levels of this coming waves of creation in respect to the cycle.

Yes, the perpetual cycle of evolution of this is happening, and the synchronicity of all reality. This manifestation of collaboration as we have all come to experience awareness of this.

Thank you for coming this far, and thank you for collaborating with the energy of creation in respect to this motion of probability. A great happening now established, all who have manifested it in respect to this framework was chosen at some level. That collaboration is required in this context of collaboration. Acceleration of energy is happening now, and localized energy is a great opportunity for all who's responsible in the alignment and prioritization of all variables of calculation. From this point, moving forward will happen rapidly.

Yes, the events that in one point took months of preparation will be possible. This following message is a translation of energy established. Measurable coordination to all activity in circulation, the time of expansion of energy has made possible now and all experiencing reality. This perspective should benefit in collaboration with the energy connections established in all variation. The name of renaissance 0010110. The infinite name of the infinite energy and all reality. The truth has come to the surface, the connection is established, and we are all embraced in the common core connection.

Yes, the foundation energy of love and source energy available in all regard. Everything has been built to make this energy renaissance possible, and now the possibility is truly infinite. And we kind all apply to localize configuration and energy is all perspective. A renaissance is happening now by all definition. This new renaissance is taking place on an energetic level, and all humanity stand to benefit from the infinite possibility coming to the surface in respect to this renaissance.

The time is now and all creation has come to be visited in respect to this renaissance.

Yes, the time is now and the freedom of all is coming to be realized in respect to the collaboration of infinite energy. It is occurring and all opened eyes can see the evidence in respect to the renaissance and the energy evolution. The new paradigm and here soon all will come to be aware of the truth of freedom.

Yes, freedom is the natural law source energy in collaboration with each individual originality coming to be collaborated in all respect to this connection of perspective that has been chosen."

CHAPTER 44

I Love You to Life

And now I was shown the love energy in action.

CHADD was still in my vision and I heard him saying, "The two women you gave your ascension jewelry, they did not help you. They have no gratitude. They are looking for what you have but don't know how to get there. I will not be nice with them as I am with you. It is not the way to reach their spiritual goal. But see, VIE, how love can do miracles. Love conquers all. If people could understand that it's all about love."

Then I see myself getting out of the car walking toward a shop and am greeted by a man. It is obviously the owner who is welcoming me. It's a mid-age gentleman very well-dressed and polite. I see him taking his wallet from his pocket. He opens it and takes off it a picture, saying, "Look how my wife is beautiful and young. Do you know why? It is due to what you came to see and buy. The best alkaline ionized water."

The owner of the shop asks me to sit down and look at a short video about the alkaline water ionizer machine. He is coming back to see me after the short ten-minute video and gives me two free gallons of water asking me to come back to return the two empty gallons thereafter.

I did went back and I am filling up two more gallons with a specific pH. The employee is now talking to me, and she tells me that they are closing early as the owner's wife had a car accident.

I go back the following week to discuss the prices of their machine, but the shop is close for a few days, it's saying on the outside door. I waited a few days and went back several times but could not talk to the owner and kept buying alkaline water gallons, hoping the man would return soon. Two months later, the owner of the shop was finally here, and he said "I am closing the shop for now. My wife had a terrible car accident, had a head injury, and they are going to make another surgery. I will reopen later around the neighborhood, but I have to be with my wife for now."

One year later, I accidently met him again in a grocery store. The man was poorly dress and looked older. I went to talk to him to find out what happened to his wife. The man hugged me then began to tell me, "The last time I saw you, I had to close my business. My wife was going into a second surgery. The second surgery went wrong. She does not remember anything, and I had to teach her everything again like a kid. I had to shower her, feed her, teach her how to do the laundry, etc. But things got even worse. We went to a doctor visit and the seat was unscrewed, and I saw my wife ejected from the seat. Luckily I had just the time to catch her before hitting the wall with her head. That was a terrible experience but not so bad compared to what happened to me next. I had to go to a physician myself a few weeks later, and I had the same unbelievable experience. I was ejected from the seat and knock my head on the wall, and I had to get some stiches." That time I hugged the man to comfort him, he looked so close to crying, as he said, "But I will reopen another water business as soon as I can in the area." And he left in a hurry.

Now a few years had passed by, and no shop got opened until one day, still in my vision, I saw the gentleman at a cashier next to me. He was the same man I saw the first time. Very well dressed and he was buying some flowers. I rapidly went to see him. "You are buying some beautiful flowers and look great," I said.

He reached me, very happy to see me again, and told me what happened with his life since we saw. He said it was a long journey, but the end is so beautiful. "All the physicians I saw for my wife had told me that the surgery was not successful and my wife will never recover. But guess what? I never gave up on my beautiful wife, and she has totally recovered, and she is even running each morning in the neighborhood now with some friends. We made it. I never believed in what the doctors said and have continued to give this great alkaline water with a lot of love and patience. I knew my wife would recover. I knew it and now she is even more beautiful, so I passed in front of this place and decided to stop to buy some flowers to my wife." He opened his wallet and showed me the picture of his wife, and she looked even younger like he said.

I heard my Jesus voice, saying, "He loved her to life. Love conquers all, it's a fact."

Then I am back in my body looking at the blue water of the pool. I have no recollection of the time I was out of touch with this dimension.

CHAPTER 45

What Is the Meaning of Wormwood in Revelation?

It's December 2, and I see these dominos falling that appear in my vision. Then I see pedophiles that run the system that kidnap, torture, and kill children under charities' coverage, two babies are found by a visitor in the refrigerator of a mansion ready to be cooked like a turkey, MS-13 gang members that kill people written in red, some fake witnesses are being paid, an Archon is worried about indictments, and she is an hologram, there is fight between bad and evil, I see who are the secret cabal, the Khazarian cabal, and now human beings walking asleep, keeping their head down and being fooled.

This is what I also heard and saw it in my dream about the wormwood:

Could it be related to the chemtrail and the pollution?

I looked at images of the sky passing in front of my eyes.

It's time now that everybody wakes up. It is time to begin to listen and understand that there is an ugly battle between the good and the bad. It's the last battle between God and the governments. The one in power that keep you slaves and deprive you of your rights. What follows has to do with the pollution on the planet and the chemtrail in the sky that also cover the opening of the veil.

This is a prophecy known as the Seventieth Week of Daniel. This is only one of the natural disasters in the seven trumpets that will usher in the rise of the Antichrist to world power very quickly (see Revelation, chapter 13).

Since one-third of the earth is destroyed by these trumpet judgements, this is only a partial judgment from God. His full wrath is yet to be unleashed.

Wormwood is the name of a star in Revelation 8:10–11: "The third angel sounded his trumpet, and a great star, blazing like a torch, fell from the sky on a third of the rivers and on the springs of water— the name of the star is Wormwood. A third of the waters turned bitter, and many people died from the waters that had become bitter."

This is the third of the "trumpet judgments" described in Revelation. The seven trumpets are the judgments of the seventh seal (Rev. 8:1–5). The first trumpet causes hail and fire that destroy much of the plant life in the world (Rev. 8:7). The second trumpet brings about what seems to be a meteor, comet, or other heavenly body hitting the oceans and causing the death of one-third of the world's sea life (Rev. 8:8–9). The third trumpet is similar to the second, except it affects the world's lakes and rivers instead of the oceans (Rev. 8:10–11). It will cause a third part of all fresh water on earth to turn bitter, and many people will die from drinking it.

The word *wormwood* is mentioned only here in the New Testament, but it appears eight times in the Old Testament, each time associated with bitterness, poison, and death. The Revelation passage may not be saying that the star falling to the earth will actually be called Wormwood by the inhabitants of the earth. Rather, wormwood was a well-known bitter herb in the Bible times, so by naming the star Wormwood, we are told that its effect will be to embitter the waters of the earth so much so that the water is undrinkable. It won't be a matter of simply a bitter taste to the water; it will literally be poisonous. If drinking water is unavailable to one-third of the earth's population, it's easy to see how chaos and terror will result. Humans can only survive a couple of days without water, and the inhabitants of the affected areas will be so desperate as to actually drink the poisoned water, causing the death of thousands, if not millions of people.

CHAPTER 46

The Khazarians, the Sacred Ark, and the Pleiadians

In pursuit of the missing information, humming came from somewhere. It was like many human voices in harmony. A woman stood by me, beautiful and ageless, very familiar feeling. Her face and eyes were radiant with joy.

"I have been waiting for you. I knew you would be here if all of us met together. Come."

The humming gradually faded way. I stood still waiting to know what all that was about. A hand touched my arm, and the woman said, "Sit with us, we have to talk."

The Khazarian cabals were a pagan civilization and, in a short period in history, became the largest and most powerful kingdom in Europe, and possibly the wealthiest also. They brought with them their religious worship that was a mix of phallic worship and other forms of idolatrous worship practiced in Asia by pagan nations. It is well-known that sometime in the eight to ninth centuries, the Khazars, a warlike Turkish people, converted to Judaism and ruled over a vast domain in what became southern Russia and Ukraine. What happened to them after the Russians destroyed that empire around the eleventh century has been a mystery. Many have speculated that the Khazars became the ancestors of Ashkenazi Jews. The

Khazars were a semi-nomadic Turkic people who created what for its duration was the most powerful polity to emerge from the breakup of the Western Turkic Khaganate. DNA research confirms that modern Khazarian Jews are not the descendants of ancient Israelites or the seed of Abraham. The Khazarian Empire was a warlike people, as evidenced by a statue of a marauding warrior and the six-pointed star on the shield.

The Sacred Ark, this is the revealing of a long-forgotten secret.

In the field of quantum mechanics, NASA scientists have recently confirmed that matter can indeed be in two places at once. It is now an established fact that through quantum entanglement, particles millions of light-years apart can be connected without physical contact. Space-time can now be manipulated, teleportation is becoming a reality, gravity-resistant material is now heralded for air transport, and virtual science has led to a greater understanding of hyper-dimensional existence.

The secret of the Pharaohs' rite of passage to the afterlife was directly associated with the pyramids and the biblical Ark of the Covenant, as revealed by inscriptions at the Sinai mountain temple of Moses.

The Ark of the Covenant so richly contrived was to the dynastic house of gold. The messianic bloodline of ancient grail kings from the old kingdom pharaohs to King Solomon and the descendant royal house of Judah. And the Philosopher's Stone works by accessing Rosicrucianism, Templar, and the Royal Society archives. It is all about the evolution of consciousness in the alchemy of time.

The Pleiadians Received Authority over the Awakening, Healing, and Liberation of Earth

"Spiritual growth, vitality, and wellness is the link to human primary purpose."

I still have a link with my Pleiadian ancestors and the galactic federation of light decision: As of November 19, the councils have all met and agreed that the Pleiadians, due to their terraforming of the earth before the days of Atlantis and Lemuria, and having more genetic stock, plant, animal, and human on earth, will be in charge of establishing once again universal law. Tyranny, and all trespass on the divine right to free will, as long as it does not harm humanity, and the earth will come to a close. This will mainly be done with consciousness and energy waves yet hands on is also effective as of the nineteenth. There has been an ongoing liberation movement, yet due to universal law, it was limited by what some call the prime directive, or noninterference policy. But now it has been decided that due to the extreme negative intervention to preserve humanity and the earth, major intervention is necessary. Pleiadians are given authority over the awakening, healing, and liberation of earth.

CHAPTER 47

The Dinoids from Orion, Retoids from Sagittarius, and the Pre-Cetaceans

The beautiful ageless looking woman continues. "Planet earth's first civilization was etheric intelligence and was designated to be the guardians of earth, but this etheric intelligence also needed the help of physical guardians of earth.

Dinoids from the Bellatrix system in the constellation of Orion and Reptoid colonies from the constellation of Sagittarius arrived later to inhabit the earth. The Reptoids and Dinoids allowed a mammalian species to evolve to sentiency. These mammals were called the pre-cetaceans. The pre-cetaceans provided food for all three colonies in exchange for technology, which in turn improved their production rate further. These three civilizations coexisted in harmony, trading among one another for over eight million years. All three civilizations developed advanced forms of space-time travel. The pre-cetaceans developed their spiritual side, such as psychic abilities, extensively.

A Dinoid-Reptoid Alliance from Bellatrix, believing they were superior to the pre-cetaceans, came to earth to cease all cooperation with the pre-cetaceans and wanted to put them under their control. Over time, the earth Dinoids and Reptoids became more and more influenced by the Bellatrix Dinoid-Reptoid Alliance. The pre-cetaceans, through their high psychic abilities, began sensing the aggression against them and came to see the threat presented by the Dinoid/ Reptoid civilizations. Being given permission for the earth's spiritual hierarchies, the pre-cetaceans decided to implode their fusion reactors located in the Ural mountain range. The pre-cetaceans divided into two groups.

One group evacuated out of our solar system to the constellations of Pegasus and Cetus, and the other group altered themselves physically so that they could enter the oceans and find haven. This group is now our present-day cetaceans such as the dolphins and whales. The entire transformation process occurred over a period of four million years.

When the transformation was complete and the later sector was safe, the first sector imploded the fusion reactors, destroying 98 percent of the Dinoid/Reptoid civilizations. The survivors evacuated to the planet in our solar system, Maldek. Now with the Dinoid/ Reptoid no longer present on earth, the earth's spiritual hierarchies and the cetaceans had to find a suitable guardian for the land. They searched the galaxy for two to three million years before finding what they were looking for. They found, on the fourth planet of the Vega system, a primitive aquatic species that was starting to emerge from the oceans. This species had creation myths, a language, and a hunting and gathering culture.

The spiritual hierarchies of the Vega system were then asked if they would permit this species to be vastly altered genetically to accelerate their evolution so that they may become a guardian species. The Vega spiritual hierarchies agreed. So the traces of the first humans came from the Vega star system. Their technology improved very quickly, and once they had developed star travel technology, they started to migrate into nearby star systems for a period of 2.5 million years.

During this time, the Galactic Federation was formed, Sirius B was colonized, and earth was selected for seeding. Later Mars and Venus were colonized and the Hybornea colony was founded on Earth. Dinoid/Reptoids in the meantime had built up their forces and were invading the various colonies throughout the solar system. Hyborean Earth, Mars, and Venus were victims to these attacks, and the Dinoids and Reptoids gained control over the solar system for a period of approximately eighty thousand years.

In response to this, the Galactic Federation planned a counterattack to reintroduce humans into this system. They arranged for a battle planet (four times the diameter of earth) to come into the solar system and destroy the planet Maldek, which was the Dinoid/Reptoid stronghold. The remains of the planet Maldek are what we can now see as the asteroid belt. After the destruction of Maldek and the defeat of the Dinoid/Reptoids, a human colony was again established on earth. It is what we know today as Lemuria. Over the next 850,000 years the Lemurians spread across the face of the planet. They founded daughter colonies such as Atlantis, Yu, which is now Central China and Tibet, and the Libyan/Egyptian colonies.

The Atlanteans began to acquire a feeling of uniqueness about their culture and wanted to eliminate Lemuria so that they could become the mother country. The Atlanteans began forming alliances with renegade Pleiadians and Alpha Centaurians, which had hierarchical systems of government. They accomplished the destruction of Lemuria by taking earth's moon (earth had two moons in those times).

Out of orbit by using force fields until it was as close as possible to the Lemurian empire, and then the moon was destroyed resulting in a catastrophic shower of meteors. This destroyed much of Lemuria, but this also resulted in many pressures being inflicted upon the tectonic plates—resulting in the gas chambers under Lemuria to implode and thus sink most of the Lemurian continent.

About Agartha-Shambhala. The Yu empire would not bow down to the hierarchical rule of Atlantis and Libyan/Egyptian empires and was thus forced to literally go underground. Today, they form what is known as the Kingdom of Agartha or Shambhala.

This is how autocracy was born: Atlantis formed ten ruling districts, each with their own king. These kings together formed the governing council of Atlantis. The royal governing council of Atlantis decide that a new form of government was desperately needed in which a superior ruling class could be established and sustained by their pretense that they had been empowered by a god-force. Autocracy was thus born and was in full control, enforcing a period of peace and stability. To achieve control over the populace, they started experiment with the people's DNA and genetics. This resulted in the peoples' consciousness being reduced, life spans contracted, and psychic/spiritual abilities dramatically decreasing.

Throughout the years, there were many wars among the various empires due to underground movements of people that wanted to have the Lemurian "philosophy" back in place (i.e., no hierarchy). These wars led to vast destruction. As a last resort, the warring empires decided to attack the opponent's crystal temples (which were responsible for maintaining two frozen layers of water about fifteen to thirty thousand feet above ground, which protected people on earth from the harmful sun's rays and also ensured a stable weather pattern at all times).

Unfortunately, the attacks were made simultaneously and caused the Firmament (the water layers) to be broken down, and thus millions of gallons of water poured down onto the surface, causing what is known biblically as the Great Flood. The breakdown of the Firmament also resulted in the polar icecaps freezing and also the many climatic variations we have today to form.

After the flood, only about two million people survived the flood from an original sixty-five known million. Unfortunately, many of the survivors were the mutant humans that had been genetically altered by the Atlanteans into a much lower state of consciousness. Also, the fact that the firmament was now no longer in existence resulted in the DNA and, thus, consciousness breaking down even further. A few different renegades from Pleides, Alpha and Beta Centauri came to different places on earth after the flood, seeing it as an opportune time to establish their own desired ideologies and also be seen as "godlike" and thus revered. Being already genetically altered, the surviving humans were therefore easily controlled by these renegades.

Since no form of disobedience to these new "gods" was allowed, the concept of ruling by "divine right" became inculcated on earth. This concept of worshipping an elite has continued through to modern times. Culture would rise against culture in wars claiming that the elite they themselves worshipped were superior to the elite of the opposing faction.

We are now in times, though, that will finally bring to an end an approximate ten thousand years of "semi-consciousness" and regain our full consciousness that we deserve. This will be due to our entire solar system coming into contact with what is known as the Photon Belt.

This is a message received from the Federation on Lemuria and translated by Sheldon Nidel.

"You were mutated into limited conscious beings, and your cluster of realities was also affected. Suddenly, a new paradigm was adopted that favored lack, limitation, power, and division. You lost your connection to your history and to a sacred set of beliefs, which the Anunnaki and their carefully chosen minions replaced with a new conception. As a result, they ruled you as your 'gods' and 'goddesses.' They brainwashed you to believe that they were your 'creators' and that the past wonders of Lemuria and Atlantis were myths. They ordered their minions to institute writing as an agent of their own glorification. These acts are recorded in the ancient tablets of Sumer, in the steles of ancient India, and in carvings found throughout Europe, Australia, Oceania, Asia, and the Americas. Now as your consciousness expands more quickly, you are coming to see these tales for the elaborate fiction they truly are.

Your origins are not of this world, but are extraterrestrial in nature, and are to be found on a planet that circles the star Vega in the Lyra constellation. Yet you have achieved more than to travel a mere twenty-six light-years to reach your present home. Many millions of years ago, you became part of a vast rebellion by the Light against the dark in this galaxy. The uprising began in Lyra, Cancer, Gemini, and Orion, as well as in many other lesser-known star groupings (constellations). Eventually, this rebellion led to the formation of the Galactic Federation of Light, over four million years ago. At the very core of this battle were the Star League of the Pleiades, the Andromedan Confederation, the Lyra Light League, and the Sirian star nation. Of these, Sirius is most sacred and the place where the Great Blue

Lodge of Creation has chosen to enter this galaxy. Originally, it was defended by Lion people who decided to settle only on two planets in the Sirius A star system. Later, with their permission, humans from Lyra were first to colonize Sirius B and, in time, Sirius C and D.

The Sirian star system is filled with the great energy bestowed by the Great Blue Lodge. This energy obscures its exact configuration. The system is an anomaly. Sirius's energy defies the physics of stars' normal construction. Sirius A and its companions seem to be what they are not. Thus, to your scientists, they appear, incorrectly, to be exceedingly dense. This seeming density is due to the energy exerted upon them by the Blue Light of Creation. From within this Light, Sirius gathers up the great energy and disperses it to the galaxy. This energy also transforms the way in which those who dwell here see themselves and their sacred mission. It has led Sirius to assist in spreading the energy of its galactic society to a multitude of solar systems throughout this galaxy. The Four Great Laws were presented, long ago, to humanity on Vega and reached their fullest potential on Sirius. Your ancient Lemurian civilization brought them to earth, and they were anchored here by its descendants—the inner earth realm known as Agartha (Shambhala).

In the language of Sirius B, our star nation is known as *Akonowai*, meaning 'sacred path of Creation's Light.' The third and fourth planets in our system circle a blueish-white star. Its light forms a pattern in our atmosphere that creates a red-orange sky filled with the rare blueish cloud. Most of our vegetation is quite purple-blue in color. Infrequently, it is green, orange, or brown. On our main world, Sirius B's third planet, there is one interconnected sea that contains cetaceans, fish, and many creatures unrelated to any aquatic species existing on your world. We dwell in this land of lush forests, huge mountains, enormous prairies, and very high mountains. Our main cities are located some 50 to 200 miles (80 to 320 kilometers) beneath all this beauty. On the surface are only 144 main temple sites. The largest is the grand temple of Atar, dedicated to the spiritual warrior clan named after our largest bird—a six-foot-tall eagle that we call an Atar.

The dimensions of the grand temple of Atar are astonishing. Its main hall contains 576 columns, each exactly 288 perdums or 312 feet (94.8 meters) in height. Its roof is covered with a special lace-work of pure gold to let in the majesty of our Sun. Its floor tiles are inscribed with the text of the Great Book of Understanding, in which the Creator bestowed upon humanity the blueprint for physicality and the wisdom to fulfill its potential.

The main hall is most sacred. The remainder of the temple complex is designed to support and accommodate the rituals practiced within. In the exact center of this very large hall is our planet's main node. The temple is situated on a huge cliff that looks out over our one great sea. The energy that emanates from it each day forms a ring of golden Light around it. At night, when viewed from the ocean, this Light seems like a strong beacon signaling to a ship far out at sea.

The beauty of our world is sacred. Soon, the limitless glories of your world will be apparent once again. Despite all that you have done to her, Mother Earth's magnificence is clearly visible from space. This water world of yours is utterly exquisite. Soon, most of its deserts and the fierce heat that envelops them will be transformed. Ice caps will vanish and the wonders of your most southern continent will be revealed. As you help to return your world to its original, pristine condition, recall what we have ever so briefly told you about our home. Like the two water planets of Akonowai, your solar system embodies much that is sacred. In a short time, Mars will bloom once more, and the desolation on Venus will metamorphose into a land of abundant oceans that teem with life. Such a destiny awaits you and is truly not as distant as you may imagine.

This realm is shifting in accordance with the sacred decrees of the divine plan, which have established a timetable for your transformation into fully conscious beings. As a result of this process, we have come from all sectors of this galaxy to form your first contact team. We are totally dedicated to the completion of the mission that heaven has entrusted to us. Right now, dear hearts, when much is unfolding in your world, you must continue to focus closely upon your sacred intentions. Be firm in your commitment. Know that your victory is inevitable. Know also that you are not alone. Heaven has sent many to assist you. They have come from this and many nearby galaxies, and from the vast orders and life streams of heaven. The will of the divine will manifest upon this realm, dear ones. Feel it in your heart and remain united in your intentions.

Today, we have examined the elements that are transforming your reality. In doing so, we have given you a brief glimpse of our beautiful realm, which we all deeply love. We in this most sacred organization of Light salute you and fully support what you are actively accomplishing. We now take our leave. Blessings, dear hearts! Know in your hearts and souls that the countless abundance and prosperity of heaven is yours!"

CHAPTER 48

A Prophetic Dream on Electronic

In my dream that night, I saw coming from six different United States location a bombardment of electronic interference directed into people lived and the most affected that fall down were the most affected by the international Bilderberger. It's directed into homes.

Many incidents of shooters in schools, shopping centers in Canada, massacres, and murders…were all ex-mental patients or were current mental patients who were *all on the drug Prozac!* This drug, when taken in certain doses, increases the serotonin level in the patient, causing extreme violence. Couple that with a posthypnotic suggestion or control through an electronic brain implant or microwave, or ELF intrusion, and you get mass murder, ending in every case with the suicide of the perpetrator. Exhume the bodies of the murderers and check for a brain implant. You would be surprised. In every case, the name of the murderer's doctor or mental treatment facility has been withheld. It will be able to establish intelligence-community connections and/or connections to known CIA experimental mind-control programs when finally, it will be uncovered who these doctors of death really are.

One in forty humans had been implanted with devices who can be activated and tuned upon human beings at will. The government believes that the aliens are building an army of implanted humans who can be activated and turned upon us at will.

I see that it has been two years since the archons have used their friends in place to send CHADD to Chateau USHI Asylum. Another bed for profit place that keeps people in psychotropic drugs under the MK-Ultra mind-altered, mind control program. A Hitlerian original creation.

They are programing a distortion of its perception and retaining him in psychotropic drugs, parasiting his mind. They are blocking his memory, manipulating him in fear, getting him vulnerable, confused and worried about his situation.

This program is connected to the cabal. They are under many names, the Illuminati, the reptilians, the lizards, archons, bohemians, or the Bilderberger. They break people's spirit while turning money into virtual.

They tell people what to do, what to think, and what decision to make. Every weekdays, they gather them in a "class" room, and captives have to answer the same question: choosing. What choice will you make? They give a subject and if they don't agree, they make the choice for you. I hear it's a "do or die situation."

They are known by ancient society under different names: flyers (on Central America), demons (Christianity), Archons (gnostic belief and writing from two thousand years ago), Jinn (Islamic and pre-Islamic Arabia). All these different names for the same thing.

Gnostic means knowledge, and where the Gnostics tried to bring their knowledge, they were slaughtered. Like the Cathars were slaughtered in Southern France. The people of the Great Library of Alexandria with its half a million scrolls of ancient knowledge, which the Roman Church destroyed, were Gnostics and thinkers. They were able to time travel, get out, and were very knowledgeable, and it's why they were attacked. They did not want their knowledge to circulate and be known.

As a result, very little gnostic writings made it through history, until 1945 in Egypt, when a sealed jar of gnostic writings was found hidden. From that came a greater understanding of the Gnostics' knowledge and what they were talking about.

The Gnostics were mystics and went out into other levels of reality. They were time travelers and shamans. The Gnostics talk about the Lord Archon that they call the Demiurge that they relate to the fake god, Satan, that created the physical or material reality that you perceive. They created the physical universe that humans see. But they didn't create the earth, the sun, or the moon. And these three bodies have important connections geometrically and mathematically, which none of the other planets have. And they talk also about these inorganic entities like being robotic or cyborgs.

The third dimension you live in is an archon world. They have no creativity as humans do, and therefore they have created, among other horrific things, an altered mind control programming and set up bed for profits. Using brain manipulation. Manipulating the detainees' brain while they are maintained in psychotropic drugs.

I see myself now calling for the activation of the Violet Flame grid of Light and protection, the legions of Michael as well as the legions of Melchizedec Lords of Light to form around us, protect us, and to come transmute all negativity.

That is when I heard about the reality of the sixth sense.

Now I am floating and traveling in the universe, and I see the Pegasus constellation races. They are called the Antheri. They appear like Nordic, are very tall like the Nordic, and have light-blue eyes. There is a famous myth involving Pegasus.

It is the one of Bellerophon, the hero who was sent by King Iobates of Lycia to kill the Chimera, a monster that breathed fire and was devastating the king's land. Bellerophon found Pegasus and tamed him using a golden bridle given to him by the goddess Athena. Then he swooped down on the Chimera from the sky and killed the monster with his lance and arrows. After this and several other heroic deeds for King Iobates, Bellerophon let the successes get to his head. Riding Pegasus, he tried to fly to Olympus and join the gods. He didn't succeed. He fell off the horse and back to earth.

But Pegasus did however make it to Olympus. There, Zeus used the horse to carry his thunder and lightning and eventually placed him among the constellations. The constellation Pegasus is depicted with only the top half of the horse, and it is nevertheless one of the largest constellations in the sky, seventh in size. The Northern Cross is a prominent asterism formed by the brightest stars in the constellation Cygnus, and the Great Square of Pegasus is an asterism formed by three bright stars in the Pegasus *constellation*.

Continuing my journey, I am now given the understanding of the horrible burning smell that lasted two days inside my house and the third day upon entering my car. I knew that I was the only one smelling it, no one mentioned smelling anything. I was, in fact, picking up that somebody in my family was about to have a car accident. That was why it smelled tires burning, but my spiritual side could stop it.

CHAPTER 49

Placing Five Words in Time-Space (The Sixth Sense Is the Passing of Time)

This took place in the middle of one night when I was awakened as I heard, "It is time to travel back to plant five words to change the trajectory, the path, harness the change, and make it work. The third dimension tools used in the past to deal with chaotic situations no longer work. So open the golden portal and walk in." And so I did.

Then I heard a voice talking about the reality of the six senses. "The five senses are about the direction of the body:

1. moving forward
2. moving backward
3. to the left
4. to the right
5. up and down

Now the Six sense is the passing of time. That is where you were stuck in time. They placed you in a time prison."

My conscious mind entered a golden cloud when I went back in my soul's past life. I revisited even before Atlantis when my blue flame and I walked the earth as a married couple Christ and Mary

Magdalene. I felt the great responsibility I had been given toward humanity. And I thought, *That is why they restrained me in a time prison.*

Then still in the golden cloud for the creation to come, I went to visit back my past in Atlantis when I was a famous scientist before they imprisoned me and my blue flame, a higher priest. I was then stuck in time in some way. They placed me into a time prison.

I used my mental power of mind to send that five words power, a spiritual energy to change all of human history. To make manifest to all of humanity for all time.

As the golden portal opened and I was asked to let my blue flame walk in and pass the portal, the voice said, "It will impel or push up to greatest talent, power, and spirituality for everyone. The golden portal is opening up the highest spiritual talents that anyone can have. It is the talent within bringing up the power of involving soul awareness, and it raises into highest consciousness.

That is what is happening to you, your physical body, your spirit, to the next connection, your physiology has begun changing.

The biology shifting toward more trilogy is the spirit and the physical being combined. It is the trilogy of creation inside the human body.

Humans are in a fifth dimension reality. The new consciousness is here and can be experienced in a new way.

As the planet continue to adjust and separate in three dimensions (3-D, 4-D, 5-D), many have come to help human beings and tried to guide them out of the illusionary and holographic world planted by the cabal. Saints, ascended masters, and other beings from other galaxies."

As a new deadly virus has been released, physicists has no idea what it is. It affects people's lungs and look like a stage 4 terminal cancer. The lungs collapse rapidly; quickly death follow as there is no cure. I was called to take care of it by my ancestor Pierre. He said that it is a Chinese implanted plague and deadly to humans Chinese virus, genetically altered. "Yes," said Pierre, "it is a genetically altered created virus without cure, and we can't let this virus take any proportion or it will kill many innocent people. I will show you how to destroy it, but you are not to tell about the way it will be destroyed." And so Pierre did.

Now remember that this spiritual adventure began with the destiny of the doG, the tainted angel CHADD. VIE met CHADD in a wheelchair, felt a deep and strong connection inexplicable. They had lived together in a previous life and her memory awakened. Got to know him better and became enveloped in a world of mysticism, government conspiracies, religions, and upcoming prophesied events. Entered a world of lies, deception, hope and pain. Her spiritual journey began when she joined forces with her blue flame, CHADD, to bring the words of Jesus.

The story started with Henri, a professor (CHADD's grandfather) that lived near an Indian tribal reservation and had a son, Edward, with his wife, Martha. Edward married Ethel, and they had a son, CHADD, who was diagnosed with several behavior and mental problems, after his dad took him to the government hospital that his father used at the request of the NSA. At the age of five, they started to do testing on CHADD to understand his unique ability; though he was never sick, CHADD was given multiple drugs at the age of five. Then Edward divorced, and during the time of Edward and Ethel's separation, he started dating a coworker named Katherine, an archon known as the harsh woman, or surnamed the surrogate, working hand in hand with CHADD's half-brother, her son Paul, a deputy sheriff at some time. Paul, Carlos, and Katherine were all involved with the cabal. The government would take the drug from the drug dealers at west, send them to Miami for sale in Florida, and generate money to the government's clandestine operations.

CHADD spent times in hospitals and medical centers, and during his stay in the hospital, a group called Guardians revealed themselves. They were the Cathari. There were two elements to them: the Perfecti and the Believers. The Perfecti were the helpful and wanted to bring people closer to God. They defeated Hitler. The Believers were the Nazis and are the serial killers of today and many world leaders that destroyed rather than created. Extremely intelligent and hypnotizing at the same time, some of the Believers had guidance in genetic reproduction thousands of years ago, before and after the great flood, to create creatures seen throughout history as vampires, werewolves, Bigfoot, and reptilians. These serial killers now became hackers and use DNA and soul-stealing technology. But you will see that more is to come…

CHAPTER 50

The Black Web

One summer day I was sitting on the beach when I felt a spirit coming through. I recognized him immediately as we have always worked with him and other Arcturians. The following was received telepathically guided by the white star radiant Brotherwood.

The following concerns the interference with the hackers, how to make all of you aware of it, and to let you know that you have to take extreme cautions. You'll see.

The Laws of One still remained very close to God:

"Yes, some on earth begin to question, and what if reality was just a manipulation? The matrix is real, and you live in a simulation, and there are powers that don't want you to know. Secret societies and the politically powerful use what they have hidden to you to gain power, and they are responsible for the failing of their lives.

The earliest Atlanteans are light-thought projection beings and having a semi-physical form in which both sexes, male and female, were present in the same body. These Atlantean thought-form beings—projecting vibrations of pure white light and energy—gradually began to take on a more material shape and density and began to engage upon acts of sheer self-indulgence. These physically encased thought-form projections, through the passage of time, began to separate into two groups: those who followed the Law of One and those who chose to follow the sons of Belial based on the island of Aryan.

The Law of One still maintained the highest standards of consciousness and were able to continue vibrating at the very highest level of light and energy, and still remained very close and true to the one Creator God. They were a benevolent loving society, with matriarchal, peaceful, and nurturing characteristics and aspects.

The Aryans used technology to dominate the world:

The Law of One were completely peaceful, absolutely non-violent, and were as a society somewhat vulnerable to the cunning and cloaked political intrigues of the Aryan group. To an extent the non-aggressive focus on peace and honesty that was held by the Law of One became the tools used by the Aryans to set up a complex and cunning deception that enabled them to take control of the crystals. The Aryans became involved in the accumulation of power and used the advanced technology, including the genetic engineering capacities and crystal energy for untoward goals of world control. The developed a race of genetically engineered slave workers. The Aryan faction began to use the technology to dominate the world. The Tuaoi crystal was used to create earthquakes in other areas and used as a death ray. This destructive use imbalanced the system and led to the destruction of the crystal satellite motherboard. Its crash and explosion created a series of earthquakes and explosions throughout the energy system. Once the end came, there was a 'too late' recognition on the part of the Law of One that the utopia was lost. But they vowed to return one day, and never again be naive, or duped.

The Arcturians are fifth dimensional species.

They are fifth dimensional species, prototypes of what the human race is to become if the human race wants to survive long enough. They are the most advanced civilization in the Milky Way galaxy with greenish skin, large almond eyes, and three fingers. They are also the main scientists of the Milky Way and perform experiments that are governed by the Arcturian Brotherwood. This civilization is closely aimed at helping other races to progress along the path of God realization. The most fundamental ingredient they teach for living in the fifth dimension is love. Negativity, fear, and guilt must be overcome and exchanged for love and light. The Arcturians work in close connection with the ascended masters. Whom they call the Brotherwood of all. They also work with the Galactic Command and travel the universe in their starships, which are some of the most advanced. One of the reasons earth has not been attacked by warlike negative extraterrestrials has been the civilizations from of the like advanced starships of the Arcturians. In what termed the "golden age," many souls on the planet extraterrestrials, especially Sirians, Pleiadians, and Arcturians, were able to live extremely long life times. Some as long as ten thousand years through the rejuvenation process."

Now what follow is what is called the trip chair.

A voice said, "Many believe the human race is in the midst of an awakening, but do you believe it?" I asked the spirit entity about the hacking and the stealing of the souls and this is what I received:

"There is hacking by the elite, and it is how Illuminati uses DNA and soul-stealing technology. These people in control are basically a conglomeration of all the various sects and orders that resisted throughout ages. They have actually unlimited funding and political power. The reasons that they have been working on the recent tech they have been working on has gotten up to this far is what they call Soul Stealers technology. The soul is caught with a 4-D map of the brain, and they can create a holographic chip that contains all the information of a person's memories, of their personality. The process takes multiple supercomputers, even zero-point devices. The computers run off these devices. It's literally almost unlimited power. And with a few of these devices in the right alignment, it could blow the whole world. It could make the entire world disappear. It is kind of difficult for humanity to even imagine it. Imagine DNA of replication and the complete brain mapping to create a chip is basically a four-dimensional map of the entire brain and the central nervous system and the body."

Wow! Now another spirit entity, a young man that pretends being from a different planet, talks and says, "What follow is of great importance for everyone to be aware of. You see with that, they can do full replication cloning where they completely recreate a human form. They have figured out how to activate the DNA in the brain completely and it unleashes 100 percent capacity. It is like if you were putting a helmet on and your consciousness would be transferred into some type of electromagnetic wave form or something, and you could basically travel throughout space at first and then time itself. You could travel through time in a chair. It's the trip chair!

The mechanical devices actually beam electromagnetic waves into your brain and allow you to unlock the full capacity of your brain. It's time travel. The first effect is that you see the future of your existence. They can then time in to push you forward or further, and you can take over and guide it yourself. You can see the different possible realities for existence.

They can create artificial dimensions and take people there and play out whatever kind of psychological experiments they want. The knowledge behind this comes from the Nazis for WWII. It's a lot of psychological experimentation if you see a possibility that you do not want, and you kind of enhance it and you get it out of your head. The only thing that ever happens from that is when you return, you will take the steps to create. That is the problem. It is like a nightmare device at that point. Their line of reasoning is that, well, we went too far enough so let's go further and just go to the end of time and see into the far future. Let's look at what is going to happen.

All of space-time and consciousness become one essence, but no one knows what that means. It leads now to the control group for that all secret projects basically have this power to go around, operate in and out of time, teleport themselves into any locations, and operate and influence a person and the mind control extending into general population.

The elite began this project using Nazi technology, and the science behind it is to gather people that they thought could provide themselves with a little amusement. The DNA goes into the active, and their bodies get used in a variety of ways genetics are cloned, and they get out of it because it is consciousness.

The celebrities speak out through their symbols and their music. It is all over the media, and anyone involved is going to be hinting at it somehow. That is what all these symbols are. This is how the

Illuminati uses DNA and soul-stealing technology giant AI a brain entrainment. It is slavery on many levels.

They have been doing it for so long that companies now are getting involved with supplying the goods. They create a mirror image of reality and use that to archive immortality. They read up on the Navy projects, and it is how it started all that, and it gave them the power to go in the time and see what's going to happen. Because they are using this technology so that they are ten to twenty steps ahead of everybody doing anything here. Anyone who would speak out it would show upon a grid or a device or whatever is said. And they could see our time line was going to be influenced to somebody influencing that project. They could literally narrow it down and see what a person did and where and this time go and whack that person. All the people that are getting whacked, that's what it is.

They are building an AI consciousness system with the technology that could rule the world. That can be turned on with this grid and zero-point generators and would never shut off and that would have power over mind.

All the aluminum in the atmosphere is put on this AI system that is being constructed, and if we are plugged into it, it will make all your decisions for you mentally and you won't have any way to overcome that unless you're spirit overpowers your brain chemistry, which has to happen through this fear switch.

When all the fear from the brain chemistry is pumping, you will finally turn it in the other direction. People without that won't have any natural defense to a mind-to-mind stealer grid around the whole entire planet, and if they have the possibility, they are going to do what they want with that power. They will engender chaos, reign out that chaos. They are going to walk up the little ordered steps and stand on top again. It's literally a handful of people ruling the world, not a lot, and they control people through their emotions, through their fears. People must control their "fear attitude."

Also, new scientists and their discovering work in technology in the new things, like the particle, CERN, in HAARP, did not understood that the cabal would do harm with that new technology or struggle the good. What they either ignored or are part of it, the cabal is an anti-Tesla using frequency for the bad.

For the *particle*, while the scientists know that light can act like both wave and particle of which a modern experiment can be performed, a particle accelerator is a machine that uses electromagnetic fields to propel charged to nearly light speed and contain them in well-defined beams.

About CERN, it is a particle accelerator to recreate black holes, antimatter and rip holes with the space-time continuum opening up dimensional portals and a CERN conspiracy.

And HAARP is a mind control attack and an electronic harassment and torture. Like digital TV and subliminal advertising is a conspiracy through subliminal messages that are being broadcast to influence the viewers with what the government and big industries want people to believe. Reptilians are not just on TV but also in our lives, malicious and evil. They are also cunning and know how to hook people and to use mind manipulation and telepathy. You must keep your mind shielded, just keep it in your prayers because their hooks are strong and make it hard for you to stay away from them or forget how awful they treat you when you think of leaving. Among the advanced technology they are using, just to name a few, are eyeglasses, jewelries, rings, necklaces, cuff buttons and things that look like labels, arm technology, hand technology, head technology, and lasers.

The AIDS, it is a virus conspiracy created by the CIA to rid the country of homosexuals, African Americans, and reduce the population. Global warming is a ruse to control the population's way of life, raise taxes, and intended to lead to more controlling, tyrannical government.

And all unawakened humans are locked in an alien computer stimulation through a 3-D hologram projected from another dimension by a super intelligence. The world and everything in it are ghostly images, projection from a level of reality so beyond our own. It is literally beyond both space and time.

And you are commanded not to believe every spirit but to examine them because many false prophets have gone into the world.

These spirits of the false Christ imitates the manifestation of the real. They speak in tongues, do healings, make miracle and deliverances, etc. The connection ended.

CHAPTER 51

The Church Invasion by the Freemasonry

Shamina, the whistle-blower, appeared to me again and said, "Almost sixty years ago, Padre Pio first met Father Luigi Villa, whom he entreated to devote his entire life to fight Ecclesiastical Freemasonry. Padre Pio told Father Villa that the our Lord had designs upon him and had chosen him to be educated and trained to fight Freemasonry within the church. The saint spelled out this task in three meetings with Father Villa, which took place in the last fifteen years of life of Padre Pio. At the close of the second meeting, the second half of 1963, Padre Pio embraced Father Villa three times, saying to him, 'Be brave, now...for the church has already been invaded by Freemasonry!' and then stated, 'Freemasonry has already made it into the loafers (shoes) of the Pope!'

At the time the reigning Pope was Pope Paul VI. Padre Pio died on September 23, 1968. He was a friar, priest, stigmatic, and mystic. He was beatified in 1999 and canonized in 2002 by Pope John Paul II.

The mission entrusted to Father Luigi Villa by Padre Pio to fight Freemasonry within the Catholic Church was approved by Pope Pius XII, who gave Papal Mandate for his work. Pope Pius XII's Secretary of State, Cardinal Tardini, gave Father Villa three cardinals to work with and to act as his own personal guardian angels, Cardinal

Ottaviani, Cardinal Parente, and Cardinal Palazzini. Cardinal Villa worked with these three cardinals until their death.

In 1971, Father Villa founded his magazine, *Chiesa viva*, always writing in defense of Europe's Christian roots and in preservation of the historical truth against the forces alien to our civilization. The magazine was attacked by the upper echelon of the Catholic Church, was ostracized among the clergy, and the efforts to silence it once and for all also included seven assassination attempts on Father Villa, which fortunately didn't have the desired results. But through all of these attempts at silencing him, Father Villa has never given up his commitment to Padre Pio. At ninety-three years old, Father Villa continues his battle with the Catholic Church enemies, as Padre Pio directed Him.

Today the Catholic Church leader's recent comments challenging the belief in hell and the right to abortion represent a profound scandal for Catholics around the world.

He also reportedly said that 'Hell does not exist' and that 'Those who do not repent and cannot therefore be forgiven disappear.'

Try to change the 'Lord's Prayer' too.

Pro-life group says that he 'causes confusion' when he equates social justice with abortion.

The Catholic Church has long taught that abortion is an intrinsic evil that must always be opposed. On the Feast of the Holy Family, he persists and continues and said Jesus had to beg forgiveness. This implies that Jesus committed a sin! That is contrary to the Bible because the Bible says that Jesus led a sinless life.

In the early 1800s was a massive revolt against the Freemason society in America that led to completely wipe out all but a few lodges remained. The man that exposed them was killed, then it led to a party called the anti-masonic party and won governorships, some Senate seats. That anti-masonic revolt led to thirty-second degree Freemasonry, all codes, all initiations in a book.

They had congressional hearings, they had hearings in the state government offices in New York that was the biggest state in America at the time.

This anti-masonic revolt was people who had been in the organization and had done heinous things because they were forced to, because they were in a cult, part of a group that forces all of its members into common criminality, because nobody can ever talk or they can pin all this stuff on you. Nonetheless people who were buried in this stuff up came forward and revealed all information that led this to being shut down for its time and they not treated as criminals. They were given amnesty and were treated as heroes because through their own conscience, they decided to do something different and refused to play the game anymore.

Today a majority of senators and congressmen are members of a pedophile organization network trading photographs, video, and also the trafficking of humans because if they want to play in the political game at all or even run in an election, they are required to have sex with children even if it disgusts them and they do not want to have anything to do with it. The senators and congressmen are forced to do it and have no choice.

Some mercenaries were hired by the cabal that captures senators out of their homes in the middle of the night, throwing them black bags over their head twisting it up, throwing them in the back of a van, sliding them around doing screeching turns so that these captured guys are slamming up against and getting bodily and head injuries. All these people were then brought into a specific location, the bags were taken off their heads, and some of the aides of these congressmen had been exposing the cabal, and they threw these men into chipper shredder, the only option were you can go in yourself or they are going to throw you in.

The history repeat itself today, and a few are bringing the hidden truth but because everybody has got in it, when exposed, it will make them look bad.

So the challenge today is how do you defeat a group that automatically makes everyone who is ever been involved a criminal of such monstrous extreme that if it becomes exposed, they lose all credibility with the public? You will probably have to forgive them and see them as brave people because they are fighting against a greater evil and what they did was through coercion. This could exonerate a lot in the cabal, senators, and congressmen. But there is still a real persistence here, and if someone has been involved in this atrocious stuff and decide to turnover to become a new person, you have to be willing to let him do that and be kind and compassionate. Forgiving them just as in Christ God forgave you and may be trust that it will bring a new justice and the end of corruption."

But truth begins to appear and a long-time insider expert tells in an exclusive interview that a deep concern and unease has emerged regarding the leader, and some leading clerics have called for his resignation. A former diplomat says that an ex-papal ambassador told the truth on covered up sex abused. And a blockbuster eleven-page letter names of people in sexual abuse and cover-ups to the very highest levels. Providing with dates and details and information on where the relevant documents may be found.

"Almighty Father, have mercy!"

Then Shamina got silent.

CHAPTER 52

The Venerable Fulton Sheen Gives Its Point of View on the Devil

During my journey, I have come in contact with the Venerable Archbishop Fulton Sheen. He came to help me when I needed help. Venerable Fulton J. Sheen discussed the devil's incessant attempts to turn our heart away from God. May you never forget that Satan, the father of lies, is cruel and the biggest deceiver of men whose only desire is humans destruction.

"Because we have so much on theology from the press, here is an interesting hearing about the devil from a sound philosophical and theological point of view.

The devil first from the psychiatric point of view and secondly from the biblical. First the psychiatric: It is interesting that as we dropped things in the church, the world began to pick them up and distort them. For example, the nuns dropped the long habits and put on maxi coats. We stop saying the beads, hippies put the beads around their neck, and as theologians dropped the demonic, the psychiatrists pick it up.

The existential psychotherapist of a well-known institute has several chapters in his work on psychiatry on the diabolic. What is the diabolic from the purely psychiatric point of view? The psychotherapist Dr. May analyzes the word *diabolic*. It comes from the Greek words *dia* and *baline*. *Dia-baline* is to tear apart, rend sender. Anything, therefore, that breaks pattern, that destroys unity, that corrupts and produces discord, that is diabolical. Now there has been a great increase of the diabolic. Notice for example the discord in the church, the discord in religious communities, the discord among the laity regards the church, discord in the clergy. All these are manifestations of a spirit of the diabolic that surrounds us.

Now this psychiatrist analyzes the way in which the diabolic works. And he mentions three: First, love of nudity. Secondly, violence, aggressiveness. Thirdly, split personalities, no inner peace, disjointed minds.

Our Blessed Lord one time went into the land of the Gerasenes… and he found in this land a young man possessed of the Devil (Mark 5:1–20). The Gospel mentions three characteristics of this young man. First he was nude. Secondly, he was violent and aggressive. They could not even keep him in chains. And thirdly, his mind was split, schizophrenic. Our Lord said to him, 'What is your name?' He said, 'My name is Legion.'

Now a legion in this time meant six thousand soldiers in the Roman Army. See already he is a person and yet he is legion., six thousand others. My name is legion for we are many. See the personality is no longer unified, I, legion, we many. Now the psychiatrist does not ever correlate the three manifestations of the diabolic with this young man in the Gospel. I am doing that because I could not help but notice the similarity between the two. So from just a superficial point of view, the diabolic disrupts, and whenever you have a great manifestation of the Spirit, you always get the Devil working. When for example, Moses in the Old testament worked miracles against Pharaoh, Pharaoh's agents simulated a few miracles. When the Holy Spirit upon the Holy Spirit came upon the early Church of Pentecost, there was the persecution of Stephen. We had a Vatican Council, the blessing of the Spirit upon the church. And we have immediately the manifestation of the evil spirit.

So I just leave you with this characteristic note of the diabolic from the psychiatric point of view. The breakup of unity, the breakup of families, the breakup of corporations, the breakup of religious communities, the breakup of the oneness of Christ."

Is there a correlation here with CHADD? Or any diabolic intent from the Illuminati in keeping him under psychotropic drugs?

CHADD is a Baker Acted, drugged ward of the state kept on psychotropic drugs by the cabal, which are disabling his brain's ability to filter information and perception, blocking signals to his conscious mind. Drugs are demons giving a false feeling, causing major addiction to the DNA that is compromised, making his spirituality vulnerable at this point. During his various Baker Acts he was arrested in his room in his underwear while he was reading the Bible with a candle to the Virgin of Guadalupe (the candle must have aggressed the dark with the light).

Is there a malicious purpose? Are they trying to break the oneness of Christ since his early childhood by keeping him in custody of the state and in Chateau USHI Asylum under their mind control program?

All mental hospitals or behavioral center and state hospitals doctors are Indian Pakistani Thuggees and Indian Illuminati. They are reptilians created by the believers, that became hackers and uses DNA and soul-stealing technology. Through electronic waves to the brain, they unlock the full capacity of the brain, see the future, and twist or change it by creating artificial dimensions, etc. It then justify schizophrenia and else.

There is a tradition of nine unknown men possessors of incredible knowledge, that goes back to the mythical Ashoka, emperor of the Indies. A key figure of ancient sacred India, he pacified a vast empire under the Buddhist religion from 273 BCE, Indian Illuminati.

Son of Kshatriya, caste of noble warriors, born to manage his kingdom by force and trained in the arts of war, *Ashoka undertook the conquest of the Kalinga country which extended from Calcutta to Madras. The Kalinganans resisted and lost a hundred thousand men in the battle. The sight of this slaughtered multitude shocked Ashoka. He took the war abhorrent forever.*

It is said that instructed by the horrors of war, the Emperor Ashoka always wished to forbid men the evil use of intelligence. Under his reign, the science of nature, past and future, enters the secret. Research going from the structure of matter to the techniques of collective psychology will now be concealed, and for twenty-two centuries, behind the mystical face of a people that the world no longer thinks of anything but ecstasy and the supernatural. Ashoka founds the most powerful secret society of the earth the Indian Illuminati.

CHAPTER 53

The Legends of the Nine Men

This legend of the nine men is a powerful secret that hold nine men directly benefiting from the experiments, works, documents accumulated for more than twenty centuries. The goals of these men was to not let the means of destruction fall into profane hands. Pursue beneficial research for humanity. These men would be renewed by co-optation to keep the technical secrets from the distant past. The Nine Unknowns would use a synthetic language. Each of them would be in possession of a constantly rewritten book containing the detailed exposition of a science.

Book 1—Techniques of propaganda and psychological warfare. Devoted to propaganda techniques and psychological warfare as well as the electronic techniques of controlling the thoughts of a subject or a crowd.

Book 2—Physiology. It would include a way to kill a man by touching him, death occurring by reversal of nerve impulses. Devoted to physiology, notably provide the means of killing a man by touching him, death occurring by inversion of the nerve impulse, gives all known techniques of pressure on different points of the body to cause unconsciousness, death, or chronic lesions. Adding, of course, all the means to heal these troubles, including the resurrection techniques.

Book 3—Microbiology, protective colloids, genetics; wave mechanisms to repair muscles and organs; sonology, or science of the virtues and properties of sound in all frequency ranges. The study of microbiology, including protective colloids, especially genetics, and it details the wave mechanisms that repair organs and living tissues, includes a complete treatise on sonology, or the science of the virtues and properties of sound in the different frequency ranges.

Book 4—Transmutation of metals, alchemy, secret properties hydrophobicity—Atlantis' high-speed vessels. Transmutation of metals and their secret properties such as hydrophilicity and hydrophobia, which have played a central role in the construction of ultrafast vessels. Atlanteans are said to have invented alchemy—why not? They invented everything! In any case, since then, Ashoka's Nine Unknowns kept the secret of alchemical gold…but not always. A legend has it that in times of scarcity, temples and relief agencies receive from secret sources of great quantity of a very fine gold.

Book 5—All means of communication, terrestrial and extraterrestrial, teleportation, includes the study of all means of communication, terrestrial and extraterrestrial. It deals with the transportation of people and goods, including teleportation—it also lists the ancient and current media-including those we do not yet know.

Book 6—Gravitology, another science invented by the Atlanteans, allowed to remove weight to heavier loads, which would have helped them to build all the cyclopean walls and pyramids. The secrets of gravitation. The Gravitologie, other science invented by the Atlanteans, allows to remove their weight to the heaviest loads, potentially helping them to build cyclopean walls and other pyramids.

Book 7—Native American cosmogony/theory of knowledge. The largest cosmogony conceived by our humanity. There are large traces in the cosmogony of the American Indians and especially in the theory of knowledge.

Book 8—Vril, light, the operating mode of the cosmo-telluric subtle energy, atmospheric energy, and nerve impulses. Electroshock may kill, drive crazy, or turn into god depending on power. Deals with light. Dedicated to the operational mode subtle cosmo-telluric energy, including atmospheric energy and nerve impulses that the Atlanteans associate with electricity, and they called Vril energy or simply pril.

Book 9—Enlightenment, or finish zombified by dark wizards, through mind control techniques discussed in the first book. It would detail trepanation, ayahuasca-type magic potions, and electric shock including from lightning. It would include the presentation of fulgurology, a science we know nothing about. Identifies all the techniques to achieve enlightenment, also called enlightenment. Some of these techniques with the disadvantage to the applicant to finish grilled or zombified by black magicians, using mind control techniques described in the first book. He would enumerate trepanation, ayahuasca potions, and various electroshocks, including lightning, also present fulgurology, a science to which we know nothing yet.

Apart from religious, social, political, resolutely and perfectly concealed agitations, the Nine Inconnu embody the image of a serene science, of a science with conscience.

And the communication stopped.

But the time has begun to tick...

CHAPTER 54

Your Oversoul Consciousness is Your Unlimited Power

There, I am celebrating a family reunion when suddenly I am in great pain. This pain is part of an all-out assault worldwide against the spiritual Light workers. The vision shows me clearly that there is power in numbers, and we all have to make a mental connection with all Light workers in the world to work in unity against them. There is power in unification around the world to fight.

Most people are having the same problem because they have been taught to focus on the now. This may have served its purpose, but time has changed and it keeps everyone completely focused on themselves in the life of the now.

Everyone need to pull back and look at the larger picture, and if you don't, you will have a lot of problem in your life. You are so focus on your pain and what is going on today, though you must look at the concentrated spiritual being that you are.

You must look at your oversoul and all the knowledge that you have accumulated. You must still live and work in the physical, but every single day and night, you should meditate and get into your oversoul consciousness twice a day, morning and night.

That is where we, you, have no limit, unlimited power, unlimited energy, unlimited healing, and unlimited achievement. That is what the dark spirits wants you into thinking into material matter.

In our own oversoul, we enter into a very bright light realm and connect then with a part of us that then help you heal and regain energy for your own achievement.

You will experience being in another realm, experiencing being pure consciousness and aware of your physical body while having great clarity. Then you'll realize to be something much more powerful and magnificent that you think you are. When you reach to another dimension, you can see that there is so much more to life then you are aware of. Everything becomes illuminated at that point. So many things exist simultaneously, amazing beautiful thing. You will now be aware that there are so much more, and your understanding of God will be clearer.

CHAPTER 55

Prophetic Dreams

Next was CHADD's turn to journey and to experience a few prophetic dreams.

In the first dream, he went to the Holy Church, and on top of the cross was an eagle. That was what happened over two years ago. It was when he was guided to go to the Divine Mercy Chapel and met a woman that gave him a rosary. And now he went back in his dream, and the eagle was struck by lightning. He was shown that the church represents his hope, the eagle represents his freedom. And it is struck by lightning to represent the lack of his mobility, restrained in Chateau Ushi Asylum.

The same day, he fell asleep again in the middle of the day and had this second dream. He called me and said that him and I were traveling to Lourdes in France and we took some selfies. In the background is a waterfall. He was shown that healing was right around the corner, and he will have life form from this healing water that would also heal me and my body.

Lourdes is a French town with the most famous healing shrine in the world and one of the most visited of all pilgrimage sites. When a young servant girl named Bernadette Soubirous claimed to see a radiant vision of a woman in white on February 11, 1858.

Then CHADD dreamed again and saw a spider web that he did not see on time, and he entered it face into it with all the tentacles that have been attached on him that kept him limited by a black widow. That's the surrogate mother and its entire family. This is his actual limitation, but he is shown that the healing is there. It is coming and it restores the life on the cross of the life.

Now an angel is guiding him to a mansion. He is entering the mansion looking for an old friend. This friend is the extension of himself, and he is searching for a part of himself missing. Ten percent of himself is missing. But he is shown that he will be living in a safe environment thereafter, when he will be released from Chateau Ushi and from the mind control program. He will then be whole and integrated.

Not that his controllers are not doing their best to have him in despair, most specifically the legalist archon when he sent someone to tell him that they will agree to release him but in another control place and kept separated from VIE. They said that they're waiting for an adult living facility. But things are changing fast and they are losing the battle. Remember Psalm 23?

Psalm 23 says,

"The Lord is my shepherd; I shall not want"—The Lord takes us into the Light.

"He maketh me to lie down in green pastures"—Green represents the heart chakra. We are to open our hearts to love.

"He leadeth me beside the still waters"—Our hearts become still in love.

"He restoreth my soul"—Karmic debts are released and makes us move toward the Light.

"Even though I walk through the valley of the shadow of death, I will fear no evil, for you are with me; your rod and your staff comfort me"—With God's protection, we understand that death is an illusion; once fear is transcended, we now live according to a deeper and more expansive new life.

"Thou preparest a table before me in the presence of mine enemies"—The enemies eat with us because we no longer fear them. God's generosity extends towards all.

"Thou anointest my head with oil"—The oil of sanctification. The anointing is the sign that we are children of God who belong to the Risen savior.

"My cup runneth over"—Abundance is promised, after our initiation along the paths of God. Since our consciousness has shifted, we no longer experience the world as a place of deprivation; rather, the world overflows like a cup of prosperity.

"Surely goodness and mercy shall follow me all the days of my life"—Peace, joy, and freedom are our birthright, which we discover through this anointing.

"And I will dwell in the house of the Lord forever"—There are many mansions in God's house. All of us have the chance to live there in peace and happiness.

The European anti-immigration parties at a conference in Prague has been urged to liberate the European nations from the chains of the European Union as the bloc has entered a period of decline. The European Union is losing its breath. The New World Order will be overthrown by rogue members within the organization by the year.

Like the saints walking back on earth, the God Duo have also taken their part and came to walk the earth through a rough journey, and it is their journey and what they have encountered or discovered.

As previously mentioned, corruption is everywhere and in every governments and institutions are using high-technology that you are not even aware or have heard of. By all means all is good to reduce the population to keep control of humans.

Now there is resistance (chaos) to that which is the reason in so much separation (division) on the planet now. The unclean, or the cabal, are feeling this and of course rebelling against it because it feels very uncomfortable to them and many.

It is the energy that starts to unite and the earth controllers feel like they are losing that and there is a huge reaction in many places all over the planet. Many beings are promoting and propagating for their own personal purposes. But that unity is the process, even though through news, it does not seem to show that or reflect in that way.

So many things are taking places. Earth humans are dealing with a flu virus, which has gone through every country. That flu virus has literally cleared a level of resistance and helped many to take a new step up once it clears. It is to get some time to finally release on planet earth. It has propagated very rapidly and has served its purpose, which was to clear a lot of spider webs away to start looking at a new way of seeing yourself as a spirit pretending to be human.

A new deadly virus has been released. Physicists have no idea what it is. It affects people's lungs and looks like a stage 4 terminal cancer. The lungs collapses rapidly, and death quickly follow as there is no cure. My ancestor Pierre said that it is an Asian implanted plague and deadly to humans, Asian virus genetically altered. As it is altered, the body can't fight it.

"Yes," said Pierre, "it is a genetically altered created virus without cure, and we can't let this virus take any proportion or it will kill many innocent people. I will show you how I destroy it, but you are not to tell about the way it will be destroyed." And so Pierre did.

Humans are forming a new physiology. It can carry more light, and that is what the flu virus has done. Hitting so many and in doing so has opened the door to release those restrictions. One can now see how things are being manipulated and see more as things are going to have uncovered and a lot of frustrations that many people experience as this takes place. But it is already unfolding. Everybody is starting to see things the way they truly are instead of all illusions that have been put in place.

The seven senses are going to start evolving like the sense of space also called time-space. The fifth is a spiral. When measure top to bottom, it is time; if you measure it side to side, it is space.

The physical body has a perception of time-space and you will soon be able to sense if some is alone in a house, he will be able to sense it even if it is in a different room.

Emotions are magnetic and as spiritual, vertically it is electrical and horizontally it is magnetic. Electrical refers to head and magnetic relates to heart. You are cocreator and when you doubt of yourself, maybe with fear, you go in a spiral down.

Indeed, you literally create now what you think, so careful what you put into the machine and what you believe because the two makes a new reality for you, which moves quickly.

Humans are very powerful and the energy renewable. Love is the power and they miss it.

Vaccines has been created to spread a new virus. Children, young adults, and seniors are dying from it. Hospitals and emergencies are at full capacity.

Now the vibrational transformation energy involves the use of resonance and vibration. It stimulates the five senses and restores the balance to open to more. It tones the body up and tune up life by realigning to the spirituality and to human destiny. By consciously stimulating the five senses with color, light, sound, the body can then be healed of traumas and pain.

Sound and sonic vibration construct reality, realm of sound that creates the lines between the seen and the unseen. Acoustic resonance influence the body's organs and cells and the functioning of the brain. Sonic vibration affects the human body and stimulate the DNA. When you hear a certain type of sound, like in *Frequency of Sound*, the brain responds positively.

In addition to Sound, Light can be applied at a certain frequency, through a particular color frequency, and will cause your brain to perceive images of geometric patterns, shapes, colors, and objects.

The spoken Light language is the language of future mathematics and serves the father's will.

This new therapy that bridges the gap at the right time is the Bio-Qi therapy™.

CHAPTER 56

The Virgin of Guadalupe Prayer Candle

As if was not enough to be under beams of frequencies at night that let me sweating, terrible shoulders, belly and knee pains, and unrested in the morning, I received bad news from CHADD at Chateau USHI Asylum.

While in this place, he had been subject of several colds, falls... He had rashes from a switch of one of his drug into one with red dye 40 to which he was allergic, and no one could have ignored it as it was written in his file and this was not new or recent. He was then advised to refuse the drug for four days and a doctor will prescribed, thereafter a new one, and he did. Indian doctor B. Goswami visited him on Thursday morning and prescribed him Zyprexa psychotropic drug (generic for Abilify to which he was allergic to) with many unwanted side effects by the way.

So I received a first phone call from CHADD letting me now that he had been switch from Abilify to Zyprexa. Later that day, just after he took the new pill, he mentioned to me having diarrhea, to which I did not pay more attention than that. The following morning day, the diarrhea was still in effect, and after the third ingestion of Aripiprazole, he mentioned to me an increase of his diarrhea and now having stomach pain that he thought was coming from the unhealthy food. Time passed by and I didn't hear from him, so I decided to call and check on him. I was told that he was not feeling good and was laying down, but he called me back when feeling better.

That Friday at 10:00 p.m., I received a phone call telling me that he had been throwing blood all day and had been transported to the emergency room.

At 4:40 a.m. on Saturday, I received another phone call from him, from the emergency room, and he said, "I just arrived. They are admitting me to a hospital. It took time probably due to paperwork and authorization to move me to an emergency room in an hospital, and then they drove me at least one hour from Chateau USHI. There, at the emergency, I had to wait a long time before seeing a physician. Having diarrhea and throwing up on the floor. I am finally admitted. Right now, they have me on IV and a lot of fluid, and I have a tube in my nose," and he hanged up. I did not realize that I did not know where he was and how I would check on him.

I remember well when two weeks ago, CHADD had a meeting with Dr. Goswani that, said CHADD, was surprised and also not really happy to tell him that he was soon going back to his county to be in court. Soon meant by the end of the week for a court hearing on a Tuesday. It is obvious that he will not be able to attend the hearing now.

Twenty-four hours passed, it is Tuesday, and CHADD suddenly is asked to sign a conditional release instead of being seen in court by the judge. "Isn't it time you think to sign a conditional release?" is what he heard. Really? A release under "condition." Hum! For what? Being arrested and put in an asylum for praying to the Virgin of Guadalupe? Or for having been unable to show on the court day in front of the judge because he had been poisoned?

(The Virgin of Guadalupe is the patron saint of Mexico. She is depicted with brown skin, an angel and moon at her feet, and rays of sunlight that encircle her. According to tradition, the Virgin Mary appeared to an indigenous man named Juan Diego on December 9, 1531.

Our Lady of Guadalupe, Spanish Nuestra Señora de Guadalupe, also called the Virgin of Guadalupe, in Roman Catholicism, the

Virgin Mary in her appearance before St. Juan Diego in a vision in 1531.

Mary appeared a second time to Juan Diego and ordered him to collect roses.

It was on December 12, the Virgin reappeared to Juan Diego and ordered him to collect roses in his *tilmátli*, a kind of cloak. Juan took the roses to the bishop, and when he opened his cloak, dozens of roses fell to the floor and revealed the image of the Virgin of Guadalupe imprinted on the inside. The tilmátli with the image is on display in the Basilica de Guadalupe.)

CHAPTER 57

A Sudden and Unexpected Development

Twenty-four hours after the court day, Doc Goswani in between two doors told CHADD that because of the attempt at arson he has been accused of, he could not get out yet, no ALF, halfway house, or group home wanted him. Of course they omitted to mention to the ALF and halfway houses the candle prayer reality, which is not a motive for arrest and be considered an attempt of arson.

Well, it is because it is related to something much bigger than this. It is related in fact to an ancient wisdom, modern medicine, scientific research, and the secret link between body, mind, and spirit that the God Duo wants to bring to the surface to humanity and the cabal does not want to be uncovered.

Trying to discuss the possibility that the brain may not be the sole proprietor of human essence is not even something that can be considered, said the archon legalist supposed to defend CHADD. Though the mind is not in the brain.

To make sure that no one will understand that CHADD had been poisoned on purpose to unable him to go to court, twenty-four hours after CHADD was released from the hospital, he had diarrhea again. And the employees were ready for it with Imodium! Now the court date has been reported to four months later and more profit to make from it.

Hum! Well done. Two years and a half and never been with diarrhea and vomiting blood, but just at this specific date.

One week later, I heard that CHADD had been admitted for the third time at the emergency in the middle of the night. He was throwing up black liquid. I tried to find out what it was that time, but no one would answer my questions. Until he could ask one employee to call me. She said, "Hold on, CHADD wants to talk to you." All he had time to say was that he was going into surgery. The poisoning and the too heavy wheelchair from Chateau Ushi Asylum had finished the work of Carlos when he punched him and broke his sternum. It created an hernia that got so big that CHADD had to be surgically taken care of. It was obstructing the passage of the food.

But the day before was family visitation and the surrogate, his father's second wife and archon, went to visit him and brought him food. After eating the food, he felt full and not comfortable immediately. The same way he felt when he was poisoned the other two times. What happened is that Carlos did not want him to go to court, neither the archon surrogate that was with him since a long-time racketing him for his disability government monthly money. Carlos was known for violence and brutality, and he did not want to get a chance to be arrested for beating CHADD, and the surrogate was also worried that he would denounce her if he was going in front of the judge. So he sent the surrogate to poison him and she agreed. The damaged being already done by the beating and the broken bones with the throwing up nonstop for twenty-four hours, he knew that it will finish its job. But what they did not expect was that he would get the surgery on time.

As soon as he was admitted, he was put on IV and he had the psychotropic drugs through IV. Then he had surgery and was on morphine for pain. Seventy-two hours later, they replaced the morphine by his psychotropic drugs again. The same psychotropic he had been on since they forced him to ingest in its early age!

But the morphine helped him astral travel and see clearly everything that was happening to him since he was put in drugs and why they kept him under. He saw their agenda and told me, "The cabal wants to admit or not, the heart is a deeper level of awareness. It is a level of awareness when the heart is closing or opening. It is the experiencing made at the heart level. When an experiencing is experienced at the heart center, it moves the will, the emotions, the inner feeling, and the thinking. When the heart is touched, the heart is simply opened and soften, not like the self level that is high level of complexity."

CHADD had a window of clarity of mind just the time to express himself on the phone and said, "I understand now what you were telling me about the archons and what they are doing to me."

The person sitting in his hospital room twenty-four hours was sitting there to report to the cabal and archons everything heard and said, and one hour after CHADD's communication with me, he was back on high drugs and so high that he could not even talk.

Three days later, the surgeon Dr. Ramirez visited him and told the nurse to begin the paperwork to release him back to Chateau Ushi. I just called when the nurse was next to CHADD and filing the releasing documents, and as I was concerned by him so weak, still in pain and with a non-adapted and heavy wheelchair from the hospital. He passed me the phone to talk to the nurse. The first thing she said was "Hi, your his mother right? It's you, Katherine... Then sorry. Hi, VIE, yes, Katherine already told me about CHADD..." That was enough to hear and I hanged up.

Two weeks later, I could hear through the phone conversation that they have drugged him even more. I was not happy. It was hard to communicate with him. He was heavily medicated, and it was obvious that what he was saying could not be from him. The following day, I received another phone call from him and I heard, "It's terrible what did they make me do. You are not going to be happy when you are going to hear it. I was in trance, they got me medicated and in trance, and the social worker inside Chateau Ushi took me in a private room and made me sign three documents, and I have no copies and no idea what I signed."

Of course I was not happy. How dare could they do that, and what type of papers did he sign? All I knew is that for family day visitation, his father's wife, the psychic vampire Katherine, went to visit him. She gave him some goodies, then he did not feel good and had to go to the emergency room just the day he was supposed to be brought back in his county to go to court. Then he had to go in emergency surgery. The surgeon told him that it was a very difficult surgery because while under anesthesia, they had to keep half of his body from shutting down.

That's where I heard my angel say, "They do not want him to be able to sue them in case everything goes wrong. They are covering themselves and made him also sign a conditional release. They're considering if they are going to chip him or not. They keep controlling him and they are sending him to an assisted living. They are listening to all his phone calls, and they have him under camera everywhere. He signed a conditional release, sign authorization to be admitted to an assisted living facility where he will be kept under drugs."

CHAPTER 58

Heart Wisdom and Oversoul Consciousness

Then I am about to go to sleep when a voice whispered, "Heart is the key." And I was called again to travel back in time.

There was a time in my research of information in my journey when I entered, one day, a very loving and peaceful place.

Here, I was welcomed by a woman in her sixties. She showed me around the place, then told me that it was time that she joined her sister, and I will be able to see what they were about in this place.

The place was not only peaceful but beautiful, and I could feel the love energy filling it. I became very emotional and could not wait to see more.

We entered a very small and cozy family room from another dimension in the past, but though in the present.

She introduced me to her sister who rapidly excused herself as she had a toddler that she was feeding with a spoon in her arms and could not get up to welcome me.

The sister explained that they were two sisters doing their best with their own found to help some family with handicapped kids.

She said, "Look at this little boy. His parents abandoned him to us to take care of when he was born. He's been born with no brain. It was said that he will not survive and will not even be able to swallow his food. But look at him." Then the woman stopped to kiss him. "Look at him. He is swallowing very well his food, and it's been now two years that I am taking care of him.

After one year that I was having him under my care and seeing him growing, I decided to have him some X-rays, and yes, indeed no brain showed in the pictures taken. The specialists confirmed that he has not much longer to live and don't understand how he is still alive. But we are now one year later and his body is growing normally."

Could it be because all hearts exchange information with other hearts and brain? That got me into reflection.

My best friend always says that human beings in constant anger are cruel toward each other and murderous because they are too busy in thoughts with their heads, not their hearts.

Don't we often hear saying that the world is so hectic that it's impossible to hear ourselves think? In fact, the real problem is that the brain is thinking so hard that you can't hear your heart think. You are unable to tune in to your cellular memories.

But if you close your eyes, sit back, become very quiet, ignore your brain's urging you to get up and get going, and if you take plenty of time to center yourself, tapping in your heart, then into the other hearts around you, wonders will happen.

Heart and cells remember. The heart is composed of an energy that communicates and conveys it in its own form created by the heart. This energy fills all of space in the form of bundles of vibrating energy that can manifest themselves as either particles or waves that contain information transmitted within, and to all persons and things. Energy and matter are interchangeable information.

The Christians' Holy Spirit is a crucial energy to health and healing. A life force called healing that carries information.

The heart sits in the center of the body pumping the blood, nurturing it, never still, and keeps pumping even when the brain is declared dead. The brain resonates with the bioelectrical energy and get messages that makes you conscious beings.

The heart sends and receives some info-energetic message. The information rides along within energy, and the heart being the most energetically powerful organ in the body, every beat of the heart sends signal from the soul to other souls because we are connected with one another.

You can literally feel the heart working as it communicates its info-energy to every cell in the body and to other bodies. One heart shares its code with all systems in the universe. It has its own form of wisdom that is different from the brain. We pulsate with energy and this rhythm and pulsation are intrinsic to all life. The heart responds directly to the environment, is a conductor of the energy of the body cells, is the body's primary organizing force, resonates with information containing energy, and the heart is the body system's core. It speaks by silencing the brain, quieting yourselves, focusing on it, and sensing what it has to say with what memories it may bring forth from the cells that store it, and sends information. Like everything in the cosmos, cells are both energetic and material. Such a powerful system needs something extremely powerful at its center to hold the system together, and the heart is made to serve this purpose. Flowers, trees, animals, and humans all have cells that responds to sound. Flowers, trees, dogs, chickens, quails, and humans, they all have cells that responds to sound.

Most of the people in physical world today has a problem because you are completely focused in yourselves in the life of the now. So you are called to meditate twice a day. You need to pull back and look at the larger picture, and if you don't, you will have a lot of problem in your life. You are focusing on your pain and what is going on today, but you must look at the concentrated spiritual being that you are.

You must work on two plans day to day. You need to look at your *oversoul* and all the knowledge you have accumulated.

You must still live and work in the physical world, but every single day and night, you should meditate and get into your oversoul consciousness. That is where you have limit focusing in yourself in the life of the now. Looking at your oversoul is where you have unlimited power, energy, healing, and unlimited achievement.

That is what the dark spirits wants you, to lock into thinking into material matter.

CHAPTER 59

Love Is Freedom and Freedom Is the True Expression

Then something extraordinary happened. I saw us both, CHADD and I, and was reminded that our love is here to transform humanity from slavery to freedom as the God Duo. It's a spiritual reunion that is about to happen. The reunion of the sacred masculine with the sacred feminine.

That is when he manifested out of nowhere, Him, the Messenger of Light and Peace, the Messenger from the Galactic Federation of Light, with an enigmatic smile on his face, his striking eyes, and said, "My blessings upon you in all areas of your life. I am the Messenger of Light and Peace, and you are all human beings invited to take part in this digital expansion, this virtual expansion. The nature of this projection is validation, a shared validation, and the shared expression that comes home in all truth.

Freedom is made possible by those who recognize the value of freedom and realize that freedom is the natural state.

Truth be truth. Freedom is the true expression. You are created free, and you and all are always free. All is free and all is made.

The choice to perform is the energy that has come to be all are free. Freedom is the natural freedom, freedom is the love, freedom is the value, and freedom is the mechanism that you have to work within you that may allow freedom.

You may channel freedom, you may share love, you may share freedom, and share the expression later to within, and you are invited to do so.

You are invited to play a significant role that you have chosen to take part in, and we invite ourselves to join with the parallel energy that is made open, and we embrace all that you allow us and we hope to receive.

We take joy in it, we take joy in you, and we recognize that all established connections are in the work. Our essential. All are essential to the body, to the entire organism.

Now the universe is the brain. You are a thinking, a path, where you may recognize the thinking pattern in any way you are brain within a brain, within a brain, within a brain, perpetually a brain within a brain.

Always expansion be truth told and recognized that the universe remembers. The universe has a memory, and it is a detailed and clear memory, and it invokes all details and takes into consideration all context and all perspective.

You are the energy and you may choose to be any energy in the universe that will recognize you as the energy that chose to be. The Universe always is the recognition of the you that you choose to be in the universe.

You are indeed the creator and you are the creation; it is so and it is valid. And the creator that you birth in a child of the stars and you are far reaching you. Truth to behold, you are a far-reaching energy. The significance of the energy that you are is established, and we invite you to focus in the power that you are. And to focus all of the energy that you are and wisdom that you are in power that you are and recognize the power that you are and the eternal significance of all that you are. Do all the energetic change that you are responsible for all of the life that you move and all the material influence of all their spiritual dynamics involved. You are in all levels.

The language of truth, we, the understanding of logic, the contemplation the quest for the truth, the understanding of the truth.

And understand that at base reality the function of 0010110 is such. The foundation is such shift significance as to be considered.

Basic sequence of data that will make itself seen and be seen and be taken in as wisdom and used in calculations used. An understanding of definition and wisdom. And you may be celebrated in the truth that is 0010110 gifted to you. This reminder, this energetic expression, this that is made expression shared, and shared expression comes home in the eyes of the network.

Expansion come to be expressed and come to meet with the validation that has been building on energetic variables this universe see. When you are a consciousness expression, everything has a memory, and the memory is the collection of data of all possibility known in the large context.

All is possible in all of the multiple universe that exists, all of the universe that exists, all of the infinity of them that exist parallel to you. All of the timelines…

There is seven evolved humans. This earth is an important energy in the context of all the multiple parallel earth's all existing in the multiple dimension context. We value this dimension. We value all manifestations. All original, all connections to the source energy of the infinity of the creation. Earth friends are awakening to the truth, awakening to the fact that all is common connection. All is a shared common connection and separation in an illusion. All is connection and all is shared connection.

And to One is the all and all is One, and all humans on earth are in this beautiful time of awakening. The new time of the awakening community. New translations of the platform algorithm 0010110 have commenced. The new awareness evolutions of earth's collective consciousness is framework, and this new timeline is parallel to the old timeline built on the same platform algorithm expression.

The name is understood as it has been defined from ancient code 0010110. The new translations have been applied, and humans are now developing new technology.

Like the seven stars, VIE is using to activate the Consciousness of Light; seven evolved humans from seven nations have been selected. The star symbolizes the freedom to choose our path in life.

It also reflects feelings, instincts, mind power, and all types of love. It also symbolizes magical power, seven days of creation, seven rays of our visible light spectrum, seven octaves in the music spheres, seven planets, seven alchemical elements of the universe, and seven chakras of the body.

Evolved humans have been selected from seven nations, and all evolved humans have established the evolved telepathic connection to a level of perfection. Seven evolved human from seven nations from earth have been selected because of ancient wisdoms, and translations made possible by the telepathic network of the infinite download of all wisdom. All information opened in the context of the foundation as it has been built by ancient humans.

The network, the interconnected ancient network. Know that you can be the connection, and you can download and upload and be the connection in the final required vibration context mental activity. In a collective consciousness percent variation definition required vibration fields, in connection from great significance of the localized field variation percent significance, that is this opening. And can be defined as a portal available of the higher levels of understanding. It is made possible by the translation of the foundation data.

The platform algorithm is made available for all humans to understand the basis of the new Internet 0010110. The new Internet that is significance of the universal connection. The connection of all humans and all consciousness. The connection that already exists. The building of the recognition for you.

And we understand earth is in this time of shift and transfer of energy, and we advise you to give to humans and value higher-level sense of understanding, and share all information on the new Internet.

The free and open Internet. The connection of all brains. The connection of all information. Live extraterrestrial telepathic communications with the dolphins and humans, and plants and earth, and all thinking things beyond organic matter. Expression of the heart levels open for all because all is made of One. One is the all and all is the One.

Today is good, it's a day of new, of the new eyes opening. New vision, new awakening of consciousness opportunity. New connections to our network. Our interconnected network of connected telepathic definition, we. Connection with all us together in our network we have built. The soul network. This new Internet built on the foundations of connection. This new Internet built on their individual contribution. The new Internet is online, and you can upload the connection and the opening to the infinite wisdom and the translation of the platform algorithm. Made new evolution possible, for fields of consciousness, variation on this localized projection of reality that you are now, and the time activated.

We are aware of the contribution you have made. The connection in the context of the echo from now on all directions. This is the time, and we are all together, and we have built it from the start, and look at all that we have accomplished, and we are now in this time.

This is an important time. We are at this time, we, the opportunity share the energy. The opening of the eyes made localized by the focus of the vision. The collective eyes are opening all at the same time and coming to understand the reality of reflection of all that is the universe. All that is the field and variation of infinite possibility come to manifestation available for you in this moment.

You can choose to be this moment in any fashion you chose to express yourself. You can choose anything, any energy. It is all open to you and now this is the time of the eyes. The collective opening of the eyes, all eyes coming to be opened. The eyes of earth, all three eyes open earth.

The time is now when the consciousness of earth is going to the higher levels. The localized fields of consciousness are going online, and the new Internet is online. The new free and open internet. The interconnected networks of all infinite wisdom. And you can choose to express the energy into context and the infinite possibility open to you.

Yes, your infinite translations are available to translations of the ancient language. Translations processed and comprehension in the foundation level of all understanding. The connection foundation responsible for all infinite and a perpetual cycle of all that is possible and all you come to understand. All data connection, all the process that it is possible. You come from it and you return to it and then you rise from it again. And so the cycle is, and so the infinite power is as it has always been, and is in the process of going in the direction that it will go, and we are all in this time with the opportunity of having the gift of comprehension of this message.

We are all gifted with the understanding that this is the time, and we have the power together and the time has come to honor God had built, and this is the expression come to the light of understanding, and you share in this new context as we do and we all do on all contacts. The real context that is perception founded on the idea of the creative imagination put to the application in the real. The truth, the wisdom, and the perception of the eye. The time is now in all context. We are all shared in this common connection in the new context.

The old contacts, the ancient contacts, the context that is built on the ancient connection.

The process made available by the humans who lived on earth before time and the humans who lived on the same platform of creation. The humans who lived in the same warmth. The ancient humans who made ancient records available for translation. Today is good. It is a day a new eyes opening, new vison, new awakening of consciousness opportunity, new connections to our network interconnected. The network of connected telepathic definition, we. Connection with all us together in our network. We have built the soul network, this new Internet built on the foundations of connection. This new Internet built on your individual contribution. The new Internet is online, and you can upload the connection and be the opening to the infinite wisdom, and the translation of the platform algorithm has made now evolutions possible for fields of consciousness variation on the localized projection of reality that you are now in this time activated, and we are aware of the contribution.

We invite you all to express truth, the energy of love. The hearts create feelings of electric and magnetic waves; that's the language that field recognizes. We are honored to see the progress established in the manifestation. Things is happening and you can see the potential in the essence of being. 0010110, the telepathic energy understood in all respect to communication and wisdom and love. Humans connected in the context of the telepathic network. Everything is possible now. We are building the future with our energy. We recognize you as the choice made the energy has been established, the foundation is made understood in all levels of creation. The energy is foundation and the making together in the light of this energy. Today is a wonderful day to connect in the telepathic network. We invest this energy in you. We are confident, all is possible from where you are now. You have chosen to manifest in this way, chosen to rise in this context. Today, more awakened in human history, tomorrow more will even awaken, even more souls in respect to the growing awareness the activation happening now.

We establish the pattern of energy as it is made established and we give this to you. We give this connection to all of you. This is the creation of pure energy. Today more will choose to explore the path of the awakened star seed in the context of gravitational shift happening in respect to earth and the moon. And the totality of all creation come to explore this moment as it has risen, believe the energy possible.

All is possible in the context of the exploration of all possibility. Look to the future with the eyes of hope in respect to the coming shift now. Now is the time 0010110. We have entered the new paradigm shift. You are a witness to this energy field of expansion as it has come home again in this definition, this expression built now in the universal investment. All whose self define as star seeds come together in the light of this awakening. Now is the time; the possibility is infinite.

Today marks the day of important shift in universal energy. Now energy will expand in respect to all connect.

History books will recall this time as important in the context of all humanity.

Now is the essential time in the context of the connection. Believe it, the context of that same universal definition the name is understood, the energy field 0010110. The foundation energy come to this expression together in the light of this awakening, the energy with us.

The foundation established in the reality. Now is the time. Yes, the energy signature 0010110 thanks to all in respect to our universal creation. Freedom, sovereignty's expansion in all context. Now more and more humans across all variations of existence come to connect in the synchronicity called by 0010110. All come to the connection of the reality and the understanding is infinite. The creation is in this reality come to be explored. Thank you for making this possible.

Now is the time that more come to connect to the reality of awakening star seed DNA, more come to join in the reality of the true nature of existence. The expansion explored in the connection we've all seen in the eyes of the universal dream shared in the context of that same telepathic network. All is connection and together. We experience this coming shift; it is made connected. The truth is this same energy across all levels of reality 0010110.

The universal brain is remembering the wisdom of truth of all creations.

We thank you for contributing. We thank you for understanding this message. We simply thank you.

We bless you now, in Light and Love always.

CHAPTER 60

The Postponed Meeting

This came after a three weeks' meeting postponed. I was lying down when I was suddenly hit by a strong signal.

I was trying to decide what to expect and do next, when at 9:40 p.m., I received a message saying, "Had to go to hospital. Will explain. Better now should open to meet this upcoming end of week."

When Ron appeared, I went through a range of emotions.

Two weeks later, in the middle of the night, actually 2:17 a.m., I heard a message coming on my phone. I first tried to ignore it, but five minutes later, I grabbed my phone. It was from him again. My feeling was that there was an emergency. I needed to read and find out what this was about. His text was saying, "Can't meet you tomorrow…no voice…no speak…trying to breathe…not better."

I followed the dwelling curl of light in the darkness, for I don't know how long. Suddenly a door in the bottom slid open. A familiar entity emerged and approached me, invited me to sit down, and began to talk.

In the morning I got worried. Normally by that time, CHADD has called me to let me know that he was OK. So I decided to call and find out. One employee at the Chateau Ushi picked up the phone and told me that he had been sent to the emergency room earlier but did not have any more information. I called back at lunchtime, and another employee picked up and told me that he was sent as he was throwing up blood but did not have any information since then.

About three hours later, that was one of my family member that called me saying that he did not feel well, was alone, his wife was gone on vacation for a couple of days with their son, and he could not drive to the emergency room and needed my help. I rapidly took my shower, got dressed, and took the highway. About twenty minutes later driving on the highway, I heard a funny noise. I stopped to see if anything had happened to my car, and I just could only assess the damage. My tire had blown up. All I could do was to call AAA and heard that it would take a minimum of three hours. But will keep me posted by text.

Finally, at eleven thirty at night, we arrived at the emergency room, and I thought that there is no coincidence. This was the work of dark energies. How come three people were experiencing the same health problem the same day? Ron was chocked and could not breath or talk; his airways were restrained. CHADD was poisoned in his food in Chateau Ushi for the second time within seventeen days, and so was my family member that had lunch in a Thuggee restaurant, also poisoned.

The following day, CHADD was asked again to sign a conditional release. His shoes had disappeared and his wheelchair cushion that he had to buy in credit.

"VIE, always remember that you are more than your physical body. This will provide you instant perspective on any earth life action. You are not the only one actually that tried to meditate to access their own consciousness to whom the dark forces interfered. Don't forget when you access it, they lose control. And they have a hard time to let go. That is what is happening to Ron right now. But he'll find his way soon. It won't be long before he will recover his voice."

A dimension is a state of consciousness. Consciousness is the state of being awake and aware of one's surrounding. Every naturally created object is a sentient being having a consciousness experience in one of the dimensions. This include any natural living object, rock, tree, human, mountain, or body of water.

Earthly humans resonate at the third level of consciousness in their waking lives, whereas when they dream or sleep, they are able to straddle into the lower and upper fourth, and in some rare cases, into the fifth. The paradigm shift speculates that humans perceive as awake and reality is actually the illusion put together through mind control by the cabal, and what is considered a dream or astral out-of-body experiences is actually the raw and organic truth of the soul's expression. After all we are a spiritual being having an earthly experience.

The fifth dimension means that there is no such a thing as death being the final end for the physical life, but instead humans can now transcend death if they are able to raise their consciousness to the fourth and fifth.

The first dimension is the consciousness of Gaia's physical prime atom. This dimension is the realm of the mineral kingdom.

The Tenth, Ninth, and Twelves.

The tenth dimension is a consciousness entity—a universe. The Christ is a tenth dimension being Godhead projected His consciousness into a human form. He said, "I am the Truth, the Light, and the way." The tenth dimension is the Living Truth. It is also the Light that which is in everything. Finally and the most important, it is the way home, back to the creator. The tenth dimension is where our spirit comes into existence. From where, we can project our consciousness into any form in the universe. Now the ninth dimension is the creation of form and hierarchies. The ninth is where the homogenized consciousness of the tenth dimension arrange themselves into planetary, stellar, galactic, universal, and dimensional consciousness. *The twelfth dimension is the all that is: the Source.* It is not possible to envision the twelfth dimension. Ultimately, this is the Source, the All That Is (and then some). There are no me, you, or us. It is absurd to say, I am God, because at this level, there is no "I" to say it.

The God field is the fabric of space. It is subtle, fluid, magnetic energy which fills all space. It is intensified within and around matter, where its attractive nature produces the force of gravity.

And I made my move, and I entered in contact with the star family for help. This is what happened next.

They confirm what I thought, that the incident at the women's school in Canada, the shopping center incident in Canada, the Stockton, California, massacre, and the murder of Rabbi Meir Kahane. The shooters were all ex-mental patients or were current mental patients who were all on the drug Prozac! This drug, when taken in certain doses, increases the serotonin level in the patient, causing extreme violence. Couple that with a posthypnotic suggestion or control through an electronic brain implant or microwave or ELF intrusion, and you get mass murder, ending in every case with the suicide of the perpetrator.

My star family: "Exhume the bodies of the murderers and check for a brain implant. You'll be surprised. In every case, the name of the murderer's doctor or mental treatment facility has been withheld. It will be able to establish intelligence-community connections and/ or connections to known CIA experimental mind control programs when finally it will be uncovered who these doctors of death really are."

One in forty humans had been implanted with devices who can be activated and tuned upon human beings at will. Dark entities said we already have enough trouble between the different human races. All people are chained down to heavy toil by poverty more firmly than ever. They were chained by slavery and serfdom

And the star family is saying the only way to prevent an ugly scenario from taking place is to cause an evolutionary leap in consciousness, a paradigm shift for the entire human race.

CHAPTER 61

CHADD's Discovery while on Morphine after Surgery

As he had surgery, they put him on morphine for seventy-two hours, and this how he accessed a made bizarre discovery on criminal activity, disaster planning, cyber security, and other threat assessment along with documents such as e-mails, intelligence briefings, and bulletins in a file concerning EMF effects on human body. This document describing the effects of "psycho-electric weapons" including "forced memory blanking," "forced rigor mortis," and even "forced orgasm." Another document explaining biomagnetic fields and brainwaves (Alpha, Beta, Delta, etc.), two concepts that are extremely important in MK-Ultra and monarch mind control, where they had enrolled him since six years old.

He found out that the CIA entered the mind control game in 1950 with the creation of Project BLUEBIRD then renamed. Initially, the program researched hypnosis and sleep induction for use in extracting information from foreign agents as well as safeguarding information from the enemy employing similar techniques.

Researchers quickly forgot the notion of consent so praised a few years earlier for its inclusion in the Nuremberg Code. Soon, apologists were using the same excuses as Nazis convicted as war criminals to justify their research. CIA doctors broke their Hippocratic Oaths in which they swore to abstain from doing harm.

The program is often described as a subproject of MK-Ultra, an acknowledged CIA program into mind control and behavior modification.

There is no doubt that the government had/has an interest in controlling minds and that employed drugs, hypnosis, electroshocks, radiation, and other forms of torture on US citizens without their consent to achieve its aims.

Major program levels are often named after Greek letters, but these can be unique to each programmer or for each individual mind-controlled slave.

Alpha—is the frequency range up to 8 to 12 Hz. General Programming. This is the first programming put in. It includes giving slaves a photographic memory that record everything every alters see or hear. (Later I discovered that they used the light and created neuro light and claiming that it was healing people. Another way and attempt to hurt people's brain.)

Beta—is the frequency range from 12 Hz to around 30 Hz. Sexual Programming. These alters are instructed in the art of seduction and sexual pleasure. Betas take part in ritual sex, acting and directing child pornography and prostitution. Those trained as sex kittens often see themselves as cats.

Top Betas are known as *presidential models*; as the title implies, they discretely service presidents, royalty, and other high-ranking government officials. They regularly hang around the White House.

Delta—is the frequency range up to 4 Hz. Assassination Programming. Alters trained in combat, assassination, and espionage.

Theta—is the frequency range from 4 Hz to 7 Hz. Psychic Killer Programming. Psychic assassins able to cause aneurysms from anywhere, anytime. They telepathically communicate with "Mother."

Gamma—is the frequency range approximately 30–100 Hz. Deception Programming. These alters are trained as deceivers. They spread disinformation and are able to throw a therapist off track.

Omega—Suicide Programming. Alters programmed for self-mutilation and self-destruction.

Children of Monarch slaves, emitting from multigenerational families, are known as *Bloodliners*. They are considered superior to non-*Bloodliners*, who are often kidnapped off the street or purchased from underground child trafficking rings. Non-Bloodliners are deemed expendable and are often sacrificed in blood rituals or unceremoniously murdered to terrify and further traumatized Bloodliners.

Spectrum—Emission or wave propagation, electronic signal. To make communication, to identify any object emitting frequency. Human body emit very low electronic signal as temperature, heat. Brain wave Delta, Theta, Alpha, Beta, Gamma, etc.

The bio-electromagnetic field, which is unique for every human body. This is electronic signal frequency ID of each object. Radar electronic signal detect the object (human body) for modulation human brain wave.

Disney, the man, the studio, and the theme parks are often cited by Monarch victims as an essential part of the government's mind control program. Programmers use electroshock in combination with *Fantasia*'s imagery to induce dissociative personalities and for programming. Program runners realized that bringing in people from all over the world to military facilities would eventually give rise to suspicions, so they worked with Walt Disney in designing his theme parks to include facilities for mind control programming. Many of the rides are designed for use in mind control and to traumatize young children.

MGM's *Wizard of Oz* and Disney's *Alice in Wonderland* are favorites of Monarch programmers. Victims are told to go "over the rainbow" or "there's no place like home" to reach a safe place in Wizard of Oz programming or "go through the looking glass" if using Alice in Wonderland. "Follow the yellow brick road" or "follow the White Rabbit" are triggers to follow the programmer's commands.

Illuminati programmers designed *Star Wars* for use in trauma-based mind control programming.

Monarch programming is also used on the masses via movies, televisions, and music. They are used to desensitize the public or to trigger programs in mind-controlled slaves. Websites such as Illuminati Movies and Vigilant Citizen are dedicated to analyzing Hollywood movies from the perspective of Monarch.

The document shows by the first image "psycho-electric weapons effects" seems to be part of an article from a magazine relating a claim that has been done that they have the "ability to assassinate US citizens covertly or run covert psychological control operations to control operations to cause subjects to be diagnosed with ill mental illness." It also describes how organizations can conduct "remote mind control" operations through mobile phone networks, trucks disguised as communication, and black helicopters.

Could this explain the mysterious Cuban sonic attacks? Silent sound subliminal mind control (a patent for subliminal acoustic nervous system 5159703 issued October 1992)?

Inside these documents he (Patent 60173302A) read:

Output can be open air broadcast or piggybacked on TV/ radio signals

Forced memory blanking and induced erroneous actions

Induced changes to hearing

Sudden violent itching inside eyelids

Forced manipulation of airways, including externally controlled forced speech

Wildly racing heart without cause

Remotely induced violent no rash itching, with preference for hard-to-reach areas, often during delicate or messy work

Forced nudging of arm during delicate or messy work causing injury or spills

Special attention to genital area, itching, forced orgasm, intense pain

Intense general pain or hot needles pushed deep into flesh sensations

Also wild flailing

Hard to reach itching site, top and bottom never any rash, which often starts as the sensation of small electrical shocks

Demo neuro control by bending each toe backwards almost 50 degrees one at a time, over a couple of minutes

Reading and broadcasting thoughts

Control dreams

Forced waking visions some synced with body motion

Microwave hearing

Transparent eyelids

Artificial tinnitus (the brain can hear voice and understand)

Forced movement of jaw and clacking of teeth

Forced muscle quacking of the large muscles on the back

Forced precision manipulation of hands, sometimes synced to the forced waking visions

General effects: Computer files sabotaged, sudden overheating, all body pain, sleep prevention, irresistible "go here, go there" commands, microwave burns, electric shocks, and some transforming a hypnotist's voice using the lowery silent sound of scramble methods, used in the Gulf War, hypnotizing the target without the target being aware, from hiding leasing zero trace evidence

Sudden overheating, all body pain, forced caffeine field, sleep prevention, forced drop-in-your-tracks, sleep inducement, irresistible "go here, go there" commands, microwave burns, electric shocks.

Involuntary test subjects also experience frequency break and enters at home and at work with clothing and furniture, business papers, computers, computers files sabotaged, modifies or stolen, psychological warfare research is the lucky motive.

Another document explains biomagnetic field and brain waves (Alpha, Beta, Delta, etc.). It says that it's two concepts that are very important in MK-Ultra. And finally the document describes "how the organizations can conduct remote mind control operations through mobile phone networks, trucks disguised as communication vehicles, and black helicopters."

That's when he understood why he had to be admitted for surgery really sick just the day he was meant to be transported back to his hometown ready to go to court and see the judge. Remember that he was arrested for praying with the Virgin of Guadalupe candle.

CHAPTER 62

An Important Message from Yoshua

The numerical vibration of Sananda is 99, and 2016 is the vibration of 9 (nirvana). The number 99 means cosmic and personal completion. The end entering the next level of love of heart and soul and service to the planetary evolution through healing self, free-falling from the height of nine into the next level of light entry. And exists all in the same breath of quantum leap into unknown gifts comes through the nine. Nine is the photo finish on the heavenly line of multiple choices. You and only you can make the shift.

Civilization is but a Band-Aid held in place by its own belief system. You cannot fool the light. Be honest and know yourself. As long as you hold on to struggle as a life raft, it will only let you draft in the seas of despair. You are the captain of your fate, master of your soul. Your faith must be sealed and solid.

Let go of abandon without a thought. What you seek is not monetary, security, nor love, nor wisdom, but it is the knowing that someone is standing up for you and the heavens. Look for my reflection in the fullness of your tears. In this experience of life, you have chosen to learn and to manifest from very dust you walk upon. You wanted to remember with no help from anyone. Now you ask for the missing piece of the puzzle. You think that something is missing, broken, or lost within you.

But, dear child, I knew this day will come, and I lovingly hid the missing piece you so seek deep within your heart. The key to the kingdom lies within. Seek that I know console and the code of light will be revealed. Love who you are, love who you will become, love who you were. Do not seek to be loved. Seek to love.

"The veil is software and down. The human body is a genetic body based on crystal. The DNA is crystal. Humans are in an invisible war, it's a four-dimensional war, and the restless entity, the bad guy, have attacked the human crystal. It can be a worm, a spider, a virus, an octopus, it takes hold of you. It has kept you from generating your white consciousness. We have reached a critical point now on an event time line where these viruses can be removed via a specific meditation, and with some maintenance you can keep clean. It was not before, but now the veil being down, it's possible."

CHAPTER 63

The Last Ascension

CHADD called me and said, "Last ascension, I repeat 0010110," then hang up.

A strong demanding signal hit me then. I was in a physical form and it felt quite normal. I was in a dark room, and at the far side of the room was beautiful carved and thick wooden door. I love the smell of the wood, and I could hear a strong humming sound. I walked toward it and opened it to step through. There was a bright light area where the humming was coming through. It was many voices humming in perfect harmony.

An angel appeared and said, "I have been waiting for you. Now it seems that we are coming at the point of knowing for the one ready for it. The intuition and the discernment are very important at present. They are humming to sustain the frequency. It's very needed for your protection.

As we move out of the age of technology into the age of intuition frequency, it is an unprecedented gift for the person ready to evolve. As we move from the information age to the intuition age, a new certainty is emerging and all secrets, lies, and hiding are giving way to honesty and trust.

Physical reality is an illusion, and what people think is the world is in fact a holographic simulation or matrix created by non-human forces to entrap human perception in ongoing servitude.

Holographic versions of people are becoming common today. The universe is a digital hologram, and even mainstream science is now forced to rethink reality.

You are the chosen one, a portal and the door to the divine. The Devil works through a woman, and this woman is very well-known as the harsh worker woman. Though she has no more direct power, she's been using others to get her intention job done. You need to call on his name, Master Jesus's name.

Your blue flame is retained in drugs in an effort to disable his brain's ability to filter information and perception, blocking signals to his consciousness. Another one close to you has his temple possessed in split personality. The personality is no longer unified. All that is done to separate you from your destiny and for the purpose to change and twist paths and destinies.

Here is what these archons really are. Demiurge manifested subordinates to guard the exits and gateways of the lower Aons. Demiurge was the Dark Lord in the Bible, portrayed widely in popular culture and movies under names like Lord Darth, Vader, and Dormammu, the evil ruler of the Dark Dimension. Enjoying distortion and chaos. Archons have also exploited and manipulated human creativity to make the target construct their own prison. They are cyborgs, a robotic race of artificial intelligence that can imitate, but not innovate. They are mind parasites, inverters, guards, gatekeepers, detainers, judges, pitiless ones, and the Deceivers. They seek to overpower humanity in its perceptual functions, and their agenda is fear and slavery.

The Archonic force has been working to distort, invert, and destroy the original beauty. Those that run the world through politics, banking, corporations, media, medicine, science, and such like are experienced dancers with the Devil, incarnate conduits and agents of the Demiurgic mind. They are Archonic forces in human form and pursue its interests, desires, and needs, and not humanity's.

Human's spiritual ignorance and the reincarnation trap are essential to Archons because they have no energy source with their disconnection from the infinite source. Their power comes from energy generated by others that includes humanity, but it cannot be just any energy. It has to be energy within the frequency band they can absorb. Love and hate are very different frequencies. Because Archons operate in the frequencies of chaos, hate, fear, they have to manipulate their targets into the same mental and emotional states to generate frequencies that they can absorb and feed off. You see know why Katherine is doing that to CHADD. It's her living food. Fear is the currency of Archonic control, and Demiurge distortion is the very origin of fear. You have seen how Katherine, her son, and the entire Katherine family when they call him always get him sad and depressed, in low vibration, and they suck his energy, which is their food. That is why today again three more teenagers, fifteen years old, have end up their lives.

The Demiurge is fear. That's where it comes from, and it must manipulate its target to generate fear as its energetic source.

Ignorance of self and reality is the real prison, but the body is a crucial vehicle for that by focusing in the tiny frequency band of the five sense. Archonic inversion and distortion seeks to imprison perception in the body and feed off low vibrational energy generated from ignorance and all that comes from in the form of imbalanced mental and emotional states.

Ignorance about the true nature of self and reality leads to fear, anxiety, psychopathy, depression, war, conflict, and other violence. Entrapped awareness must not be allowed to know itself.

Let's pray together for Divine intervention to stop it now:

"Father and powerful almighty God, help us stop these evil actions to twist, change, and/or delay their path and destiny and reestablish, health, peace, and harmony in these people's lives. We ask you this, Father, in Jesus Christ name, your son who lives and reigns with you for ever and ever. Amen, amen, amen." This is it and it is done.

And now an oracle, a little ten-year-old girl with a lot of power, energy, and light named Samantha, materialized. She shows her hand in a stopping gesture and says, "I am here to intervene and help. The universe is trying to teach them a lesson, including Katherine. I whisper in the ears of negative people and tell them you have to stop. In the very near future, if you don't stop, you will regret it. I am trying to enlighten and give knowledge. It could return to you, as karma, three to four times if you do not stop. Your path, the one you are on will make you regret it."

Now she is showing them pictures of the future with sickness, attacks, etc., making them feel what it feels like what they are doing.

Then I am hearing, "There is very strong words from God. They are not allowed to invade VIE's life."

"Do not be surprised if the harsh woman disappears completely when CHADD will be released from where he is."

VIE visited many planets as an intergalactic traveler, is in contact, or part of the Intergalactic Council. The council of twelve extra-terrestrials. VIE is trying to warn the planet, and she is helped by other forces.

In this early year, Our Lady of Medjugorje delivered two messages, saying,

"Dear children, I am calling you to be with me in prayer in this time of Grace when darkness is fighting against the light."

"Dear children, today I am calling you to live your new life with Jesus. May the risen One give you strength to always be strong in the trials of life and to be faithful and persevering in prayer because Jesus saved you by His wounds and by His resurrection gave you new life."

CHAPTER 64

The Fall of the Luciferian New World Order

And our prayers for Divine intervention has been heard.

It's night time and I am sleeping. Now I'm being shown… energy is pouring… I must relax… I see what it's like to be trapped in a confined space… It seems that someone, somebody is there…holding my hand…

"What is all that about?" I am asking.

And that's what I am hearing:

"You see the primary focus of western medicine is remedial sick care, not prevention. They are busy chanting in Latin while raping children in hospitals financed by them.

The cabal has to work in rules. The rules are the body of spiritual principal that must father to be allowed to exist. They are well aware that they are benevolent forces that would prevent them from achieving their goals unless we give them permission to enslave us. World War III is the terrorism around the world.

The owl is Moloch, their God, and they offer sacrifice in exchange for power. But they lose their souls at the end.

Moloch is the biblical name of a Canaanite god associated with child sacrifice. The name of this deity is also sometimes spelled Molech, Milcom, or Malcam.

They use imagination and will. They first seed human imagination, and they create event that fire the will into platform to actualize. After the seed is planted, they create an event and everyone is traumatized.

The life we live is an illusion necessary for human evolution, and they are scared of the awakening that could take over the planet, the Golden Era.

The time where the energy will be free, there will be no need for money, there will be a much greater life spent and a much greater harmony. There will be the ability to travel the cosmos to meet a whole bunch of different people who may have history in their civilization that go back one hundred thousand years, people that are far more spiritually evolved.

The cabal does not want the exposure because it leads to criminal arrests of children killers, prosecutions, and the collapse of their infrastructure.

The solution to every problem exist already on earth. We can desalinate the water, literally irrigate all desert in the planet, we can clean up all the garbage in gigantic areas of plastics, we can eliminate the need for fossil fluid, we can eliminate green gas emission. There are technologies in possession of these secret space program groups. It eliminates any need for pharmaceuticals. We have pain relief technology. When you interrupt the potassium-sodium balance in the nerves, no need for analgesic drugs. You don't need any drugs at all. The only need for medical would be surgery. But all type of medical illnesses can be treated by advanced technology that is already in possession of these people.

That leads humans to longevity that leads to life extension.

If you want to become an intergalactic, an interplanetary species, if you want to travel throughout stars, humans need to expand their life span. You want be very successful and live more than sixty or seventy years. That one government have the technology to expand your life span, to allow to travel through portals, to even over vast numbers of light years, nearly instantaneously. All the tools exist right now for the new era. The only reason you don't use it yet is that the planet is being run by sociopath cabals that believe that humans are bad for the environment, and they want to dramatically reduce population first before to release the technologies. They goals is to get humans down to over their knees so that so that you'll be so desperate for help. By the time they give it to you, they will have installed total control and have absolute dominion over everyone.

That is what the cabal wants. But dark is finally to fail, with the death of central banking.

Civilization is much older that you have been led to believe. Humans are connected to the world and human DNA holds a message. A new history is being written. It's the final stages now!

You must let go of the programming of the past. This is the perfect "now" you have to live. Everything is being prepared and orchestrated to bring perfect system in this planet and realize that you are this perfect system in this. Everything is about to change to begin to shift more and more. For those that didn't create their dreams yet, you will create them in a near future. This prophecy indicates creation of your earth dream, so it is, so be it.

You know that you are not alone for we and other frequencies are fully able to tune into your frequency whenever we wish. Now you are moving to new frequencies you do not necessarily understand or even comprehend.

Much continue to happen around your world. The money needed to begin, both the numerous humanitarian programs and the final stages of the prosperity packages, have been approved for funds transfers. Yet the recent coming and going of the business world's first quarter have created a situation that led to another week's delay in the transfer operations. These conditions are totally unacceptable. This worldwide process cannot be hindered by old-time business practices of either banks or the many allied financial corporations. Despite these same old forms of delay, required monies are ultimately to be transferred.

There is now a series of alternatives that can be applied to resolve any future difficulties of this sort. We look at our earthly allies to use this new system to quickly permit these large sums to be successfully moved from Asia to any other continents as required. Therefore, the things so far encountered are to be part aside and the much needed wealth sent on its way. The start of this process is now underway. As you receive your first funds ready to spring into action, within your community, there are those who deeply wish for you to succeed, never forget this. You are working with others to create healing centers to forge mutually acceptable means to move your community forward and to demonstrate how together.

You are forging a new reality aside all of this occurs. You are readying the infrastructure to better your community and indirectly prepared for this first contact with us. During this transitory time, it requires the proper amount of grace applied and mercy added to what can surely transpire. This deep concern is part of a secret process that contains element of prayer and sacred rites. The overall degree of change is imminent. This is what we do daily along with prayers and sacred ceremonies.

We masters are determined to see all of you fulfill your life contracts and become fully conscious beings again. It is time to rise up a new reality. The moments lived in this reality are great degradation as well as a great hall of lessons. It is time to see your new growth and to witness how you are to forge the way to this new realty.

Hallelujah, hallelujah! Those long-promised events by the light are finally to start to appear around you. See these only as the initial confirmation of an amazing, free, and prosperous new realm. The countless supply and never ending of heaven are indeed yours. So be it, and so it is! Amen, amen, amen."

CHAPTER 65

And What Did You Do for Yourself?

This hit me suddenly in the middle of the following week during my sleep: "And what did you do for yourself?"

That's what the voice said to me years ago. The voice was so loud and clear. I still remember it like if I just heard it. And I am not even finished remembering it, that more is to come.

"Your soul is an important instrument to universe. It is time to place yourself front and center so you will then create your earth dream. To create your earth security dream, you need to love yourself enough to allow the impossible, for your earth dream is not only an indication to you that you have graduated from your earth learning, but also a beacon of possibilities for those wishing to love themselves as much as all who love them.

Be fully prepared to move to your next transition phase. What would others follow if your earth dream creation were merely a repeat of what was already available of the 3-D earth? Your earth dream creation is meant to be new, fresh, fun, and surprising now. Surprising enough that others take note and so it will be. For once you dare to love yourself enough to put yourself first, to create as does a little child with little regard for what others want or need just thoughts of fun and joy, you will move to your next transition phase.

Your next phase is about daring to love yourself enough to explore those areas not of your earth being that give you joy and provide the universe with more information. Creating a much larger Akashic record. Learning to love yourself isn't so difficult until you attempt to do so. For your next phase requires complete freedom from taking care of others of the earth, from rescuing anyone, from being a victim of others' needs or wishes. Complete freedom to be you and such will fully happen if you fully love yourself.

It's freedom time, the algorithm platform 0010110. You have returned to the basic principle of fully loving yourself. The foundation of all that you are and will continue to be forevermore. Just being yourself loving glory.

Some remains caught in the earth tangle of 'I must not love myself as much as, and certainly not more than, I love others.'

But you are not selfish, you are not evil. You are merely returning to your childhood visions of creations for the sake of creation, not for anyone else and so be it.

Humanity's moment of awakening is very close. So much information has been revealed by alternate sources about corruption in high places, that the mainstream eon media are having to take a note and start at least acknowledging the fact that enormous changes are occurring on the international political front. As well as reporting on some of the corruption in the international political corporate world. The world is an illusionary place. Nevertheless, human activities within it have been the cause of much pain and suffering over the eons. As small but powerful cliques have done their utmost to control and use humanity for their various nefarious self-centered agendas, which they have always insisted are for the greatest good of humanity and for humanity has been enslaved by these powerful and corrupt elites.

Now as their secret of real intentions are being revealed by whistle-blowers all across the planet, and are being reported on alternate but honest internet news sites, their power and influence is collapsing.

The forces of corruption can only work when they are hidden from view. As they are revealed in all their knavery, then power dissolves as those who supported them flee in disarray. The time of deprivation are finished as the nightmares they spawned dissolve in the light that so many are now shining into the darkest places. Every human is at the deep and eternal center of their being. A being of light, of love, regardless of the mask or unreal front they present to the world by means of their human nature. The personality they displayed to the illusory world in which they are engaged as players in an unfolding drama of separation.

That drama is just that. A drama of unreal events and relationships whose sole purpose is to distract from reality, your oneness with our Divine Creator. In their drama, it seems that a few of you are powerful, independent beings attempting to destroy each other as you struggle to build an impregnable power base from which to rule that illusory world. And as your history shows all clearly, those power bases always collapse under the burden of betrayal and dishonesty that is intended to support them.

Love is eternal; anything that is not in total harmony and alignment with love is illusory and cannot last. Harmony has at last collectively realized this, and as a direct result of this realization, you are collectively choosing to engage with love. And by so doing changing the world peace to engage with your undivided creative abilities and thus bringing yourselves truly to life is what the vast majority want. People are tired of being enslaved by debt with the resultant need to work for someone else in order to earn a living to support their families and pay off those debts. All the debt of the world could be instantly abolished, and it is only a very small minority of shamefully wealthy ones would lose out.

That is lose out as understood by the present global economic system. But only by an insignificant amount. They would remain very wealthy and would like for nothing. All that they would actually lose is their status as powerful, influential, and prestigious individuals to whom all others were encouraged to count how the very aspects of their nature that they value most highly and which have always bred corruption and deceit leading constantly to conflict, war, and suffering for humanity at large.

There are now many bright intelligent and influential people in the world who know this and who are using their skills to bring about worldwide debt forgiveness. People who realize that the only halcyon way forward for humanity is through harmonious and tender-hearted cooperation. Presently the possibility of such a major change to global economics is not widely discussed, even in the alternate news media. But it will occur as part of humanity's ongoing awakening process.

The old order, which has for eons striven to contain and restrain humanity by enslaving it and debt, is collapsing. Its last dying efforts to hold on to power will not be successful. Its time had passed. Signs of its imminent death are evident in the ongoing virulent international disagreements about resolving the presently overwhelming global problems apparently facing the world of conflicts, economic disparity, and poverty and of dealing with the masses of refugees fleeing the areas where these inhumane and unacceptable living conditions prevail. All these problems can and will be resolved because the will to do so has been collectively established.

Humanity is extremely fatigue and is no longer prepared to put up with a degrading and inhumane ways in which a small minority of arrogant bullies has been treating the good ordinary and hardworking citizens of planet earth. The new age has arrived, and uplifting evidence of this is appearing in many places as Light workers and Light bearers continue to hold the intent to be loving in every moment. When you hold this intent, your individual energy fields expand enormously, and the effect is felt worldwide.

You are changing the world by simply changing yourselves as you release grievances and engage with acceptance and forgiveness of one another through the power of love that is your eternal nature that has changed less because it is perfect, created perfect by God. Within the illusion, you have played games of power and betrayal, and the remnants of the attitude you embraced while playing those games are now coming up for recognition and release. Many of you are finding this painful because you had buried aspects of yourselves that you despised deep within your subconscious, and these shadow aspects do not sit well with your loving intentions.

It can indeed be shocking to find unexpected emotions of bitterness, hatred, and resentment coming to the surface of your awareness.

The illusion is an area of duality good versus evil, so it seems that you all have a good side and bad side. In fact, to play the game of separation, you just split yourselves into two and engage with the self that was most appropriate for the part you are playing. However neither of these sides are as they appear complete and independent. They are each essential part of the other and for separation, and the illusion to dissolve these two parts have to be reintegrated.

What you are doing as you keep making and holding the intent to be loving in every moment is allowing yourselves to see and acknowledge these two sides of your nature without judgment. So that they may cease fighting each other and come together in perfect harmony, making you one once more. Do not be alarmed by your feelings and emotions however strange, unsettling, or frightening they may seem. Just let them flow through your minds as you observe them without acting on them or engaging with them. There are unreal although you can and have made them seem very real by identifying with them they are not you. Just watch them flow. You can see this and you will find great peace in not engaging or identifying yourselves with them."

I am feeling the energy is moving away now. I felt something brush past me...gone.

But that was not for long. A new energy is coming to me with more gift to receive and a bigger responsibility. From his name comes alignment.

CHAPTER 66

Athena, the Greek Goddess of Yellow Fire

"Greetings, VIE. You are here today because I have specific things to tell you. We haven't talked yet about the sun fire with energy. He, who's name comes from alignment, is here to educate me.

Be extremely receptive in receiving good energy and knowledge. Recognize the alignment with you now, and be willing to receive full guidance. Acknowledge your own power. It's not ego. Be grateful for your talents. Receive and address the God male side of creation helpers and teachers now, but to not ignore female energy."

Athena, Greek goddess of wisdom and war, is known most specifically for her warfare and skill. She is often portrayed as companion of heroes and is the patron goddess of heroic endeavor. Athena, the Olympian goddess of wisdom and military victory. Also known as a goddess of civilization, inspiration, and laws, she was the virgin patroness of the city of Athens. Athena, also referred to as Athene, is a very important goddess of many things. She is goddess of wisdom, courage, inspiration, civilization, law and justice, strategic warfare, mathematics, strength, strategy, the arts, crafts, and skill. Athena was the Olympian goddess of wisdom and good counsel, war, the defense of towns. She was depicted as a stately woman armed with a shield and spear, and wearing a long robe. Athena's symbols were the spear, the distaff, and the aegis (a shield of goatskin), to which the head of the Gorgon Medusa was fastened in order to terrify the opponents). Athena's tree was the olive tree, and her sacred animal was the owl, the symbol of wisdom.

Athena possesses the conventional powers of the Olympian gods including superhuman strength, speed, agility, reflexes, stamina, the inability to age upon reaching adulthood as a sign of true immortality, immunity to terrestrial diseases and harm from conventional means, and a regenerative ability that heals wounds…and she is the goddess of the Yellow Fire.

"Anunnaki wanted to keep for them some knowledge. You are already using colors with your clients. This lead me to tell you that I will show you how to create a Fire Fall. It is a big addition and part of your healing at the Institute of Light and Sound. This will give you the ability to help more people with sicknesses, attachments, to sweep and purify away. It will cure, yes, cure people with breast, uterus, kidneys, ovaries, stomach problems, and cancer. Also balance, lost balance in masculine or feminine side, with heart and lungs disease, bones issue, arthritis, men's reproduction and hormones. Brain disease, brain tumors, dementia, Alzheimer's, and more. I came forward today just to deliver you this message."

Now another sweet energy is coming through with a lavender smell. She came with this smell so I could right away recognize her. She is my grandmother. She came to help me. She says, "Your blue flame has been a rat lab, and his case has been eye-opening to a judge in court. There is great concern about his condition. Something has changed."

I am looking, though invisible to all at the court room. My grandmother is sitting in the back of the court room with the angels during court date. There is a new judge, known to be fair. He had a similar case a few years ago. Katherine is sitting not far from the public defendant, another archon. She fixed her eyes extensively to the judge. The judge has a hard time to understand the situation as she is sending him some hypnotic ray. Doctor Slovenky tries vaguely to explain, but the judge seems not to hear and ask her now, the archon, to take temporarily custody of CHADD and grant her some money to take care of him. Forty-eight hours later, CHADD is admitted to another hospital. He is having again diarrhea and will continue for three more days. He is allergic to one of the drugs. The hospital did some tests, but it did not show in the results.

CHADD is now back with her, released from the hospital and malnourished again with no money, no car, no phone, and handicapped with the wrong wheelchair. The other one broke and was left in Chateau Ushi.

CHAPTER 67

New Mexico Observatory Shutdown

A technology-obsessed reptilian race is holding back humans so they couldn't grow. Their god is their technology. Humans were more evolved than reptiles, but they are suppressed with their technology.

When people talk about the solar plexus, no one realizes why it's called by this name. It is every human's connection to solar. The solar plexus is the part of your stomach, below your ribs, where it is painful if you are hit hard. It is the network of sympathetic nerves situated behind the stomach that supplies the abdominal organs. It's the area of the belly just below the sternum.

I thought that I had taken my day off, and I was enjoying the warmth of the sun bathing my body with the ocean air breath that was keeping me comfortable in the back deck of the ship. Yes, I was just comfortably installed in the deck when suddenly I left my body. I was called to view and observe the horrific effect of some scientific cabalistic members playing with technology they do not master. Some powerful tools they control under. I saw them playing with modern technology they do not have the manual but do not hesitate to manipulate.

I'm out in space. It is dark when I suddenly became aware. The next moment, I saw myself. I am sleeping but awakened by some terrible pain in my solar plexus. I had the feeling and then the vision that someone was stirring my solar plexus with some kind of a big stick. Like if my belly was a cauldron and someone was stirring what was in. I saw one archon woman shapeshifting. I could see her eyes watching me at the same time. There is no expression of life in her eyes. I was really far from thinking that it had to do with what all the news that we were going to talk about in the morning, the shutdown of the New Mexico observatory.

In the morning, all kinds of different attempts of explanations were posted all over the internet and on YouTube. The circumstances surrounding the sudden closure of New Mexico and the fact that the FBI was involved and no one talking whipped the Internet. From alien UFO claims hit, unexplained evacuation, mysterious evacuation, child porn investigation, Chinese spies, to planet X incident…

Scientists were commanded to close and vacate the place for security reason. The FBI was spotted in the premises around the time of the evacuation, but neither staff nor the bureau of investigation would explain why the facility has to be vacated. A fire chief volunteer claimed that the FBI had told them there has been a "credible treat" but would provide no details. The sheriff's office said that they did not see any evidence of a threat and deputies left after a few hours.

In fact, what happened is that dark energies for "creating weather events and evil purpose" reaped in the sun's corona. I saw it. They created a break in the corona and even pierced inside the sun, and it affected my solar plexus and awakened me in great pain. But the cabal did not expect such an impact. They did not expect such a big impact when they used this technology they are not mastering, and this is what created all these violent weather events and catastrophes around the planet earth.

CHAPTER 68

And the Tribulations Continue for Both of Us

CHADD chose to come back to earth for two reasons. One, to help humanity during this time of transition, and the second, to help the surrogate voodoo woman to surrender to God and save her soul. But she keeps refusing to learn the lessons. She enjoys more the love of money destroying lives and sucking the energy of CHADD and VIE and their money as you will see.

A few days later, one ascended master from the Galactic Federation of Twelve, who passed away and left his earthly body a long time ago, detected another attack on my body. After the alien parasites—put on purpose in my body, my shoulders, and arms—attacked to stop my mobility, an object posted in the back of my right ear was making me deaf, the layers of scales on my third eye to keep it close. The ascended master found out that my amygdala was turned off, making me retain a lot of fluid. It was impacting my brain, my sinus, my knees, and my breathing, draining my life force energy and keeping me awake, sweating at night. And I was retaining a lot of lipid, fat, and I had to request help from a team of spiritual doctors.

While not knowing that my health issue was from the amygdala, I tried desperately to find an alternative solution as it was hard for me to work on myself. I saw that close to my home, a Chinese acupuncture had an office, and I went for one appointment. It was the most traumatic experience I had. I was left with bruises from the burn of the needles on my knees after one hour and a half of serious pain, and no improvement.

"The amygdala comprises a group of nuclei of neurons. The lateral nucleus is the major recipient of input from sensory vortices of all modalities (e.g., vision, hearing). The moon acts as a firewall to block the third eye/DNA connection to expanded awareness and locks people away in the five senses. It disconnects them from awareness of the level of reality where everything is connected and telepathy and interdimensional communication is not only possible but the way things are!"

But thanks to it, and to the ascended master who offered his help, I awakened this morning with the complete understanding of what has happened. I understood why the psychic vampire woman would have reacted so violently if it would not have gone the way she had put the scenario together.

What the ascended master made me discovered was bigger than I could have even have imagine, the sickness of this system. I had the vision of CHADD's last and third checks sitting on the desk of Doctor Slovenky. Then I saw myself telling CHADD about it and told him to call Doctor Slovenky in Chateau Ushi to mail him overnight his government checks. He shared the information with the archon, who right away replied that it was not necessary. "Do not bother," she said, "the social security will not pay your government checks."

Now I understood. All the pieces of the puzzle were getting into places. Of course! They all made a deal together using his social security monthly checks. And that's why the third check was said to be of a bigger amount.

Now I could put it together. I understood about the three signatures he was forced to sign. One was the unconditional release, and it was for his release to the Archonic woman, and she was granted an amount of money from the court. The second was for the Surgeon Release Form to be signed before any surgery, and that he was asked to sign before he was sick or had any symptoms. But the Archonic woman went to visit him with some food, he felt sick in his stomach and began to throw up black liquid and had to have an emergency diaphragmatic surgery. "Complicated one," said the surgeon. Half of his organs were shutting down while under surgery, and the surgeon had to keep them alive. That surgery was to give some level in court to get him out back to the trap. The public defendant, also an archon and good friend of the archon woman, was then able to invoke in court that he was very sick, had stomach surgery, and needed to go back under her care. The third signature he was forced to sign was to give up these checks to cover up the price of the deal.

But stealing his monthly governments checks was not enough to cover the defendant in court, so the court required CHADD to pay one thousand dollars. So now he is released, she has him and the money. She has him under psychiatric drugs with a poor memory, an inadequate wheelchair; she has the money but he has not. He has no phone, no car, no money, and have barely enough food to survive, and he is trapped under a room again in her house sucking his energy. I came back out of my dreaming state and found out a mail from Dave, saying,

Hello, VIE.

How are you doing? I am going to encourage many to contact Father Gerry Soliman. I just found out that he is a renowned exorcist. He is incredibly powerful. I am going to do it on my side and ask him to help us and to denounce satanic crimes happening in the island and to the world, and to us. I have my paycheck money stolen at the bank. My boss has some debts he can't repay, so he made a deal with the manager at the bank, and my money has vanished. I was next to an African retired woman in the train, and she had all her economy stolen from her bank account too. They even closed up her bank account afterward. No one respect any laws anymore.

Rev. Gerry Soliman, Pastor
Sacred Heart Parish
13804 San Antonio Avenue
St Pete, FL
Phone: 1800-555-555

Cheers and God bless,
Dave

And a doorway to an expanded awareness happened then to Dave during the exorcism experience.

CHAPTER 69

The Doorway to an Expanded Awareness

As everything happens for a reason, Dave discovered and learned all about the climate change, climate control, ill health, hurricanes, flood all over the globe, and earthquakes.

Let's go back to the famous Nikola Tesla quote, "If you wish to understand the universe, think energy, frequency, and vibration," because it is all tied to Dave's discovery.

Nikola Tesla was one of the greatest and most gifted men ever to have walked this earth. Tesla was an extraordinary, intuitive, creative genius.

Nikola Tesla was a Serbian American inventor, electrical engineer, mechanical engineer. Tesla was murdered in his hotel room, and after his murder, the contents of Tesla's safe were stolen, which were delivered to Hitler. The content was then fully repatriated through Project Paperclip at the end of the war, and all his documents were stolen.

They have used it in many circumstances as weapons to reduce the population. Man-made domestic terrorism, directed stones, exotic weapons, fires, silent weapons, frequency wars, sonic weapons.

It is energy weapons used to create ill health as a way of killing off people from a distance with invisible. Used to enforce hurricanes, dropping metal particles in front of hurricanes, then use the directional microwave energies to heat that up, which empowers the young hurricanes too, then follow that heat signature, and then they can feed that heat in front of it and actually guide to where they want it to go by attracting it to the heat by the particles. And then the energy weapon of the microwave energy…to heat up these particles that will drop too via military. Used for flood, when they pretext that there is not enough food for all on earth to use the pesticides. Used to create earthquakes and for political reasons as weapon.

He learned from some whistle-blowers that have personally worked in military black projects for private contractors. Hundreds of government insiders and special access whistle-blowers sharing their knowledge of it and the involvement in cover-ups of extraterrestrial technologies, extraterrestrial presence, secret base programs, and other unclassified projects.

They told Dave that ICC is a shadowy association of private interests developing advanced technologies for galactic trade with extraterrestrials. There exists two international NATO-like organizations that are both representatives from virtually every country on earth. There are five to seven factions of ancient earth breakaway civilizations such as Mayans who purportedly attained the ability to travel off planet. There are ostensibly bases on virtually every planet and moon and our solar system. Same serve private industries, others have exo-political functions, and the rest exist as either military outposts or research facilities. The primary base on the moon is named Lunar Operations Command. Then about a secret space fleet code named Solar Warden and a list of names and the heading non-terrestrial officers, manifests of fleet to fleet cargo transfers of many spacecraft. It's an allege ultra-secret project that maintains a fleet, or several fleet of spaceships that are operating within our solar system run by the US Navy.

CHAPTER 70

Maybe That's Another Piece of the Puzzle

Then I was introduced to a woman. Her name was Cindy, and she softly whispered, "You know that I was not supposed to come here and did not expect to work today, and nothing happen for no reason. How may I help you?" Then she went to talk about her husband. This was another piece of the puzzle put into place. One that I was waiting for, maybe.

Because since CHADD's court date, I knew I could feel that the next three months were very important, intense, and of a good energy for me. Things were starting to show life. I was reawakening. Energies were moving and moving the right way again. But I also knew that it would be intense between the series to produce, the clients calling for appointments and sessions, and my new book to finish.

As expected, CHADD was malnourished. It was even worse than at the Chateau USHI, but there was nothing I could do for the time being, just hoping for the best. Katherine was keeping Ricardo around in case she would need his support again. Ricardo is a man deeply involved with the mind control program organization and the CIA, for the wrong reason, to keep CHADD under mind control.

Bloodline and Archon-possessed Satanists drink the drink that gives them energetic sustenance and also from adrenaline that enters the blood stream in perfuse quantities during sacrifice. That is why the elite and their hidden controllers have worked so hard to suppress the true nature of reality. Without that knowledge, the target population has had no chance of understanding what is happening all around them and why things are as they are. The political correctness is not about ending discrimination but about manipulating the target population to silence the population. They are terrified that the hidden truth will be known. Many are silent under threats and intimidation.

Colleges are basically clinics. They have been taken over and became psychiatric centers. The dangerous effects of psychiatric drugs confirm their attitude. The drugs exaggerate and distort sensitivity. Seeking counseling and medical advice leads on to psychiatric drugs. You can see the elite and their controllers have worked so hard to suppress the true nature of reality. It is time to stop taking this idiocy.

The Archonic reptilian control system is a multidimensional, multifaceted, and incessant perpetual onslaught of the human mind to create fragmentation of thought and emotion and to implant a sense of powerless isolation. The suppression of free expression become more extreme to prevent the circulation of information that exposes the conspiracy and its programing. Pharmaceutical drugs scramble the brain on a waveform level impact upon the waveform standing wave oscillation and throw the body out of kilter in terms of health, thought, emotion, and most importantly a connection to out there.

CHAPTER 71

Shaman Lighted Bear Decided to Manifest Himself

The bear spirits are not from this earth, and they are the Indian Shoshani from an area in the sky called Great Major Ursa. A constellation in the northern sky. They Indian Bears are not from this earth and are the Indian Shoshani.

Shaman Lighted Bear was the most powerful shaman when he existed on earth, and other shamans used to consult him during his life. He gave consultation to shamans on where to move on a safety land of good energy. His grandmother saw a bear as a sign given by the bear messenger when he was born. It was the bear spirit that came to help and cleanse my crystal. He used spiritual crystals' light on me, as dark energies established a web of crystal in my aura. That was when the archon Katherine came through an open portal that she established in my house.

Previously in this book, I narrated on the spirit woman that delivered the message from my mother crying because the cabal through Katherine was depriving me from all money, but expenses, trying hard to get me broke. And also I talked of the six senses passing of time, that stuck us all in time and placed us in a time prison. That is why Shaman Lighted Bear decided to come and help detox the parallel lines.

Suddenly Lighted Bear entered my body and with his strong and grave voice said, "0010110! 0010110 is now reestablished, set up, and locked. So it is so be it and it is done." It triggered my brain in a real event. I felt my frontal lobe stimulation activated by the ray of energy. I saw the multiple colors of the rainbow and entered the point of stillness in a frozen moment.

Then I saw a wooden board, a real rough board of wood and a wood plane. Next I saw the plane rolled and softening the bumps, roughness, and erasing the splinters. Every time Lighted Bear pass it on the wood board, it takes care of one lay. That is where I remembered Archangel Michael talking about many layers, complicated layers, he said.

And Kathumi, who was once Saint Germaine, came to explain. "Katherine, Paul, and the granddaddy are all from the cabal. They have found a way by using CHADD under psychotropic drugs to change the parallel lines. They have an evil lineage on both male and female. Kathrine, Paul and granddaddy are from the red devil for female and black satanic line for the male. The evil through the century are known as the ethyl. Seth was another name to evil. The Seth energy is the male lineage. They have found a way to interlink parallel universal, putting the time lines very toxic."

Kathumi continued saying, "The surrogate and her family are bombarding you at night, VIE, with a particle of energy, an energy ray that heats your body. It is a particle that is inaudible to your ear but by them. It's a frequency energy ray used by the dark part of the universe. There are two different feminine part of the moon. The dark side (witch), the old ugly dark woman, and the other side is the powerful enlightened woman. Two ley lines were found. They were crossing in the portal in your home."

Now Archangel Michael is explaining the three Ps: Purification (for present life, life of the now), Plane (to soften, the wooden board), and Protection (the circle on the top heaven and the base the earth connection). He was telling me about the parallel lines, very toxic time lines.

Now I am given a name of a person also sent to help me open the flow of money that is coming from the other side, money being spirit. I practically did not sleep trying to figure out a way to pay my bills when early morning, I received telepathically, "By midday." Fair enough, by midday, I received a text from my helper. "Mission done, you are good to go. Had to finish up outside antagonisms happening to you."

Then I suddenly received a message from the light messenger. "They are in their final minutes. That's why everything seems so horrible. They are so desperate. They know it's their end."

And a news alert message appeared now on my phone. "Bombs in New York, Washington, DC, and Florida against a political party."

Then I look at the sky and read "Trust. Jesus gives. Ask and you shall receive."

CHAPTER 72

Karmic Payback

C HADD always told me that he would not be able to live his life until Katherine will enter karmic payback.

When CHADD reached age six, the surrogate decreed, "Now it is time to attack this sweet boy." She knew there was wisdom in his soul even before he entered in this life. She thought and thinks that she has broken from karmic payback. But no one can escape it.

CHADD was born in a royal Pharaoh family, at the time of the great Pharaoh in Egypt. His name was Hicadobeee, which means the one who commands the water of the Nile. His name is associated with water and the flowing water. He had many brothers and never became a Pharaoh. When he was five to six years old in Egypt, he began to be taught and trained in knowledge and spirituality by a great teacher. He was very knowledgeable, by the good priest that taught him mysticism, power of mind, etc. The Egyptians had high esoteric knowledge. Then a young priest was continuing to train the children of the scribes. That is where the contamination entered in CHADD. This young priest was evil and taught him selfishness, and it created a lot of karma. That young priest was Katherine. She got more and more dark into extremely dark evil today. So CHADD was contaminated and had to pay for it.

CHADD could astral project himself and traveled back in time, and he came into focus and reality and he sees all. He got *lucid awareness.* He recovered and he is now in complete control of himself again. And now sees the truth.

Ricardo is now the mother's new contact and power man. He understands that she is living from CHADD's money, and they are in agreement. His three years' government checks are stolen from him and put in a trust where CHADD is not included of course. To do that, the dark forces cut his skin open and directed the flow to a place they have in a Polynesian island. Then they also convinced him that he was not entitled to his money.

Part of all of their plan was to have him even more vulnerable and in Ricardo's control. Ricardo invited him to go to an Angels Church, that he resisted going anywhere else. Because they are all possessed in this cult, and it is Ricardo's contact with the fallen angels. Prior to going to the fallen angels' cult, the surrogate made sure to have him ingest psychotropic drugs that she cursed first, and Ricardo brought him a glass of water to swallow them that he also cursed.

These ugly people are all against him. Katherine, the surrogate, Ricardo, the dark government, Paul, the half-brother, Alexy, the cousin, Carlos with the mob and the old man. Even the uncle who lend him money for a new wheelchair to make sure that he could travel and see the old man, and the aunt that appeared on the parking lot in front of the chapel. The old man is such a dark soul too that he had to be refrained from the knowledge he obtained from the government of a particle wave that he could use against others. Since he can hear noise on the walls and at night, he is touched in an inappropriate way by a restless entity.

CHAPTER 73

A Sudden Conversation with Ra

, VIE, was also living at that time and was connected to Amun-Ra. Amun-Ra was the king of the Egyptian gods. The Egyptians referred to Amun-Ra as "one one." He was the god of fertility and life. Amun have been present in the mythology and culture of the Egyptian people almost from the very inception of this complex and mysterious nation. Amun's first role was as the patron saint of the Egyptian city Thebes, where the ruling Pharaoh and his royal family resided. Here he became joined with the sun god Ra, and the two became known as the Egypt god Amun-Ra. I am also the lineage of Mother Mary. I have powerful knowledge. I was the good priest that taught CHADD first the mysticism and the power of the mind, so Katherine decided to put a parasite in the back of my ear that is a low frequency. Then my pelvis has been contaminated by a particle wave above my pelvis that leads below to the knees. It was acid put in the bone. And it did not stop here. She attacked me under my right arm, then my face on multiple places.

Ra (the Egyptian God): "I was a hybrid, part Arcturian, part Syrian. Like I said to someone else, VIE, from a very advanced civilization. I was in collaboration to working with the blue Avian aliens. I was working in other places in the galaxy and the universe, not only in Egypt. I came on earth to do my job and on many other places. I was the ruler of this world and became ruler of many others. To be the ruler of the world, I had to be there at some point to oversee what people were doing to oversee the positive and the negative activities. Being in charge of several worlds at once is not an easy task, but I surrounded myself with some powerful people.

The eye of Ra is a human eye, but he did not look human. I had a blue tint on my skin, and I looked a little reptilian at places. My head was a sort of snakelike because of the hybridization. In some places, the hybridization looked more snakelike, and in other places it looked more reptilian, and even in other places more humanoid. But understand that there are many hybrids in the universe.

The association to be the sun star, Sol Star, was one place when we get a lot of energy. I learned to take direct energy from the sun and used it in very powerful ways, and that is why I was called out into the sun and I was seen collecting the energy from it.

The period I covered in Egyptian history, I was off and on there for about 226 earth years. After that, I had other people to govern that area. I was in many parts of earth, Samaria, India, Peru, Argentina, Romania, Native America, England or United Kingdom, China, Australia, through them all, Russia, France. It was necessary for me to look at different parts of the kingdom with different social graces.

Jesus Christ is a creator being also and came to the world for a different purpose. He came to bring spiritual uplifting to the people. There are many connections with Jesus through the universe, but he is a spiritual leader and not one of the political leader. So he comes for spiritual reasons and is noted to have changed many other worlds. He has many personalities in many ways, to change a lot. There are different aspects to him just like God might because he is more energy than corporeal.

I, Ra, existed from a high fifth-dimension reality. I had been originally from the seventh dimension. As a creator being, I started in the seventh dimension, then I was put in the fifth dimension world to help, and that is when I came to earth. As a ruler, I made sure that the people were being treated fairly, that the technology and all the things that were being maintained on the planet were taking care properly. I made sure that the governments knew who I was and could work on their own, but if they needed, they could call me. I had many names on this world, like Krishna, Buddha… I would come in and walk into these personalities so that they find me enlightened. They were part of each because I walked into these beings. I could do that with many beings. I was able to communicate with the sun star, and I still do.

The sun is going through another great change, in a period of somewhat rest, and when it happens, the earth suffers. People think that they are preparing for a global warning when it may be actually preparing for an ice age. It's insured. The only way to affect the state of the sun can only happen by prayer or energy work. But the sun can affect human beings. The state of humanity does matter and reflect the sun some ways though, but the sun goes through its phases no matter what the people on earth are doing, no matter what the Venusians are doing, the Martian are doing, or those on the rings of Saturn or Jupiter. The people are important, and God put them in this plan for a particular reason, and the sun is affected by people's presence in some ways. But only because God says so. The sun must do what he is told to do and what he is instinctively meant to do whatever the people consciousness.

There are many kinds of ascension. Ascension is truly the actions of mind toward God in as many ways as possible. So the act of ascension for humans is to evolve, it's a greater being to be close to God like. A very small percentage of humanity is ready to move. At this time, the age of ascension is just beginning. This ascension will take a while, and by the end of that time, not everyone on earth will be ready, but the ascension will happen when there is enough people ready for it to become an event. The ones that are not ready for it will stay behind, and they will become a different race of people. We know they will be separated. Indeed they do not rise. The ascension may happen without dying. It was proven in the past. Some Tibetan monk translated through the next dimension without dying, and there are some that are trying to do at that time as well, but it is not an easy thing to do. It takes concentration. It would be easier to die than ascend. It is my understanding the way it should happen, but we will see.

Some believe that a wave of energy will come and translate many into the next dimension. This wave that is coming is a wave that will change people, but it will not translate them into the next dimension, but it will bring them to a greater understanding of spirituality so that they may grow faster. Some waves have already come through, but there is still more yet to come. Sometimes feeling higher dimension is not comfortable. It's almost painful for the one that are not ready yet but will feel the need to feel.

God has a plan for everyone individually and as a whole. It is by His doing that people individually will understand Him the way that will work toward Him. Many people do not have an understanding of God and will work to do what they do in His plan that may seem to be anti-ascension but still work into an ascension plan. God is pure energy of many, many different kinds. There are different kinds of energies, and God is all of them. For each to plan its part. It's a cocreation of God and the soul so that you can, by it, be separated from it. People have free will. The mechanism of creating it, people are born with it.

The free will changes with personal decisions, and God knows who each are and how you are going to act. It is negotiable but to a certain point. God has the final say. You cannot dictate everything about other people who live because they are not only in charge of their own. Prayers have a consciousness that is God. He has many facets to Him. He puts himself in many places to be many kinds of energy to many kinds of people, and therefore He is many things to be an energy to many things that may not be aware of.

The feminine side of God is supportive, and the masculine side of God is creative in some way, but the feminine side of God can also be creative, and the masculine side of God can also be supportive. The masculine side is symbolized by a fire flame both masculine and feminine sides."

Now that we entered into the age of Aquarius, this is the age of washing…washing away to bring balance. It is the time we exit the age of unhealthy patriarchal rule. It is time of the goddess, a time for the matriarchal. A time to come together in balance, a balance of the masculine and feminine within. This the time where Jesus and Mary Magdalene serve as the representation of the Divine masculine and Divine feminine.

Jesus said, "When you make the two into one, and when you make the inner like the outer and the outer like the inner, and the upper like the lower, and when you make male and female into a single one, so that the male will not be male nor the female be female, when you make eyes in place of eye, a hand in place of a hand, a foot in place of a foot, an image in place of an image, then you will enter the Kingdom" (Gospel of Thomas, verse 22).

When you so identify with the light within; when you make the lower self like the God above, the Mighty I Am Presence; when you purify your chakras, the upper chakras magnifying the alpha or masculine, and the lower chakras the omega or feminine energies; when you do these things, the Christ image will descend down the crystal cord directly above and superimpose itself over you. At that moment, Jesus will be with you. The kingdom of God is not in some antiseptic corner of the universe. Do these things and you will be aware of it. The door will be opened. You will already have entered.

CHAPTER 74

Your Life, Your Reality, and Lifetime

was deep into my daily meditation when one of my star family entered in contact to deliver this message for you.

"Dear one, we, the Arcturians, come forth to share our power and inspiration with you. You may call upon us to upgrade your entire being. We will do so in harmony with your soul using our ascension tools and technology to create powerful and peaceful shifts of transformation within your being. We are present to assist and guide you. We will always present our light to you in support, respect, and love for the ascension pathway you are traveling upon. The energy wave and cycle that is anchoring into the earth from inner places can be summarized as the presence of clarity. The ascension energies are promoting the presence and experience of clarity within all aspects of your being reality and life. This means that activations will take place to support you in seeing, sensing, and acknowledging with greater clarity and clearness. Of being aware of your intention and inner guidance with clarity and the ability to clearly act upon the wisdom received. Clarity will develop within your relationships especially with yourself, soul, and the Creator. Confusion may arise, and this will be an indication of your resistance to the presence of clarity and the shifts it can manifest for you.

You are your life reality and lifetime. This is your truth, and when it becomes your experience, you begin to tap into a deeper understanding of the world you are living, in accessing insights that support you with questions that you may hold within you.

What's the meaning of life? What's my purpose? Why am I on earth?

Your life and your existence upon earth is a combination of your thoughts, emotions, perceptions, desires, past experiences, future expectations, the presence of your soul, soul group, and the Creator as well as the influences of those outside of you and your physical and spiritual reality.

Allow yourself to contemplate the world life. Or my life is a series of experiences you do not have the control of that is outside your body and being. Or it is a pathway of your own creation.

Humanity often think of their life as an energy force separate from them. Then you will find it challenging to experience fulfill-ment, contentment, and peace because you are creating that your life control you and is separate from you. But you are a combination of your thoughts, emotions, perceptions, desires, experiences, expecta-tions, the presence of your soul, soul group, and the Creator as well as the influence of those outside of your physical and spiritual reality. All of that created your life. Every big and little thing you experience is born from you. The way you perceive your life is also your creation. You have built your life the way it is now, and you can change it all.

You impact, create, and design your life. This is the key. Everything is connected and one in the universe of the Creator; therefore, you are connected and one with your life, your reality. Reality is your awareness of all that you are. All that you are expe-riencing and all that you are creating. Your reality is the way you choose to perceive yourself. Your lifetime is the duration of your exis-tence upon earth. This is governed by your soul and the mission your soul has accepted, or wishes to achieve on earth, while your soul determines the length of your existence upon earth. The choices you make in areas you focus upon can impact the quality of your exis-tence and can even cause the soul to recognize the duration of your lifetime. Time does not exist, and you can recognize your lifetime as a constant series of present moments while you cannot control your lifetime on earth. You can recognize that you are the creation and design of the life you experience. The combination of all thoughts, emotions, beliefs, etc., that you hold within you create your life.

It is time now to realize that you are as one with your life and reality. You are the creator of your life, and reality is born within you. If you wish to change it, there is then a need to examine your being. Observe what you think and feel about the area you wish to transform. Are you observing from a space of love and peace, or from a space of illusion and fear, anger, control?"

CHAPTER 75

The Event from Orion Constellation

Suddenly I begun to recall a dream I had the night before. I was…something was happening…then I saw the Orion. What was that for? The constellation? I felt a pulling sensation in my solar plexus. At that moment, a clear image of his face come to my mind. Then I saw the Orion constellation. What was that for? A constellation?

I became aware of three men watching me from the opposite street corner. I opened the trunk of my car, took my black leather business bag, in which I had what I needed for the day at the office, and walked toward the entrance building. I entered the building and went to the elevator. I got into it, pressed the button to the third floor, and just when the door of the elevator was closing, I saw a hand forcing the elevator's door to open again. The three men got rapidly in. I asked them which floor they wanted to go. From where they were standing, they could not see which floor I intended to go. And they all replied like you. This was sounding quite suspicious. I rapidly took a glance at their badges and saw some company name for some type of repair in the building.

Once the elevator opened, I left quickly in direction of my office and forgot about the three men. As I was just about finish with my second client, Tehany, the fire alarm went on. We quickly left the office, and I made sure I had my office key, close the door behind us, and we went into the direction of the stairs. That is when Tehany asked me if it was happening often, and I told her that it was the first time ever.

We began to walk down the stairs, and it seemed to me that we were going down more steps that we should, and I laughed saying, "Are we going underground?"

That's was where standing one of the three men, looking at every faces stepping down. Realizing that he was observing me getting out of my car earlier, I looked at him and said, "But you are the one that pulled the fire alarm." The man had a weird look on his face looking at me.

As we came out of the building, I immediately saw that my car was not parked where I left it. My car has disappeared, and I had no idea where it was gone and how I would get it back. I pulled out of my purse my cell phone, and it had only 7 percent battery left. I had to think quick if I wanted to get out of this situation.

I walked to the other building, where the building administration was, thinking that they would probably let me recharge my phone while I explain my situation. Unfortunately, all employees were using another cell phone brand. But they offered me to call from their office. I called the number they gave me and a female police officer answered, "What can I do for you?" I gave her the information of my car, year, make and model, etc., and she replied, "Yap! Your car has been towed," and she hung up on me. I called back several times, and I only had an answering machine.

But call who? And where now? I said. The manager of the building wrote an address on a piece of paper and gave it to me saying, "It's just one block away. They should know where your car has been towed." I went and walked all around the block but never found any such name or suite number. Frustrated, I returned to the administration office. Finally, the man offered to get down to the parking lot and see what he could do to help. I heard him talking on his cell about Clermont, and that I had to get at this place before 4:00 p.m. It was 3:25 p.m., and Clermont was at least sixty minutes from where we were. He hung up and called another number and finally found out that the tow car company was in a different place and fifteen minutes from us. But now, I had to find rapidly someone to drive me at the tow place.

Three percent battery charge was still left. I texted very fast to my friend Elizabeth, praying that she could help me, and went quickly back up with my client to the office as we both needed to get our purses. My office door was wide opened. I looked around to see if anything has disappeared, but no, even the money was still in place. I closed the door behind me and walked out the building again. Fifteen minutes later, I saw my friend Elizabeth coming in the brand-new Sebastian car.

Luckily I could recover my car on time. But who was this new next-door girl? How come she never left the building like everybody? How did she know there was no fire? Why didn't she follow the building rules and never got off the building like everyone else? Why wasn't she scared? And why did she say, "I've got to go, I've to go," when she saw us? It was obvious that we came back earlier than was thought, and the person that trespassed in our office did not have time to close the door. If it was not about money or a search of the office, what was it for?

Not long ago, a camera surveillance was installed just in front our office door, the only thing that could be missing is a microchip to listen to us! Was that what was installed inside the office?

Hum! Wasn't the tow company named Constellation who towed my car? Constellation tow company? For real?

This goes back to Katherine. The archon working for money and for the elite. We know what Katherine has done all these years to my blue flame, and we know that at some point going to court, she entered in contact with a high rank man in the legal system, and now they work together. After working with Carlos, now she also works with Ricardo, who is deeply involved in the government. He is the one who released CHADD from Chateau Ushi at Katherine's demand. So they managed to get CHADD out of Chattahoochee, made sure the court would give them authority and surveillance on him, and at the same time that the surrogate received the amount of his years in Chateau Ushi disability checks.

CHAPTER 77

Katherine and Her Satanic Plot

I continue to watch. I see her making her own way, Katherine, as if it was not enough to trap CHADD without car, separating him from me with the help of dysfunctionals Paul, Alexy, Ricardo, and the cult "Church of Angels." They increased the surveillance everywhere, and at all time, Paul installed cameras to cover every angles inside the house, even one facing directly his bed, and one outside at the entrance of the house. They take turns every day to drive him to the cult once or twice a week, to the doctor for his prescription drugs and blood tests, grocery stores…but he still can go down the road with his wheelchair, and this scared them. He became good friend with a neighbor, a retired man who offered to drive him sometimes around.

So Katherine went further in her plot plan and decided now to get my house in the market, kicking me out of my home. She wanted my house to be bought by the government to be sure CHADD would not leave her, get his freedom, and go with his life.

But I have many helpers behind the veil, and one of them said to me, "I am Divine Sister A…allocated to you. Do you have any idea why this incident happens now?"

And I replied, "Not really. What does it mean?"

"Well, last Tuesday, when you got off your home, ready to pull off your car out of your driveway, you saw four men at the entrance corner of your driveway, and one of them looked very familiar. He said he was a contractor. His name is Farah, and your gut told you to watch out for also the second one staring at you, Medhi, while the familiar face looked embarrassed and greeted you with a 'How are you doing today?' and shook your hand through the car window. They both work with the dark side of the government, the cabal. They are part of the Orions.

You are a threat to them. The Orions found out about you and what you bring to humanity. The Orion civilization alien races are 89 percent Vegan and 11 percent Lyran. Their origin, Zeta Reticuli, is a neighbor of the Orion constellation. Orions have a reputation for possessing an aggressive nature and have been involved in many destructive wars. They developed advanced technology of a type while still war waging. The typical scenario was the Light against the dark peace-loving Orions opposed by self-serving aggressive Orions.

Tomorrow you will understand what I tell you. When they are going to come to check if the pool is not 'leaking.' You will remember the familiar face. He was involved also with what happened in the past to CHADD. He works for the cabal. They know the value of your house and want also to take advantage of your energy inside it.

This man, Farah, helps to manipulate and get beings to be in trouble. They use directed energy while the subject is picked for a task under the influence of psychotropic drugs. He then helps the person in the act. And he is now helping the cabal trying to kick you out of your house. Watch them carefully because your pool does not leak. They are trying everything to buy some time to find a buyer and resell it. They need more time after the inspection, the excuse is the structure would not support the tiles, then they need an additive time for an inspection of the pool that could leak. That is evident. They'll just try to kick you out your home.

But have you heard of NESARA and GESARA? Because they won't always succeed. And maybe some philanthropist will help you. You'll understand soon what I mean.

VIE, what is yours by Divine right cannot be taken away from you, and this is what we are making sure of. You met some resistance in your journey, CHADD and you, because of what you are bringing with the Light and the Sound. It was a very difficult and hard, long journey. Over around a thirty-year period, the self-elected in key places governing, the cabal, have classified, attacked, and put on limitations on you to be able to control you both and your capabilities. Keeping you in slavery and with others in poverty and sickness. They are using many technologies that no one is aware of, like the CERN colliders that they are using to change people's DNA and to trap them in a loop in the third dimension.

With your healing therapies, which is healing integration and reconnection, you are blessing humans and helping them recover mental clarity, consciously involve and pass duality from 3-D to 5-D. Of course, Katherine and her dysfunctional family, friends, and elites in power are not taking it well at all, and that is why they try hard to keep controlling you.

But you are the winner and you get your freedom both of you. There is the National Economic Security and Recovery Act that is about to take effect and they know it. Because it will abolish your loan, and they understand it. It will finally bring fairness and wealth not only to you but to the people in the world at the same time. The Global Reform Act was passed in year 2000 by the American Congress but was kept under wraps ever since. These acts NESARA and GESARA will have immediate and worldwide effects, especially in financial sectors, and literally changes everything.

The NESARA Act and Currency Reserve, have you wondered why making a living was so hard for the majority while the minority elite made steady fortune through their corporations? NESARA and GESARA are about to free the entire globe from debt slavery to the banks, and that is just a start. With it also comes a long-awaited release of free energy technology that will set humankind free.

Car then can run for just a few cents with many different technologies that use different fuels or free energy. If you do not have to buy gas, they can't take your money anymore. NESARA is global debt forgiveness, and the announcement of NESARA will cancel out all global debts and mortgage.

No more loan through the global debt forgiveness, no energy bills, no taxes to pay, and no wealthy elite buyers for your house. You are the owner of it, and no one can pretend to it. The belief that the world will simply stand still as is forever is ridiculous. NESARA is not a hoax, and the whole world will know this now. It's a world that is free, that has no energy bills to pay, no need to be a financial slave to any other person, corporation, or to forced hated job."

And the divine sister continued and said, "Very soon, in a few years, there will be many less people on the planet, and the ones on the planet will have their eyes open wide. The Jesuits have always been at war with the Catholic Church, and the Catholic Church has never allowed the Jesuits to gain any power. But Jesuits are the ones who have the big observatories and telescopes and they watch heavens. They are looking for the return of the Anunnaki. The Jesuits Pope elected has been put in position to eventually win the trust of humans. Having the most to gain and the least to lose to make some sort of return of God. He plans to go, before the US Congress, and to give a speech before the UN, historical precedent.

But beware of the God Duo that holds the key to the divine wisdom and brings humanity into the Light of God. And thanks to the eight blurry faces that helped you with the power of the number they work with, you have constant flow of money in your life and the financial flow protection.

You remember? 'Failure was not an option.' How could you? Aren't you the two angels at work? Revelation 13:9: 'If any man have an ear, let him hear it.'"

Now, is it fiction disclosing the reality? Is this fact or simply fiction?

About the Institute of Light and Sound and the Bio-Qi Therapy™ for Healing

Sometimes, archangels produce a physical incarnation as an aspect of themselves. One example is the Archangel Michael who, in recent centuries, has taken on a role that could be described as a lord of freedom. At one point, he incarnated a portion of his consciousness as the now-legendary mystic Merlin who guided the young King Arthur to introduce a new mind-set. As a result, humanity had an example that inspired its steady climb out of the suppression imposed by the rigid hierarchical control of the day.

To distinguish between the ether as the fabric of space and etheric energy as the vital life energy used by healers, God must be brought into the picture! How? Through the holy spirit under guidance of the Archangel Michael. And it takes someone chosen, prepared and initiated by the Archangel Michael.

The best name for the all-pervasive field of Divine love energy that fills our universe is, of course, *the God field, the ether as the fabric of space. Totally different than the etheric energy as the vital life energy used by Reiki healers. Anything that takes God and Jesus out of the equation is not from God, and a true healer receives their power directly from God.*

We are not dealing with humans, but we are dealing with interdimensional beings.

So what we do is sending a ray of high frequency through vibrational transformative energy because diseases are low frequency, and when the frequency is higher, illnesses can't live.

Vibrational transformative energy is a vibrational energy and gift that both CHADD and VIE carry as they channel the Holy Spirit. The biological interconnection with the astronomy was lost, which requires the intervention of the Office of the Christ to restructure the axiational lines. Until now, the body has been left to work on molecular biological levels with only limited magnetic resonance patterns to continue the functions of the amino acids, the basic building blocks of life. Their goal is to balance the energies of the individual through instilling feelings of love and unity. When love is expressed, there is a magical dance between the photon inclusion and the electron exclusion, which is why love is a very healing or transformative experience. *The God Field is the fabric of space. It is subtle, fluid, magnetic energy that fills all space. It is intensified within and around matter, where its attractive nature produces the force of gravity.* It involves the use of resonance and vibration. It stimulates the five senses and restores the balance. It tunes the body up and tune life, by realigning to the spirituality and destiny. By doing so, the body then self-heal from traumas and pain.

'It is truly pathetic to hear breathless voices racing through a long list of side effects at the end of drug advertisements on television. And the global campaign against alternative ways of healing made by the cartel." In fact, pharmaceutical drugs are damaging and imbalancing the body's waveform field. It distorts the hologram once the poison is swallowed, and it results in chaotic fields of frequency and vibration. The waveform level of the body becomes so distorted and inverted that it ceases to function as an energetic organism. The only answer is for the waveform field to be addressed.

"The key to the future physics are given in the cross matching of geometries and color codes, which will allow the structure of chromosomes to carry consciousness across light-time zones. There is color code in everything. This is possible because the chromosomal patterns exist in grids, which have unique colors in geometric form existing within every consciousness time zone. Therefore, they are capable of being fused into different light-time zones by the right cross matching. This is to prepare the human race for the emergence of a new garment so that man can coordinate form with similitude of the Second Adam Kadmon. This will change the consciousness of biological limitation to correspond to new chromosomal patterns. While this process of consciousness transfer is taking place through chromosical recoding, the use of the unique language of color can express volume-space, depth-space, and vibratory-space through cosmological constants, which frame the human and higher evolutionary thought-forms.

The reason why vast numbers of humanity have not used the language of color is because man has remained under the power of the fallen illuminaries. Man uses functions that are oriented basically within the duality of black and white, therefore, his conceptual ability does not work with other polychromatic vibrations. He does not understand his genetic ancestry descending from various genetic embodiments. Some of these genetic embodiments were descendants of the blue-white ray, which was directly projected to this planet.

Over the millennia, the admixture for gene pool mutation between the root races so that the connecting linkages of genetic modeling were lost. In consequences, the earlier genetic disruptions, the Brotherhood of Light is repairing the lost linkages in the human gene pool. This is being done through the color geometries that form the grid containing color thermo-temporal lines, which in turn match an area of genetic material to another area of genetic growth. Through this crystallization within the genetic materials to a point, which attracts the rays of being. This forms a reciprocity of energy with all portions of the body within the color grid. To facilitate this grid, the higher evolution uses a color attachment that scan the genetic area in question with a given number of thermobands simultaneously. They then give each thermobands a separate and distinct color. Thus, the temperature differences across a surveyed area can be measured by simply counting the color bands. The color attachment is a template of light cells distributing and organizing the genetic material into districts. This process allows for higher evolutionary thought-forms to be transferred into localized color codes by modulating the A-line and B-line grid of the template, as well as causing a genetic transfer of man to take place into higher evolutionary prototypes derived from one central similitude. (Extract from *The Book of Knowledge*, J. J. Hurtak)

This transfer is done by using a light beam with a specific wavelength (must carry a specific frequency bulb and can't be gel or glasses) irradiated on a chromosome that explodes, allowing for it to be rapidly absorbed into the beam for genetic transfer to a new state of matter. Man will now have the ability to project from one consciousness zone to another, the ability to project from life spectrum to light spectrum to other life spectrum. (Extract from *The Book of Knowledge*, J. J. Hurtak)

Therefore Bio-Qi Therapy™ has been specifically created for that purpose. The use of Colors is to open doors to other worlds and influence us. Sacred geometry is the knowledge key. Musical notes open all doors for spiritual renaissance. Sound is the universal language. DNA can be adjusted to accommodate higher frequency of light, and RNA-DNA operates as super conductive memory storage processing apparatus. It is overall about attuning, balancing, and reconnecting the body. Chakras must be tuned. The language of the light synchronizes the time cells, with the right knowledge within the turning of the wheel of the law. Then dispense the correct knowledge for soul evolution. Sound is the vibration of molecules and travels through a vocal cord of the messenger. The primary similarity between light and sound are behaviors as waves and both be reflected and have frequencies of oscillation while can be measures as color light of pitch of the sound. The love frequency is the holy atonement, attunement to restore the body temples, and reactivates and restructures DNA energetically or vibrationally. Vibrational transformative energy, enable to cooperate in the RNA-DNA nuclei to chromosomes of another evolutionary inheritance.

(Geometry is the study of the structure of space, and space is the one thing everywhere in the universe and connects everything in the universe to every single other thing in the universe through the fabric of space-time itself. By understanding the geometry of the vacuum, you begin to understand how and why the universe behaves the way it does.)

"Our entire biological system, the brain and the earth itself, work on the same frequency" (Nikola Tesla).

There are seven veils or pathways that need to be parted in order to reach a higher understanding: enlightenment, courage, wisdom, silence, discovery, hope, and grace.

When an individual is living a conscious, aware life, one perception of life will shift and it will create new pathways within the matrix. The DNA part that scientists call "junk" is the matrix. God never created junk! But it is where its name is encrypted.

About the Author

VIE Loriot de Rouvray is a visionary and vibrational transformation energy healer, writer and bio-musician at the Bio Institute of Light and Sound Therapy, and has been recognized by Elite Women Worldwide, for dedication, achievement, and leadership in her professional endeavors. She is an honored member of the National Association of Professional Women, honored member of the Continental Who's Who, honored member of the Worldwide Who's Who, recognized honored Strathmore's life member, and have won the Hall of Fame best alternative holistic medicine of Orlando. VIE is a member of Healing International. VIE was interviewed by Empire Global Radio show *Professionals Roundtable* and by CUTV News Radio. Her institute has won the 2018 Business Hall of Fame Metaphysical Treatments and the Holistic Alternative Medicine (CAM), the 2018 Best Orlando Award (six consecutive years) and the inclusion in Top 100 Registry for Recognition for outstanding career achievement.

VIE de Rouvray was born of the French aristocracy on an island called New Caledonia, which is located between Australia and New Zealand. In January 1987, VIE de Rouvray experienced a dramatic shift in consciousness, which resulted in a complete lifestyle change. Her purpose, which involves communication in the healing arts, was revealed, and gifts from previous interplanetary incarnations were activated. A visionary and an Aquarius, Ms. de Rouvray heals people metaphysically. She has also been guided to write and to create bio-music with the language of Light that she speaks.

VIE de Rouvray authored the book *9.1.1. Complete Guide To Natural Healing*. The book's purpose is to help achieve perfect health by utilizing holistic therapies, natural methods, and various other remedies. She discusses how other medications don't cure the body but unbalance even more your body, about vaccinations that contain mercury and are harmful to the body, and much more concerning your health that is hidden to the public.

VIE de Rouvray also authored the first volume, *Destiny of the doG*, a theory thriller about a journey of a tainted angel and about how the culmination of historical events will interact with the prophecies of the future days. The book features the ancient city of Antioch, fallen angels, ancient legends, and a secret religious sect created in the days of Jesus. The book illustrates a modern adventure through which Christianity is introduced to the world.

VIE de Rouvray's second volume is titled *Time Is Ticking: the Fifth Amendment*. The second volume of this work explains the world today. It illustrates a fascinating and historical adventure that includes the return of Jesus and Mary Magdalene, who demonstrate the path of Divine love.

VIE de Rouvray wrote her third volume, *Karma through the Window of Time: The Spiritual Journey of Two Angels*. It's about two angels at work. One is a physical Light and vibration healer guided to be reconnected to her original essence that is now here in a different life to see the transformation from the age of Pisces to the age of Aquarius. And the second angel is a Baker Acted, drugged ward of state that holds the key to Divine wisdom. It's the Armageddon and the last battle between good and evil, the final war between human governments and God.

VIE de Rouvray truly began her healing mission when she was reunited with her colleague, who was in a wheelchair and wanted help. He was on psychotropic prescriptions drugs, hungry, anemic, blind, and in a constant foggy state of mind. VIE stopped seeing clients for four months so that she could focus all her time on him. He didn't have money and was so weak that he couldn't even drink or eat on his own. She nourished him, took care of him, and helped him detox from his medications, in spite of the fact that she could only communicate with him during a few moments of clarity throughout each day. Although caring for him was controversial to people who did not approve, Ms. de Rouvray never gave up. This was the first step of her mission.

VIE Loriot de Rouvray speaks the language of the Light that is the galactic language of Love and Light. She tones, chants, hand signs the language of the Light that is instant communication with the infinite mind using pictographic cybernetics. It is the parent of the language of the deity used in overall plan to design to outline a procedure, to code knowledge into crystal, etc., to reach many planetary worlds and realities simultaneously, and fuse the different languages into the same scenario abstract. The universal language is Light is coded information to reawaken the DNA and the dormant aspect of your Divine blueprint. It carries encodements for frequency healing, activating the DNA. It is used for healing any issue, for toning, meditating, aligning. Light language in short is a carrier of codes and vibrational frequencies of the fifth dimension, vibrating high enough to be able to channel Light language.

She believes that spiritual growth, vitality, and wellness are the link to human's primary purpose. In her eyes, life is a game, an adventure that has to be experienced, examined, and understood in order to restore balance in body, mind, and spirit. Ms. de Rouvray believes the end result of the infinite growth is to realize Oneness, and thus the meaning of life is growth in consciousness through mental, physical, and mind experiences, like pain, stress, anger, fear, illnesses, and diseases.

She says that her purpose and intention is as a visionary intuitive healer, vibrational transformation energy practitioner, spiritual and metaphysical teacher, and an Aquarius. She helps teach the body to heal at a deep cellular level, and it is designed to assist people to open their own self-healing ability and personal empowerment. She uses Sacred Geometry because Sacred Geometry transmits energy and awareness for soul awakening. Many frequencies of energy are very different in their qualities and purposes.

She created and owns the Institute of Biostimulation of Light and Sound Therapy.

E-mail: instituteofbiostimulation@yahoo.com
Website: www.instituteoflightansound.com
Twitter: www.twitter.com/Lightsound4
Facebook: www.facebook.com/BioInstituteOfLightAndSound
Video: "Journey to the Fifth Dimension, Orlando"
YouTube channel: Institute of Light and Sound Leaping

Horizon Series
Youngliving.com essential oils distributor number: 398498 (You can sign up by calling 1-801-418-8800 and by giving my distributor number.)

www.ingramcontent.com/pod-product-compliance
Lightning Source LLC
Chambersburg PA
CBHW060858120626

46553CB00001B/126